MOTORCYCLE TOURING
An International Directory – 1989/90

A Whirlaway Book

Whitehorse Press, Boston

Copyright © 1989 by Kennedy Associates

All rights reserved. No part of this publication may be reproduced or transmitted in any form or by any means, electronic or mechanical, including photocopy, recording, or any information storage or retrieval system, without permission in writing from the publisher.

Cover and interior design by Tsuneo Taniuchi
Cover photo courtesy of Desmond Adventures, Inc.

A Whirlaway Book. Published in March 1989 by Whitehorse Press, 154 West Brookline Street, Boston, Massachusetts 02118, U.S.A.

Publisher: Daniel W. Kennedy
Marketing Director: George N. Bradt
Research Director: Barbara A. Campbell
Editorial Director: Sandra L. Fraley
Editorial Assistant: Max Canis

Whirlaway and Whitehorse Press are trademarks of Kennedy Associates.

ISBN 0-9621834-0-7   ISSN 1041-5734

5 4 3 2 1

Printed in the United States of America

INTRODUCTION

Motorcycle Touring: An International Directory – 1989/90 is dedicated to our readers, those who are already touring enthusiasts and those who are becoming. We want to play a part in getting you on the road more often and in more exciting places, on group tours and on independent adventures. Our job, as we see it, is to make motorcycle touring more accessible to you.

First of all, thank you for buying this book. In cooperation with a number of generous tour operators, we want to show our appreciation by offering you a discount on some of the tours described in this book. As you read about these enticing trips, notice that some offer a Reader Discount. If you take even one of the tours in the discount program, you'll receive from $25 to as much as $55 off the price of your tour. To qualify for the discount, you must register for these tours before March 31, 1990. Other limitations may apply depending on the individual operator. Contact the tour operator directly.

We're also excited about several future projects at Whitehorse Press. One is to publish a directory of motorcycle touring clubs and associations, both domestic and international. If you are affiliated with a motorcycling club or association and would like to have it included in our directory, please drop us a letter at the address below.

We also plan to publish a series of regional touring guides for motorcyclists interested in touring alone, or in small groups, at home and abroad. The series will be called *Great Motorcycle Routes of the World*.

We want you to help us identify the best routes and describe them for other touring enthusiasts. If you have seen some wonderful scenery, had a good time, and traveled independently, we want to hear about your trip. If you have good photos to augment your story, so much the better. We'll pay for any material we publish.

Rather than sending us a full account of your tour, first write for our Guidelines for Writers. Tell us briefly where you toured and when. Also, we want to hear about tours you are planning for the future. And, please tell your touring friends about this project.

Let's not forget about this book. We need your help to make sure that every annual edition of *Motorcycle Touring: An International Directory* is as complete and accurate as humanly possible. Perhaps you know of another motorcycle tour, a motorcycle rental agency not included in this edition, or another company specializing in motorcycle transport services. We would appreciate hearing about anything you think would be of value to future readers of this Directory. We want feedback about the tours you have taken, to provide a better subjective gauge for future participants. Please send your comments — pro and con. We may be able to use some good photos of your trip if they show the character of an area or a particular tour in an interesting way. If you send pictures, we prefer black and white prints or 35mm slides. Please do not send us your only copy of anything. We cannot return photographs. However, we will send a free copy of the new Directory to anyone whose contributions we use.

We want to learn more about you — what you like and what you want from motorcycling. You can help us by filling out our Reader Survey in the back of this book. In addition, we've provided a Reader Service Card so you may request more information on as many as five tour operators. Just fill out the card and send it to us, and we'll be happy to put the tour operators in touch with you.

As you will soon see, there is a ton of information in this book. The nature of travel tours is volatile; things are changing all the time. While we have tried to be complete and accurate, inevitably there will be omissions and errors of various kinds. Schedules and prices are current as we go to press but are subject to change at any time by each tour operator.

You should use this book to get an idea of the kind of trips offered in various parts of the world. When you have narrowed your interest down to a few tour operators, contact them for current information about dates, prices, and other details. This book is not intended as a substitute for the information you'll receive from the tour operators, but rather as a guide to those you'll want to learn more about.

In presenting matters of price, we use the $ sign alone only for United States currency. For other countries' dollars, such as Australian dollars, we wrote $35 AUS. We kept the same units of currency used by the respective tour operator: Deutsche Marks, New Zealand dollars, and so on. Since these currencies fluctuate relative to the U.S. dollar, we felt it was better not to convert them. Still, to give you some idea of the relative values (as of late January, 1989) here are the conversions for currencies found in this book:

One U.S. dollar = 1.83 DM (German Deutsche Marks)
One U.S. dollar = $1.61 NZ (New Zealand dollars)
One U.S. dollar = $1.19 CAN (Canadian dollars)
One U.S. dollar = $1.08 AUS (Australian dollars)
One U.S. dollar = £0.56 (British pounds)

One German Deutsche Mark = .55 U.S. dollars
One New Zealand dollar = .62 U.S. dollars
One Canadian dollar = .84 U.S. dollars
One Australian dollar = .87 U.S. dollars
One British pound = 1.77 U.S. dollars

It is worth mentioning that many of the tour operators are relatively small enterprises; they are dealing with a small number of tours and a small number of guests. One traveler more or less can make the difference between a tour being canceled, being held, or being overbooked. They (and ultimately you) will benefit greatly by early contact to let them know of your interest in a particular tour. You should book early once you've made your decision. If you wait too long to contact them, a tour may be filled or canceled before you even get to them. They can be very flexible in their planning — scheduling overflow provisions or keeping a tour — if they just have a little advance warning from prospective travelers.

One final note: Don't forget. We want to hear from you, often and on any subject pertaining to motorcycle touring. Write to us or call us at:

> Whitehorse Press
> 154 West Brookline Street
> Boston, Massachusetts 02118
> Phone: 800-842-7077 or 617-482-3350

PREFACE

This is the first year of publication of this Directory; putting it together has been extremely enjoyable. I first thought about publishing this book while my wife and I were on a motorcycling trip to the European Alps in the fall of 1988. It was our first experience motorcycling outside the United States and our first experience traveling with a motorcycling tour group. We were absolutely overwhelmed with the natural beauty of that area and the appropriateness of motorcycling as a way to see it.

Perhaps just as important in forming our impression was the exquisite care that had been taken by the tour operator (Desmond Adventures) to make sure things went smoothly and that we all had a good time. As Tom Desmond put it, "Our job is to do all the work so you can go out and play every day." And that is just the way it was. We met some wonderful people on the tour — Canadians and Americans who toured with the group, as well as Europeans we met along the way. It was the best vacation trip we've ever taken.

When we came home and began looking for information on other tours we might take in the future, there was no single place we could look that contained the information we needed to get a flavor of other available trips. I thought it ought to be easier for more people to learn about this wonderful way to vacation. Being a pretty determined individual, and having spent a good part of my career building computer systems for publishing, the next step seemed obvious to me. You are holding the results in your hand.

My hope is that you will find this book valuable in planning your next motorcycling vacation, and that you will want to go to one of the many exciting places you'll find here. Motorcycling is a wonderful way to see the world, to meet other people and to have the vacation of a lifetime.

> Dan Kennedy
> January, 1989
> Boston

CONTENTS

Tour Operators	1
Guided Tours	**39**
Canada & Alaska	41
U.S.A.	57
Mexico & Caribbean	75
South America	97
Great Britain	107
Western Europe	117
Eastern Europe	161
Mediterranean Area	171
Africa & Near East	191
Asia & Indonesia	223
Australia	247
New Zealand	271
Motorcycle Rental Agencies	283
Motorcycle Shipping Facilities	307
Rides and Rallies in the U.S.	309
International Weather Chart	322
Index	323

TOUR OPERATORS

Here are the people who make it happen; wonderful folks with drive and vision and a love of motorcycles, travel and people. They knit together motorcycle routes, travel arrangements and schedules; handle endless details so their customers are free to enjoy unencumbered pleasures of the road.

Adventure Asia

China Worldwide Travel, Inc.
#603 - 1112 W. Pender Street
Vancouver, B.C.
CANADA V6E 2S1

Contact: Mr. Bill Leininger, Director
Phone: 604-687-7435
FAX: 604-687-2639
Telex (USA): 7601023 RIA UC

Background:

Adventure Asia (AA) is the newly formed adventure tour concern under the parent company of RIA Travels. RIA has 18 years experience in Asian specialty travels. Tom Manton, president and motivational force of RIA/AA, was the first motorcyclist to ride cross-country from Singapore to Britain. He accomplished this in 1957, at 17 years of age, on a Norton 500. To our knowledge this ride has never been duplicated.

In 1985 Manton organized the first motorcycle tour of China. Then, in 1987, he organized the Ride to the Roof of the World expedition to India, Nepal, and Tibet-China. This attempt was eventually halted short of the goal. Rioting in Tibet closed the border to the expedition team and made reaching the base camp of Mount Everest impossible.

RIA/AA has continued to operate package tours in Nepal. For 1989, tours are scheduled to Nepal and northern India, as is a repeat attempt at Tibet and Everest.

Why Asia? Manton and his team have extensive experience in these regions and as true motorcycle enthusiasts, realized that riding these areas is the best way to experience the country and its people. Their motto: Travel the unbeaten path and provide a first class access to adventure.

Services Offered:

- RIA/AA is a tour company specializing in group tours, both standard and customized. No "Fully Inclusive" tours.
- Adventure Asia has an eight-minute video for $25.

Alaska Motorcycle Tours, Inc.

P.O. Box 622
Bothell, WA 98041-0622

Contact:
Mr. Timothy McDonnell, President
Phone: 800-642-6877 (within Washington state: 206-487-3219)
FAX: Not available
Telex: Not available

Background:

Alaska Motorcycle Tours began in 1987 when Tim McDonnell and his brother, Duke McDonnell, a motorcycle fan for 20 years, realized there was an opportunity to show touring enthusiasts a new destination. With 18 years experience in the travel industry and 13 years of living in Fairbanks, Tim's knowledge of traveling in Alaska was extensive. Duke's knowledge of motorcycling and Tim's expertise in travel made a great match.

They wrote and designed their first brochure and mailed it to motorcycling enthusiasts all over the United States. In March of 1987, the reservations started coming in. To fill their need for an office manager with extensive Alaska experience, they hired Vonnie Dahl to maintain and service all of their clients. Then in May they hired Vic Aye as their tour guide. Vic's a delightful man with ten years of motorcycling experience and three years experience driving a motor coach in Alaska.

Alaska Motorcycle Tours' first season in 1988 was a success. In 1989, previous riders will return for a second tour to relive their great Alaska adventure, in addition to many new, excited riders. Alaska is a great land to see by motorcycle.

Services Offered:

- Guided tours of Alaska.
- Alaska Motorcycle Tours can also arrange ocean cruises from Vancouver to Anchorage, or Anchorage to Vancouver, through the Inside Passage.
- Special rates for round trip flights from Washington, Oregon, California, and Arizona.

4 TOUR OPERATORS

Australian-American Mototours

Craig and Kerry Keown

RR1 Box 38
Waitsfield, VT 05673

Contact: Craig or Kerry Keown
Phone: 802-496-3837
FAX: Not available
Telex: Not available

Background:

Kerry Keown, as "dinky di, true blue, and fair dinkum" an Aussie as you can get, grew up on the east coast of Australia. She learned the area as her father, a law officer, was promoted and transferred from post to post. After traveling her native country, she spent five years crisscrossing the world. Her journeys included a year in New Zealand, a couple of years in Europe, and extensive travel in North America. She met her husband, Craig, at Sugarbush Ski Area in Vermont. Craig, an aeronautical engineer from Penn State, had left the business of building space satellites to become a professional skier. His hobby was motorcycling.

They married soon after meeting. The wedding was in Australia. Together, Craig and Kerry started Australian-American Mototours.

They have built up their clientele steadily since 1983. They now run five tours around "Oz" each year; two in the Australian fall (our spring) and three in the Australian spring (our fall). Craig and Kerry are dedicated to making Australia more available to Americans and are proud to be among Australia's most experienced hosts.

When they're not guiding their own personal tours in Australia, you can find them motorcycling in Vermont's summer and skiing in Vermont's winter.

Services Offered:
- Scheduled, guided tours of Australia.
- Customized tours for individuals or groups including a wide range of special interests.
- Motorcycle rentals and purchase/resale arrangements.
- Expert and experienced Australia and New Zealand travel arrangements including air, accommodation, and vehicle hire.

Australian Motorcycle Touring

Geoff Coat

46 Greenways Road
Glen Waverley
Victoria 3150
AUSTRALIA

Contact: Mr. Geoff Coat
Phone: (61) 3-233-8891
FAX: (61) 3-233-1407
Telex: Not available

Agent for U.K./Europe:
Twickers World
22 Church Street
Twickenham TW1 3NW
ENGLAND
Phone: (44) 1-892-7606

Agent for U.S./Canada:
Adventure Center Inc.
5540 College Avenue
Oakland, CA 94618
Phone: 415-654-1879

Background:
Australian Motorcycle Touring is owned and operated by Geoff Coat, who accompanies every tour. Geoff, now in his 40s, retired from the Australian Army as a Major and then went on to become national sales manager for Mercedes Benz buses. Among other talents, Geoff is a qualified watchmaker, has a long-standing love of motorcycles, and is a first-rate motorcycle mechanic (a valuable talent to have in the Australian outback). He has been president of the BMW Motorcycle Club of Victoria. He and his wife, Maxene, have toured extensively in Australia and the United States. Geoff knows Australia well and he knows how to see the best of the country by motorcycle.

Services Offered:
• Organized tours in Australia.

Beach's Motorcycle Adventures, Ltd.

Rob Beach

2763 West River Parkway
P.O. Box 36
Grand Island, NY 14072-0036

Contact: Mr. Robert D. Beach
Mrs. Elizabeth L. Beach
Mr. Rob Beach
Phone: 716-773-4960
FAX: 716-773-0783
Telex: 6854139 GIBCO UW

BEACH'S
MOTORCYCLE
ADVENTURES, LTD.

Background:
Bob and Elizabeth Beach made their first motorcycle tour of the Alps in 1969. After two years of research and planning they began their Alpine Adventure tours in 1972. Starting with two tours each summer (June and September) they soon expanded to three and the next year, because of the demand, conducted four tours. Since 1981 there have been a minimum of four tours annually. Their son, Rob, joined the business in 1978 and is responsible for the design, layout, and operation of all non-Alpine Beach tours and, on occasion, conducts an Alpine Adventure.

In addition to their long-standing Alpine tours the Beaches offer motorcycle tours in Australia, New Zealand, and Great Britain and have also conducted motorcycle tours in South Africa.

The Beaches lead unstructured trips which allow everyone to set his own pace and they encourage the tour members to explore on their own. There are free days where cyclists can mingle with the locals on foot, or tackle a long ride in a unique area.

The tours are all personally conducted by Bob and Elizabeth Beach and/or their son, Rob. Bob has owned 61 motorcycles and has been an active rider for 47 years. He has been awarded the BMW Motorcycle Owners of America (BMW MOA) 250,000-Mile Medallion and has more than 100,000 miles of Alpine riding. A BMW MOA Ambassador, his membership number is #91 and he is past president of the BMW Riders of Western New York.

Both Bob and Rob are members of BMW MOA and BMW Riders Association. Rob teaches sport-bike riding and holds an Expert Road Racing license. After 13 years of street riding Rob is now rapidly approaching the 100,000-mile mark.

TOUR OPERATORS 7

Services Offered:
- Scheduled motorcycle tours to: Australia; Great Britain (England, Scotland, and Wales); the Alps (Switzerland, Italy, Germany, Austria, and Liechtenstein); and New Zealand (North and South Islands).
- Purchase of new motorcycles with delivery in Europe.
- Motorcycle and automobile rentals.
- Customized tours for special groups.
- Shipping of motorcycles to/from Europe.

Bike Tours

Kurt Weidner

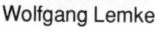

Wolfgang Lemke

Einsiedeleiweg 16
5942 Kirchhundem 4
WEST GERMANY

Contact: Ms. Eveline Veenkamp
Phone: (49) 2764-7824
FAX: Not available
Telex: Not available

Background:
Seven years ago Kurt Weidner fell in love with Australia. He decided to combine his three passions, motorcycling, touring, and organizing in his

8 TOUR OPERATORS

profession. Today, Mr. Weidner's company, Bike Tours, takes explorers all over his beloved Australia throughout the year.

As a traveler, Kurt knows how to see the country and its people best; as a motorcyclist, he knows how to make a journey easier for the rider without intruding on personal freedom. The theme of independence carries over to the trips. Camping out in the wilderness, cooking on the fire, and outdoor life are not always perfectly comfortable but are always unique experiences. Over the years, Kurt developed a group of loyal riders. It was his customers who asked for tours of North America starting last year. Bike Tours is run by Kurt's closest friends while he leads all the Australian tours. The booking office remains in Germany.

Services Offered:
- Scheduled tours in Australia, Bali, northwestern United States, Canadian Rockies, and Alaska.
- Customized tours in those same areas on special request.
- Videos of North American trip (90 minutes, 15 DM) and of Australian tours (180 minutes, 15 DM) are available. For mail delivery, deposit the charge in advance in the company account number 3809653800 at the Volksbank in Littfeld, Branch Number: 46062106.

Bike Tours Unlimited

Nancy and Vic Perniciaro

P.O. Box 1965
San Pedro, CA 90733

Contact: Mr. Vic Perniciaro
Phone: 213-833-2671
FAX: Not available
Telex: Not available

Background:
Bike Tours Unlimited was born in 1984 when Vic Perniciaro and his wife toured Europe on a motorcycle with a German tour operator. The idea for the trip was great – but Vic and his wife had a miserable time, mainly because they felt the trip was not well executed. Vic thought he knew what American riders really wanted in a motorcycle tour of Europe, and that he could do a better job of organizing one than the agency he used. He quit

his position as an operations manager for a large company and set about doing his research for the new business. He rented a motorcycle in Italy and spent many 20-hour days exploring roads, restaurants, cultural and artistic attractions; planning the routes he would use; and the things he would show his guests. Afterward he returned to the U.S. and began making meticulous shipping arrangements with airlines so that his traveling clients could bring their own motorcycles with them to Europe.

By now, Vic has taken dozens of groups through Europe and Mexico. His trips are aimed at people who want an easy paced view of the cultural side of places they visit, rather than those who might want to focus just on riding.

Services Offered:
- Organized tours to Mexico: *Cyclecruise*™.
- Organized tours to Europe: *Piggybike*™.
- Organized tours to Daytona Bike Week and to New Orleans: *Motorail*™.
- Motorcycle shipping services across the U.S. by AMTRAK.

Bosenberg Motorcycle Excursions

Mainzer Straße 54
D-6550 Bad Kreuznach
WEST GERMANY

Contact: Mr. Leon A. Heindel
Phone: (49) 671-67580
FAX: Not available
Telex: Not available

U.S. Agent:	Around the Globe Travel, Ltd.
1417 North Wauwatosa Avenue
Milwaukee, WI 53213

Contact: Mr. Walt Weber
Phone: 800-234-4037 or
414-257-0199 (in Wisconsin or Canada)

Background:
Bosenberg specializes in a heady combination of a meticulous, all-inclusive land package and travel in some of the best wine and Alpine regions in Europe. Their tours feature the good life – excellent motorcy-

cling, small groups of seven or eight motorcycles, superb dining, and the guidance of multilingual leaders who love the sport and know the area.

The Nahe region in Germany produces the effervescent Riesling wines. In deference to their environment, Bosenberg tours begin and end at Bad Kreuznach, West Germany with opportunity for wine tastings and a river cruise on the Rhine.

Leon A. Heindel, owner-coordinator, named the company for a beautiful hill near Bad Kreuznach. Tours began in 1988.

Roland Huske is the resident wine expert. When he isn't touring on his Moto Guzzi, he earns his living as a master photographer. Gerhard Wilk is the mountain expert with over 15 years experience crisscrossing the Alpine ranges and passes looking for the perfect curve.

These leaders smooth out the details of travel, guide you to the most tantalizing routes, and suggest ways to satisfy your individual needs on tour. Before departure, you receive a complete information packet containing high quality maps, detailed routes, descriptive regional brochures, and hotel addresses and telephone numbers. All details of the land package are handled in the same thorough fashion.

Services Offered:
- Scheduled tours in the Alps, Austria, and the French/Alsace-German wine regions.
- Assistance with air travel arrangements, air shipment of your own motorcycle, car rentals for friends and family, and lodging for self-guided tours and extended stays through their U.S. agent.
- Full rental services for BMW motorcycles from Frankfurt and Munich, West Germany.

California MotoTours

Kjell and Maria Westberg, Lars Bjorkvist

2170 Avenida de la Playa #B
La Jolla, CA 92037

Booking Agent:
Ms. Izabella Miram, Terra Tours
Phone: 800-444-9554 or
619-454-9551
FAX: 619-454-3549
Telex: 495-0609

Background:

California MotoTours was formed by Kjell and Maria Westberg and Lars Bjorkvist to promote the best tours possible for an international clientele to tour the western United States.

Kjell and Lars come from Sweden; Maria is a native Californian. Kjell and Lars have always been avid motorcyclists, having spent their vacations touring through the European countries to Spain to enjoy a few weeks of sunshine. Together they bring many years of riding experience to the company, and many friends throughout Europe now come to ride with them.

Maria is also an avid rider who has lived and worked throughout Europe and the Middle East for a number of years. She also brings many motorcyclist friends from other countries to experience the fabulous roads and scenery of the West. Maria, who knows the West intimately, has put together the best highlights of the West for the motorcycle touring enthusiast.

The three directors bring a most interesting personality to the company, giving the people who join them an enlightening experience. Personalized service, plus well planned and executed itineraries, bring riders from all countries back to join them again and again.

For Kjell, Lars, and Maria, their satisfaction comes from the camaraderie that is formed between people who come from different countries. "It's something you cannot make happen," says Maria. "But each time a group comes together, special things happen. There are always plans for a reunion in Europe or back in the U.S. It's this special feel that sets our pace and gives the personality people look for."

California MotoTours is evolving rapidly now. They expect to have soon a new base of operations in southern Colorado. From that facility, they will be within one day's ride of many great national attractions: Zion National Park; Bryce National Park; Lake Powell; Monument Valley; Grand Canyon; Mesa Verde National Park; Taos and Santa Fe, New Mexico; Canyon De Chelly; and Indian pueblos and ruins.

Services Offered:

- Organized tours in California and southwestern United States.
- Customized tours in southwestern United States.
- Motorcycle rentals connected with their tours and also to riders not connected with the tours. See the separate listing under Motorcycle Rentals.

Coach House Tours

Jack Evans

70 Coolidge Street
Ashland, OR 97520

Contact: Mr. Jack Evans
Phone: 503-482-2257
FAX: Not available
Telex: Not available

Background:
Jack Evans, a youthful 41 and the owner of Coach House Tours, originated from Philadelphia, graduated from Syracuse University with a degree in journalism, and hopes to freelance in the future. Jack started reading *Sports Cars Illustrated* and *Cycle World* in 1960 and has a lifelong love of motorsports, both two- and four-wheeled variety.

In 1981, after working for two airlines, Jack and his wife, Pam, opened the Coach House Bed & Breakfast Inn as well as Coach House Tours. Jack started the Isle of Man Insiders Tour from his love for Britain and Ireland, especially the Isle of Man. The island itself is breathtaking, and the Tourist Trophy races each June around the challenging 37 miles of open roads and city streets are unique in all bikedom. The T.T., having started in 1907, is the world's oldest motor racing fixture, bar none. Jack's stable of bikes includes a BSA Gold Star, Triumph Bonneville, Norton, Yamaha XS650, and a Triumph Spitfire four-wheeler (for when it snows). He loves Celtic music, Guinness Stout, and lively conversation.

Services Offered:
- Scheduled, guided tour to Britain and the Isle of Man.
- Jack runs a bed and breakfast inn in Ashland Oregon. He loves hosting people and showing off his vintage British bikes.

Desmond Adventures, Inc.

Karin Millette, Tom Desmond, Randy

1280 South Williams Street
Denver, CO 80210

Contact: Mr. Thomas E. Desmond
Phone: 303-733-9248
FAX: Not available
Telex: Not available

The AlpenTour

Background:

Tom Desmond began serious motorcycling in the late sixties. He spent time touring all over the United States and Canada on a variety of different motorcycles. After selling his business in 1978, he traveled extensively throughout the world and then moved to Europe in 1979 to see the Continent. He picked up a motorcycle in Europe in the spring of 1979. Feeling there was no motorcycling anywhere in the world that compared to the Alps, he decided to share his experiences with his motorcycling friends at home. In August 1979, he conducted the first AlpenTour™. Years of research in the Alps have paid off. He takes great pride in showing his charges the most interesting spots to see and to ride. There are plenty of both in Europe and Tom seems to know most of them. In the 1988 season alone, some 350 people joined Tom for a spin through the Alps. They just keep coming back.

Recently, Tom and the AlpenTour™ have enjoyed an explosion of press coverage heaping praise on virtually every aspect of his operations, stressing his careful planning, professional execution, attention to detail, and thorough knowledge of the area. (See *Rider,* January 1988; *Motorcyclist,* January 1989; *BMW Owners News,* June 1988; *BMW Owners News,* February 1989.)

Karin Millette, Director of European Operations for the AlpenTour™, has lived and traveled extensively throughout western and eastern Europe on and off for seven years. She was raised in Munich, West Germany and

Colorado and was therefore able simultaneously to pursue her love of foreign culture, history, and the mountains. Karin received a degree in International Studies from the University of Colorado while ski racing and instructing, tutoring German, and working for a local paper as a writer and photographer. After studying at the University of Regensburg in West Germany for one year she spent two months at the Dante Alighieri Italian Language Institute in Rome, thereby solidifying her fluency in several languages.

Her first introduction to motorcycling came in 1978 as she attended the annual Pike's Peak New Year's motorcycle hill climb. She became hooked and bought her first bike that spring: a 350cc Yamaha. That summer she learned all the great motorcycling roads in the Rockies.

As acting tour guide for the AlpenTour™, Karin has since developed a taste for the BMW K75S and Kawasaki Concours but she rides everything from the Suzuki Katana 600 to the Yamaha FJ1200. Karin oversees all hotel relations and is responsible for their customers' satisfaction with all aspects of the tour. She loves her work, especially the interaction it affords with fellow adventurers like herself.

Services Offered:
• Scheduled tours to Switzerland, Austria, Italy, Germany, and France.

Tom Desmond hosting his daily AlpenTour™ trip review meeting

TOUR OPERATORS 15

Edelweiss Bike Travel

Coral and Werner Wachter with aspirant travelers

Steinreichweg 1
A-6414 Mieming
AUSTRIA

Contact: Mr. Werner Wachter
Phone: (43) 05264/5690
FAX: (43) 05264/58533
Telex: 534158 (rkmiem)

U.S. Agent:

Armonk Travel
146 Bedford Road
Armonk, NY 10504

Contact: Ms. Linda Rosenbaum
Phone: 800-255-7451 or 914-273-8880

Background:

Werner Wachter does not take no for an answer. When he contacted Intourist about a motorcycle tour of the U.S.S.R., they replied that it was impossible. Werner began intense negotiations with the huge agency responsible for all tourism in the Soviet Union to prove that (a) an organized motorcycle tour has nothing to do with Marlon Brando's tour of Hollister, California, and (b) these tours bring in real Western money. This year Edelweiss Bike Travel features three tours of the Soviet Union: *Soviet Union Tour '89, First Motorcycle Tour, Caucasus,* and the *Baltic Tour.*

Werner is a determined and resourceful man. Undoubtedly, that is why he is one of the world's leaders in organizing guided motorcycle tours.

Ten years ago, he left his career as a successful Austrian businessman to start Edelweiss Bike Travel. He began with the usual European jaunts: the

16 TOUR OPERATORS

Alps, the Mediterranean, the Isle of Man. Since then, Edelweiss has expanded their world and developed a growing number of loyal clients.

Werner and Coral Wachter, his lovely English wife, present a program that offers the uninhibited freedom to ride in a safe and hassle-free tour. Edelweiss strives for the best routes, the small scenic roads, the unexpected vista, and the hidden shops.

Services Offered:
- Scheduled tours in Europe, the U.S.S.R., Asia, and North America.

Explo-Tours

Joseph Geltl (center), with guides Peter and Anneliese

Arnulfstraße 134
8000 Munich 19
WEST GERMANY

Contact: Mr. Josef Geltl
Phone: (49) 089-16-07-89
FAX: Not available
Telex: 1631 btxd/089161716 1+

Background:
Joseph Geltl, 37, originally planned to become a teacher of physics and geography. However, on summer holidays he began to explore the countries around the Mediterranean Sea including the Near East and Morocco. Morocco lead him to the Sahara desert where his real passion took hold. He combined his enthusiasm for motorcycling with his love of the desert and Africa. Fortunately and happily, he married a woman who shares his enthusiasm for Africa.

Six years ago he founded Explo-Tours and began organizing motorcycle tours through Africa. Mr. Geltl's first clients were geography and geology student groups. His tours are designed for hardy adventurers with enduro cycle experience.

Services Offered:
- Scheduled enduro tours of Northern and Central Africa.
- Motorcycle rentals for members of tours.

Fritz Horvarth Trial-Tours

Weinbergstraße 15
7704 Gailingen
WEST GERMANY

Contact: Mr. Fritz Horvarth
Phone: (49) 07734/1241 (after 8 p.m. local time)
FAX: Not available
Telex: Not available

Background:
Mr. Horvarth organizes courses in off-road driving for beginners as well as advanced drivers. He is an expert trial-rider, OMK vice champion 1980. He offers trial tours in France, Spain, Portugal, Italy, and the Canary Islands throughout the year. These trips are fun and help customers improve, or learn, enduro and trial skills. He provides Honda TLR 250 four-stroke trial machines.

Prices include lodging, breakfasts and dinners, trial motorcycles with servicing, trial training, and guided trial tours. Protective clothing is available for a small fee.

Below are the dates of his tours in France, Scotland, and Spain:

Dates and Prices:
- Ardeche, France
  April 5 through April 7, 1989 .... 500 DM
- Vogesen, France
  April 22 through April 23, 1989 .... 250 DM
- Scotland
  May 1 through May 6, 1989 .... 1,350 DM
- Haut-Provence, France
  May 29 through June 6, 1989 .... 870 DM
  June 5 through June 9, 1989 .... 870 DM
  June 26 through June 30, 1989 .... 870 DM
  July 3 through July 7, 1989 .... 870 DM
  July 24 through July 28, 1989 .... 870 DM
  July 31 through August 8, 1989 .... 870 DM
- Pyrenees, Spain
  August 8 through September 1, 1989 .... 950 DM
  September 4 through September 8, 1989 .... 950 DM
- Vosges Mountains, France
  Weekend dates available .... 250 DM

Great Motorcycle Adventures

Les French

8241 Heartfield Lane
Beaumont, TX 77706

Contact: Mr. Les "Gringo" French
Phone: 800-642-3933 (within Texas: 409-866-7891)
FAX: 409-832-1474
Telex: Not available

Background:

"Gringo" has been exploring Mexico and motorcycling since he was 13 years old. Prior to forming Great Motorcycle Adventures Gringo owned and operated an adventure tour company specializing in archaeological and photographic expeditions throughout Mexico and Central America. "I've been fortunate enough to have introduced hundreds of people to the beautiful and varied cultures of Mexico," Les says.

"Our guests are surprised to find that Mexico is not a big desert, but rather a wonderfully diverse country of snowcapped mountains, fertile valleys, vast savannas, breathtaking gorges, and lush tropical seashores housing many different cultures," he says.

Les has spent a good part of his life having fun with adventure activities: he's a certified sky diver, a certified scuba diver, a certified airplane pilot, a certified boat captain (to 300 tons), an experienced motorcyclist (touring, hill climbing, trail riding, drag racing, and enduro racing), and auto enthusiast (drag racing, quarter midgets, stock cars). And if that weren't enough, he also has spent a good deal of time studying Meso-American archaeology, specializing in the Mayan civilization. He's sure to be a fascinating guide.

Services Offered:
- Organized guided tours and trail rides through Mexico.
- Gringo will also arrange custom rides for groups.
- Motorcycle rentals for his trail riding guests.

mhs Motorradtouren GmbH

Hans-Urmiller-Ring 59
D-8190 Wolfratshausen
WEST GERMANY

Contact: Mr. Herbert Schellhorn
Phone: (49) 81 71 12 38
FAX: Not Available
Telex: Not Available

Background:

mhs Motorradtouren was founded in 1987 by Herbert and Wolfgang Schellhorn. Wolfgang has been a Suzuki dealer for more than ten years in Wolfratshausen, near Munich.

Herbert is a car mechanic with experience also in motorcycle repairs. After his apprenticeship he studied business and engineering at the high school in Munich. Starting in 1984, in addition to his studies, Herbert worked as a tour guide for a large company organizing motorcycle trips. During that time he toured Austria, Switzerland, France, Italy, and Kenya. In 1987, he decided to start his own company. Based on his good reputation as a guide, many previous customers participated in the new mhs Motorradtouren trips. As a result of the careful preparation and follow-through which are hallmarks of every mhs Motorradtouren trip, their guests keep coming back for more.

They are very selective about their tour guides. Each must speak several languages, he must be an experienced motorcyclist and mechanic, he must be smart and polite, and he must be an expert on the region of the tour he's leading.

mhs Motorradtouren's specialty is their complete program covering the many interesting parts of Italy. Mr. Schellhorn is a specialist in that area. He not only knows the land and its people, he knows the roads, the churches, the sights, hotels, restaurants, and a lot more.

Mr. Schellhorn takes pride in perfect preparation and organization of tours before leaving; the insurance package; the excellent choice of routes; and of course, the knowledgeable and concerned direction of their experienced leaders.

Services Offered:
- Scheduled motorcycle tours to: the Alps; Italy; Austria; Germany; Great Britain (England, Wales, and Scotland); Luxembourg; the Ardennes; Turkey; and Canada.
- Motorcycle rentals to tour participants.
- Passenger Service. On all the tours which use an accompanying club bus (for transporting luggage), nine seats are available for companions who

are not riding motorcycles and want to go along. It's comfortable for both of you, without additional charge on the passenger travel price.
- Customized motorcycle trips for companies, clubs, and associations from five to fifty persons.
- Additional hotel and transportation reservations for tourers, before and after scheduled tours.

Motorrad-Reisen

Postfach 44 01 48
D-8000 Munich 44
WEST GERMANY

Contact: Mr. Hermann Weil
Phone: (49) 89 39 57 68
FAX: (49) 89 34 48 32
Telex: 5218511

U.S. Agent:

Motorrad-Reisen
P.O. Box 591
Oconomowoc, WI 53066

Contact: Ms. Jean Fish
Phone: 414-567-7548

Background:

Hermann Weil loves motorcycling and enjoys introducing people to natural and cultural resources – an unbeatable combination for the owner of a motorcycle touring agency. Even though the variety and scope of Motorrad-Reisen demands that Mr. Weil spends time off the road negotiating new programs, he still prefers tour guiding to any other activity.

Motorrad-Reisen (M-R) offers enough variety to suit the person who wants a few days of recreation in connection with a business trip, as well as a couple who plan an extended holiday. M-R specializes in a variety of tours illuminating the Alpine region and also offers other trips to China, Turkey, Kenya, and Tenerife.

Tours feature relaxed riding with a bilingual guide. More experience, more adventure, and more fun are the leading principles of Mr. Weil's motorcycle tours. Guides are anxious to introduce aspects of the culture not available to most tourists and respond to individual requests. Safety is a primary concern for all M-R tours. All touring managers carry a two-way radio to help in emergencies.

Each tour features cultural aspects. Cuisine and environment are selected with "heart and mind and are always in the traditions of the culture," according to Mr. Weil.

Services Offered:
- Scheduled tours to Austria, the Alpine region, Germany, Italy, France, Tenerife (Canary Islands), Kenya, Central Africa, U.S.A., China, and Turkey.
- Customized tours out of Munich and in the U.S.A.
- Motorcycle rentals in conjunction with tours and for those who want to tour on their own. Rental includes collision insurance on the motorcycle with $400 deductible, riding suit, luggage case, and spare parts.
- Purchase of BMW motorcycles for delivery in Munich.
- Rental of accessories and cycle wear.
- A full spectrum of travel services including arrangements for shipping motorcycles, booking flights, and making other land arrangements in conjunction with tours.

Motorrad Spaett, KG

Rüdesheimerstraße, 9
8000 Munich 21
WEST GERMANY

Contact: Mr. Paul Spaett
Phone: (49) 089-57937-38
FAX: (49) 089-57017-69
Telex: 5216823 mosp

Background:
Motorrad Spaett is one of the oldest and largest Honda and Yamaha motorcycle dealers in Germany. The company was founded in 1951 by Josef Spaett, the father of Motorrad Spaett's two chiefs, Peter and Paul. In the beginning it was a two-man company. Now, after 38 years, they have about 50 employees. In 1963 they sold their first new Honda, and in 1965 their first Yamaha. For a few years Kawasaki and Suzuki were also listed in their program. Since 1969 they have imported motorcycles on their own. Today, they are the biggest shop in Bavaria, and their spare parts department is the biggest in Germany.

Peter, 46, and Paul, 42, run the business now. They have both visited the United States and Canada several times. Both are married and have children interested in motorcycles. Peter, the father of three boys aged nine to thirteen, stays close to the office and is also an expert with motorcycle technicalities. He took part in the first motorcycle tour to China in 1984. Paul is the more practical part of this team, dealing with customers and helping the service department. He holds the title of master in automotive engineering for motorcycles. Paul is the one who guided the first tour to Turkey; both of his sons (10 and 12 years old) accompanied him.

Services Offered:
- Scheduled tours to Turkey since 1988.
- Tours through Europe during the season.
- Sales and service of new and used motorcycles and accessories, clothing.
- Motorcycle rentals.

Pancho Villa Moto-Tours

9437 E.B. Taulbee
El Paso, TX 79924

Contact: Mr. Skip Mascorro
Phone: 915-757-3032
FAX: 915-562-1505
Telex: Not available

Background:
Pancho Villa Moto-Tours (PVMT) began modestly in 1981 when Skip Mascorro ran his first motorcycle tour. At that time, he was president of Caravanas Voyagers, a large recreational vehicle travel firm running as many as 60 caravans to Mexico each season. After that first trip in 1981, motorcycle touring began to occupy more and more of Skip's time and eventually he left Caravanas to spend full time on motorcycling.

Today, Pancho Villa Moto-Tours runs a wide variety of tours south of the border in Mexico and New Zealand, including a number of customized tours for motorcycling clubs. In 1988 he recruited Graeme Crosby, world class road race champion and winner of Daytona, Isle of Man, and numerous Grand Prix races, to head up a tour of the western U.S. by a group from New Zealand. Skip's tours have generated tremendous loyalty, bringing many riders back four or more times to travel with him. By all accounts, Skip is a colorful character and a delight to ride with.

Services Offered:
- Scheduled tours to Mexico and New Zealand.

- Customized tours specially designed for riding clubs and touring organizations.
- Motorcycle rentals for participants of any PVMT Mexico or U.S.A. tour.
- Motorcycle rentals available out of El Paso, Texas for individual travelers.
- Slide presentations for clubs, rallies, and motorcycle functions.
- Volume sales of used motorcycles to foreign markets, including shipping.
- Mexico motorcycle insurance for tour participants.
- Preparation of necessary visas and vehicle documents for entry to Mexico interior.

Prima Klima Reisen GmbH

Tour guide Peter Schmidt

Hohenstaufenstraße 69
1000 Berlin 30
WEST GERMANY

Contact: Mr. Peter Schmidt
Phone: (49) 030 216 10 82/83
FAX: Not Available
Telex: 186381 pkr d

Background:

Prima Klima Reisen (PKR) was founded by four friends in 1983. They started as non-professional adventurers, individual travelers, coach drivers, and sport trainers. In the intervening years, their business has grown so that PKR now owns seven tour buses, with which they offer various trips through Europe for young people. They also rent luxury tour buses for traveling bands and movie production crews.

Their specialty is individualized tours, such as enduro tours in Cyprus, bus trips through India, and jeep trips through Venezuela and Morocco. They also are planning a tour through India with '50s style Royal Enfield Silver Bullet 350cc bikes (made in India).

24 TOUR OPERATORS

Peter Schmidt, responsible guide for the Cyprus motorcycle program, has been with PKR since 1985. He studied education, psychology, and art at the Free University of Berlin and has worked several years as a press photographer, coach driver, and tour guide in many European countries.

Services Offered:
- Scheduled motorcycle tours to Cyprus and India.
- Surfboard and equipment rental, all watersports (diving, water skiing).
- Self-catering guest houses.
- Informal hotels.
- Motorcycle rentals.
- Coach tours through Europe and India.
- Jeep tours through Venezuela and Morocco.
- Guided walks.

Rocky Mountain Moto Tours Ltd.

Dave Blackwood (left) and Nick Moar

Box 7152 Stn. E
Calgary, Alberta T3C 3M1
CANADA

Contact: Mr. Nicholas Moar
Phone: 403-244-6939
FAX: 403-229-2788
Telex: 03-821172

Background:
Rocky Mountain Moto Tours began in 1987 as most adventure companies start: Nick Moar and David Blackwood enjoyed motorcycling so much, they decided to commit themselves to it one hundred percent. Not just for their guests' enjoyment, they do this for their own pleasure as well.

Nick Moar spent most of the seventies motorcycling around Australia and North America. If there was a back way to get there, he found it. After completing his education, Nick worked for a helicopter skiing company in the rugged mountains of British Columbia. It was there he realized how much people from other places wanted to experience the rugged and unspoiled beauty of western Canada.

Lifelong friend David Blackwood was a fellow motorcycle enthusiast. He found time to head up monthly tours of the northwestern United States and Canada while following the Gran Prix motorcycling circuit. They formed a natural partnership.

They cater to an international clientele and riders of various styles and ages. Their adventure holidays explore some of the most diverse geography in North America.

Services Offered:
- Scheduled, all-inclusive seven-day tours of Alberta and British Columbia.

Sahara Cross

Jürgen Greif

Landfridstraße 6
7910 Neu-Ulm 4
WEST GERMANY

Contact: Mr. Jürgen Greif
Phone: (49) 07307-31445
FAX: Not available
Telex: Not available

Background:
Jürgen Greif, the founder of Sahara Cross, traveled to Morocco during the summer of 1978 and fell in love with the country. To fulfill his desire to learn more about that part of the world, Jürgen and his wife returned later and traveled for a full year across Kenya, Egypt, and the Sudan. On that trip, he learned much about the country, where to go, and things to do. He decided then that he wanted to share his experience with other adventure travelers. A passionate motorcyclist, Jürgen began formulating plans for a motorcycle touring company. He observed there were a number of other motorcycle touring companies with whom he would be com-

peting. So, to distinguish his tours, he decided to focus on the Sahara, an area he knows and loves.

Since the inception of Sahara Cross in 1985, he has offered six tours each year, with never a serious accident or negative incident. In spite of his attention to safety, his tours maintain an element of adventure, often trying new routes and destinations. At this time Sahara Cross is the only motorcycle tour operator working in Egypt.

Services Offered:
- Organized tours to Egypt.
- Organized tours to the Sinai.

Smoky Mountain Motorcycle Vacations

Gary Dagiel

200 Upper Herron Cove Road
Weaverville, NC 28787

Contact: Mr. Gary Dagiel
Phone: 704-658-0239 weekday evenings
FAX: Not available
Telex: Not available

Background:

Gary Dagiel knows motorcycles from the ground up, having worked his way through college as a motorcycle mechanic in Bowling Green, Ohio. He also knows the beautiful motorcycle routes in the Smoky Mountains. Seven years ago, Gary and his wife made a major lifestyle change as they moved from Pennsylvania to North Carolina, an area they consider paradise, to start their own business. They now run Smoky Mountain Plantscapes, Inc. from their 42-acre farm. During that time, Gary has covered over 25,000 miles riding in that magnificent part of our country.

The inspiration for Smoky Mountain Motorcycle Vacations came during a spirit-cleansing sunset ride to Craggy Gardens, just up the Blue Ridge Parkway from the Dagiels' home. Gary decided right then he wanted to share his riding experience with other motorcycle travelers. He has been running tours through the Smoky Mountains since 1987.

Services Offered:
• Guided tour of the Smoky Mountains.

South Pacific Motorcycle Tours Ltd.

	18 King Edward St. P.O. Box 158 Masterton NEW ZEALAND Contact: Glen and Maureen Bull Phone: (64) 59-84490
Reservations and information:	A.A. Travel (Wairarapa) Ltd. P.O. Box 457 Masterton, NEW ZEALAND Phone: (64) 59-82222 FAX: (64) 59-82485 Telex: NZ 3982
U.S. Agent:	New Zealand Central Reservations Office 6033 W. Century Blvd., Suite 1270 Los Angeles, CA 90045 Phone: 800-351-2323 (Outside California) 800-351-2317 (Within California) FAX: 213-215-9705

Background:
Glen and Maureen Bull have been actively involved in motorcycling for over 35 years. Glen is a founding member of the Wairarapa Motor Cycle Club. He has ridden extensively overseas. Maureen is a noted motorcycle author. Together, they bring a personalized approach to tour operation that is hard to beat. The Bulls host a home-cooked meal to welcome and to say farewell to tour members. Seeing their large collection of vintage motorcycles is part of the fun.

Glen and Maureen are extremely flexible. Since New Zealand has relatively mild weather, they tour year-round. Their regular tour is 14 days. They can adapt the tour to specific groups or rent Gold Wings to individuals. They will arrange a one, two or three week tour and are happy to provide maps and tour suggestions.

Services Offered:
• Scheduled tour of New Zealand.
• Customized tours for specific groups.
• Motorcycle rentals for those riders wishing to tour on their own.

Southern Skies Travel

Jan and Terry Bryant

P.O. Box 109
Mornington, Victoria 3931
AUSTRALIA

Contact:
Ms. Liz Sannen (Booking Agent)
Phone: (61) 59 751 505
FAX: (61) 59 751 599
Telex: Not Available

Background:
Southern Skies Travel is run by Terry and Jan Bryant who have 15 years experience in the motorcycle industry as Honda and Suzuki dealers in an outer Melbourne suburb. They traveled the world extensively. This inevitably hooked them on motorcycle touring so they now combine pleasure with business by running tours full-time. In the Australian summer, between November 1 and April 30, they offer two different tours in Victoria and one in Tasmania. Any of these can be combined. Between May 1 and October 31, the tours switch to the outback of South Australia and western New South Wales. Terry would like to run these tours all year, but the summer heat in the outback makes this impractical for comfortable touring.

Terry is as close to the genuine Aussie as it is possible to find and he'll have riders saying "G'day" to strangers in nothing flat. Like all Aussies he's open and friendly, and treats everyone as an equal. He has a great love of the countryside and his knowledge of the highways and byways as well as the Australian bush is encyclopedic.

Services Offered:
- Standard escorted tours all year.
- Customized tours.
- All land arrangements, including pre- and post-motorcycle tour arrangements, accommodation, and transport.

Te Waipounamu Motorcycle Tours

P.O. Box 673
Christchurch
NEW ZEALAND

Contact: Mr. John Rains
Phone: (64) 03 794 320 or (64) 03 427 503
FAX: (64) 03 842 345
Telex: Not available

Booking Agent: Starquest World Tours
1120-87 Avenue S.W.
Calgary, Alberta T2V 0W1
CANADA
Phone: 403-252-4641
FAX: 403-229-2788

Booking Agent: Schnieder Reisen
Schomburgst 120
2000 Hamburg 50
WEST GERMANY
Phone: (49) 40 38 02 06 33
FAX: (49) 40 38 89 65

Booking Agent: Mr. Volker Lenzner
TransCyclist International
CPO Box 2064
Tokyo, 100-91
JAPAN
Phone: (81) 3-402-5385
FAX: (81) 3-402-5358

Reference Information:	Te Wai Tours West
Rt. 1, Box 130
Carmel Highlands, CA 93923

Contact: Mr. Al Jesse
Phone: 408-624-0829
FAX 408-646-5365

Background:

John and Maria Rains both speak the native language of Maori and between them have university degrees in New Zealand flora and fauna. They have lived in every corner of the country. John has vast experience motorcycling around New Zealand, and enjoys showing visitors his beautiful country.

In 1985 John and Maria established Te Waipounamu, named after the Maori word for the Southern Island of New Zealand. Translated, it means "greenstone water", and to the Maori it was the most valuable object they possessed. John and Maria feel the same way about their island home.

It is a constant source of amusement to his guests that John is always running into someone he knows, or vice versa, wherever he goes in New Zealand.

They provide friendly assistance to their groups and individual travelers.

Services Offered:

- Guided tours of New Zealand.
- Motorcycle rentals, in conjunction with guided tours and also for independent use.
- Rental of motorcycling helmets, gloves, and rain suits.
- A short video showing what to expect regarding motorcycles, scenery, and general information is available from Starquest World Tours. Please send $5 to cover postage.

Team Aventura

Karlsebene 2
8924 Steingaden
WEST GERMANY

Contact: Mr. Christoph del Bondio
Phone: (49) 08862-6161 or
(49) 08807-8360
FAX: Not available
Telex: Not available

Background:
Team Aventura is a new touring organization, founded in 1987 by Christoph del Bondio. Mr. del Bondio organizes two-week tours to Peru and Turkey, including motorcycle rental. (Refer to separate tour listings.)

In 1989, Team Aventura also will conduct tours in the Alps and the Sahara (North Africa). Because we learned of these tours only days before our press date, we are including some very brief information for them below. We hope to have more complete coverage of Team Aventura next year.

Dates and Prices:
The Alps: Difficult Roads! (does not include motorcycle rental):
- July 30 through August 9, 1989 .... $800
- August 13 through August 23, 1989 .... $800
- August 27 through September 6, 1989 .... $800

Sahara (does not include motorcycle rental):
- November 25 through December 17, 1989 .... $1,700
- December 31 through January 21, 1990 .... $1,700

Services Offered:
- Tours to Peru, West Turkey, East Turkey, the Alps, and the Sahara (North Africa).
- Motorcycle rentals are included with all tours, except to the Alps and Sahara.

Tee Mill Tours Ltd.

Steve Millard, Julie Norris, Reg Thomas

56 Tooting High Street
London SW17 0RN
ENGLAND

Contact: Mr. Reg Thomas
Phone: (44) 01-767-8737 (24 hours)
FAX: (44) 01-682-0138
Telex: 945307 (TEEMIL G)

Background:
The company was formed 18 years ago by Reg Thomas and Steve Millard. It was founded to organize tours for motorsport events worldwide, such as Grand Prix races. Activities for touring riders were introduced in 1983; since then the company has built a sound reputation in the services it provides. The company's ultimate aim is to provide worldwide services for the touring motorcyclist.

Services Offered:
- Guided motorcycle tours of U.S.A. and Canada, Africa, and Thailand.
- Motorcycle rentals in: New York, Los Angeles, Miami, and Vancouver.
- Personal motorcycle airfreight to the continent of North America for U.K. and European touring riders.
- Insurance for riders.

Tours, S.R.L.

VENEZUELA EN MOTOCICLETA
Venezuela on bike

Edif. Res. Los Sauces
Entrada A, Piso 8, Apto. 1
Valencia
VENEZUELA

Contact:
Mr. Werner Glode or Mr. Martin Glode
Phone: (58) 41-213007 (office) or (58) 41-213752 (home)
FAX: (58) 41-342950
Telex: (58) 41-45116

U.S. Reference:
Mr. Karl Raedisch
Phone: 215-675-8094

Background:

Tours, S.R.L. was established in 1983 by Werner Glode and his two sons with the objective of showing fabulous Venezuela to motorcyclists. Mr. Glode moved to Venezuela in 1954 and set up a private accounting practice there. He first got interested in motorcycles about ten years ago, when one of his potential clients gave him a BMW 60/5 with 1800 km on it as a gift. His three sons immediately supported his interest and explored the many great motorcycle treks in Venezuela with him. His middle son Martin, 24, recently graduated from the University of Carabobo with their first group of bilingual tourist guides. Martin plans to develop Tours S.R.L. further.

Because the tours are an extension of their own hobby, riding and touring, the Glodes restrict each tour to a maximum of six motorcycles. Mr. Glode says that accompanying visitors is a hobby for him and claims not to be a professional tour operator.

Services Offered:

- Scheduled tours to Venezuela.
- Customized tours: upon request during their rainy season (May through September), into areas not covered by their formal tour programs.
- Motorcycle rentals (Yamaha RD 350 only) to those riders wishing to tour on their own; full-value security deposit required. For all standard and customized tours the following security deposits are required: Yamaha RD 350, $250; BMW R100 and Honda GL 1000, $500.

TransCyclist International

CPO Box 2064
Tokyo, 100-91
JAPAN

Contact: Mr. Volker Lenzner, Chairman
Phone: (81) 3-402-5385
FAX: (81) 3-402-5358
Telex: Not available

Volker Lenzner

Background:
Headquartered in Tokyo, TransCyclist International (TC) started in 1979 as a mail box touring club for the exchange of information and mutual aid among motorcycle travelers. It is a non-profit motor travel organization based on the international motorcycle traveling experience of its founder, Volker Lenzner. TC strives to encourage better mutual understanding among people of the world through travel, with motorcycle travel being the form allowing the greatest freedom of expression. Volker Lenzner is a West German who has worked and traveled in West Germany, South Africa, Australia, the Pacific, and Japan.

Services Offered:
- TransCyclist offers organized, guided, adventure tours, usually involving other outdoor activities (river rafting, horseback riding, etc.) to Australia, Canada, China, Japan, New Zealand, Venezuela, South Africa, Italy, Spain, West Germany, Israel, North Africa, Peru, Mexico, and the U.S.
- Motorcycle rentals, buy/sellback arrangements, purchases, shipping, exchanges.
- Video workshops for touring and other topics.

- Yearbook, newsletter.
- Club aid programs for long-distance motorcycle travelers.
- International Club Shop for the exchange (or purchase) of rare models, parts, etc. through TC's worldwide network.

Special Note: All tour customers are automatically entitled to full membership/insider-status in the TC organization and to benefits from its worldwide programs. When requesting information, TC asks that you send a self-addressed, stamped envelope and one international reply coupon (available from the post office).

Von Thielmann Tours

Sabine von Thielmann

Michael von Thielmann

P.O. Box 87764
San Diego, CA 92138

Contact: Ms. Gina Guzzardo
Phone: 619-463-7788 or
619-291-7057
FAX: 619-291-4630
Telex: 910 335 1607 MESA SERV SDG

Background:

Von Thielmann Tours was established in 1957. Originally founded in Munich, Germany, the headquarters of the tour company is now in San Diego, California.

Even though Von Thielmann Tours organizes and offers various types of special interest tours, including a complete travel service, their specialty has always been motorcycle tours.

Von Thielmann Tours has successfully conducted motorcycle tours in more than thirty countries throughout the world. Many of the tours have been guided personally by the president of the company, Michael von Thielmann. In 1984, he was the world's first tour operator to receive official permission to operate motorcycle tours in the People's Republic of China on a regular basis. In 1988 the Soviet Union granted Mr. von Thielmann permission to bring motorcyclists to the Soviet Union. Since 1983, he has added tours of New Zealand to the program. European Alpine countries are included in the most popular tours, but specific destinations change from year to year because of the high number of tour repeaters who wish to travel new scenic areas when they return again and again.

Michael von Thielmann was born in Germany and raised in Munich, Bavaria, where he received his Master of Business Administration at the Munich University. Even though he now lives in California, he spends much of his time in Europe and other countries, preparing and organizing tours.

Services Offered:

- Scheduled tours operate in various parts of Europe, in New Zealand, People's Republic of China, Mexico, Jamaica, Argentina, and the U.S.A.
- Customized tours. Special tours, for clubs as an example, can be arranged any time and for any budget.
- Tour members join from many States and several countries; travel and flight arrangements are made accordingly.
- Video tape presentation of tours.
- Motorcycle rentals for tour participants and also for those traveling on their own. See section on Motorcycle Rentals.
- Motorcycle shipping.
- Motorcycle purchasing services:
    1) in Europe: European Delivery Program, tax free vehicles (BMW), and used vehicles (BMW and Japanese).
    2) in California: new and used motorcycles.

World Motorcycle Tours

14 Forest Avenue
Caldwell, NJ 07006

Contact: Mr. Warren Goodman
Phone: 201-226-9107 or
800-443-7519
FAX: Not available
Telex: Not available

Warren and Flori Goodman

Background:

In 1972, Warren Goodman won passage to Europe for himself, his wife Flori, and his trusty motorcycle as a reward for booking numerous ski tours with Lufthansa Airlines. Mr. Goodman intended to retrace his World War II route through the Alps. Inadvertently, he founded yet another business.

"I figured if we could do it, so could anyone with a sense of adventure," Mr. Goodman said.

He started World Motorcycle Tours in 1973. Two years ago, Warren and Flori gave in to their desire to be full-time travel people. They concentrate on luring other mature travelers to this daring way to travel combating two myths at once: the motorcyclist as outlaw, and the senior citizen as sedentary spectator.

At 65, Mr. Goodman barely qualifies as a senior. However, his enthusiasm for speed and mountains reawakens the dormant adventurer in others like his wife Flori who gave up her nursing career for travel.

The Goodmans lead two motorcycle tours a year and offer a variety of services for the touring enthusiast including their specialty service – shipping clients' motorcycles overseas uncrated to save time and expense.

Each year, they return to the Alps where their 16 years experience makes them welcome visitors. This year they extended their concept of luxury living for motorcycle tours to the Iberian Peninsula.

Services Offered:
- Organized tours of the Alps and Spain/Portugal.
- Customized tours for groups and individuals.
- Shipping motorcycles to Europe for tourists.

Wüstenfahrer

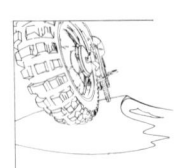

Bahnhofstraße 7e
8011 Baldham
WEST GERMANY

Contact: Mr. Thomas Troßmann or
Mrs. Antje Vogel
Phone: (49) 81 06/77 99
FAX: Not available
Telex: Not available

Background:
Wüstenfahrer was started in 1986 by Thomas Troßmann, journalist and photographer, to organize expeditions to the most beautiful and untouched parts of the Sahara. Mr. Troßmann is a reporter and photographer for the German motorcycling magazine, *Tourenfahrer;* there, he published his accounts and photographs of motorcycle tours all around Europe. In addition, he published two books, both in German: one, a counselling book for people who want to travel by motorcycle in Africa (*Motorradreisen zwischen Urlaub und Expedition,* published by Därr); the other an adventure report (*Wüstenfahrer,* published by Schneider Publishing).

Because of his extensive experience traveling in the Sahara, readers of his books and articles asked him to organize motorcycle trips there. The Sahara is a unique part of the world, one with great natural beauty but one which is very difficult to tour without expert guidance. Mr. Troßmann removes the difficulties from these trips, leaving only the pure fun of driving and pure fascination with the Sahara.

On Wüstenfahrer tours, Mr. Troßmann will be your highly qualified and experienced guide.

Services Offered:
- Organized tours to the Sahara.
- Motorcycles for rent; details upon request.
- Four-color prospectus may be ordered at the address above.

GUIDED TOURS

See the world by motorcycle. This is the universe in its breadth and complexity. These tours cover the globe and offer incredible variety in length, level of difficulty, and level of luxury. There is a journey here for every taste and disposition — from a tour that includes some of Europe's four-star hotels to one that features hard riding and camping in the Sahara. You can catch a tour for any season or any location — if you hurry. There are no excuses to stay home.

GUIDED TOURS – CANADA & ALASKA

ALASKA

On the road: Alaska

Alaska

Tour Operator:
Alaska Motorcycle Tours, Inc.
P.O. Box 622
Bothell, WA 98041-0622

Contact: Mr. Timothy McDonnell
Phone: 800-642-6877 (within Washington state: 206-487-3219)

Length of Tour: 7 days, approximately 1,300 miles.

Dates:
• Departs every Saturday from May 27 through September 16, 1989

Trip Begins and Ends at: Anchorage, Alaska

Highlights:
Stay in deluxe hotels with sumptuous dinners each evening as you explore Alaska's wilderness by day. Start your journey with a drive to Alyeska, America's choice for the Winter Olympics. You'll follow a spectacular route to Fairbanks in the heart of Alaska's gold rush country. Pan for gold with a prospector. Visit the Great One — at 20,320 feet Mt. McKinley is North America's highest peak. Explore part of the two million acres of untouched wilderness that surrounds this magnificent mountain. Spend your final night in Anchorage, a city of 200,000. You'll appreciate the luxury of this personalized tour for six cyclists and their riders. Optional tours are offered in Anchorage, Fairbanks, and Denali National Park.

Price (includes motorcycle rental):
• Two riders, double occupancy .... $1,300 per person

Price Includes:
Six nights in luxury hotels; six dinners; tour guide; baggage transfers; gratuities; motorcycle rental and fuel; and sightseeing where applicable.

Motorcycle Provisions:
1988 Honda Gold Wing

Luggage Provisions:
Motorcyclists will carry their own baggage. Extra luggage may be stored in Anchorage.

CANADA AND ALASKA — Arctic Tour

"Honey, do you really think we should wait . . ."

Tour Operator:
Edelweiss Bike Travel
Steinreichweg 1
A-6414 Mieming
AUSTRIA

Contact: Mr. Werner Wachter
Phone: (43) 05264/5690
FAX: (43) 05264/58533
Telex: 534158 (rkmiem)

U.S. Agent:	Armonk Travel 146 Bedford Road Armonk, NY 10504 Contact: Ms. Linda Rosenbaum Phone: 800-255-7451 or 914-273-8880
Length of Tour:	23 days, covering approximately 4,500 miles
Dates:	June 15 through July 5, 1989
Trip Begins and Ends:	Vancouver, British Colombia

Highlights:
Adventurers and explorers, answer the call to the Arctic circle. Conquer the last frontier in motorcycle riding. Begin in Vancouver, the beautiful city nestled between the mountains and the Pacific coastline. Plunge into the interior of British Columbia through Indian villages, lakes, and woods. Ride through breathtaking mountain ranges. Watch for bears fishing for salmon. Follow the Klondike Highway through the heart of gold rush territory to Dawson City, a happy compromise between a modern town and an historic site. Join with other adventurers and gold miners in a grand party to celebrate midsummer night. Master the Dempster Highway — almost 500 miles of unpaved road with one gas station midway and natural beauty around every corner. Touch the Arctic Circle. Return through Alaska on the Top of the World Highway with views above the tree line that go for 100 miles before they meet snow covered peaks on the horizon.

Price (does not include motorcycle rental):
- Single rider, double occupancy $3,475
- Motorcycle passenger, double occupancy $2,975

Price Includes:
Hotel/motel accommodations for 22 nights; breakfast and dinner every day except on ferry; all ferry fares; welcome and farewell party; tour guide; daily route briefing; tour gift.

Motorcycle Provisions:
BMW and Yamaha motorcycles are available for rent. Or you may ride your own touring, street, or enduro motorcycle. Ask agent for types and prices on motorcycle rentals.

Luggage Provisions:
No luggage van accompanies this tour.

Special Notes:
Healthy, strong riders are welcomed on this trip. You must be able to ride up to ten hours a day on gravel roads. Tolerance for cold and hot temperatures is also a must for this trip.

ALBERTA AND BRITISH COLUMBIA

Big Sky Tour

Ah, the peace, the solitude . . .

Tour Operator:
Rocky Mountain Moto Tours Ltd.
Box 7152 Stn. E
Calgary, Alberta T3C 3M1
CANADA

Contact: Mr. Nicholas Moar
Phone: 403-244-6939
FAX: 403-229-2788
Telex: 03-821172

Length of Tour: 7 days, approximately 2,200 km

Dates:
- June 4 through June 10, 1989
- June 20 through June 26, 1989 *
- July 6 through July 12, 1989
- July 22 through July 28, 1989
- August 7 through August 13, 1989
- September 8 through September 14, 1989 *
- September 24 through September 30, 1989

* These are the premium tours and include an upgraded selection of first class accommodation and dining at such world renowned places as Chateau Lake Louise and Banff Spring Hotel. There is a $300 surcharge for these dates.

Trip Begins and Ends: Calgary, Alberta

Highlights:
Leave the tamer life and plunge into the rugged, spacious landscape of Alberta. Skim through the foothills of the Rockies. Enter ranching country — the last frontier of the working cowboy. You'll travel the homelands of the Blood Indians near the Montana border and Waterton National Park. Grizzlies live in the hills; deer and mountain sheep wander across your

pathway. You'll drive the renowned Going to the Sun highway in Glacier National Park before you leave the Big Sky Country. Explore the Kootenay Mountains. Descend to the orchard- and vineyard-rich Okanagan Valley. Visit sparkling Shuswap Lakes. Watch the sun rise over the towering Rockies. Journey through some of the last virgin timber stands in North America. Explore Banff National Park. Ride a gondola to the top of Sulpher Mountain for a breathtaking view of the Rockies. Course through the Kananaskis Mountains, home of the '88 Olympic alpine events, before returning to Calgary. You'll have a taste of all western Canada's different landscapes and lifestyles on this tour.

Price (includes motorcycle rental):
- Normal tour, double occupancy, per person .... $1,875 CAN
- Normal tour, single occupancy, per person .... $2,235 CAN
- Premium tour, double occupancy, per person .... $2,175 CAN
- Premium tour, single occupancy, per person .... $2,735 CAN

Notes:
Because of the type of riding and somewhat isolated accommodations on this tour, double room occupancy is encouraged. These tours are for single riders only, due to the kind of bikes used and the somewhat rugged roads traveled.

Price Includes:
Pickup at designated hotels on first morning of tour; the use of a fully insured 600cc or 650cc dual-purpose motorcycle; all gas and oil; six nights deluxe and, if possible, unique accommodation (double occupancy); all breakfasts and lunches; two special interest excursions; and the services of an experienced tour guide.

Motorcycle Provisions:
Honda XL 600 or Kawasaki KLR 650 dual-purpose motorcycle equipped for touring.

Luggage Provisions:
A van accompanies each tour for luggage and other needs.

Special Notes:
Spend three nights on either a remote guest ranch or in a western style town with old-fashioned boardwalks. Almost one-third of the tour is on isolated gravel routes. Due to vast uninhabited areas, you'll travel together for safety and comfort. Maximum tour size is six. Riding pace is moderate with some higher mileages to reach remote destinations.

ALBERTA AND BRITISH COLUMBIA   Bugaboo Tour

Tour Operator:	Rocky Mountain Moto Tours Ltd. Box 7152 Stn. E Calgary, Alberta T3C 3M1 CANADA Contact: Mr. Nicholas Moar Phone: 403-244-6939 FAX: 403-229-2788 Telex: 03-821172
Length of Tour:	7 days, approximately 2,550 km

Dates:
- May 27 through June 2, 1989
- June 12 through June 18, 1989
- June 28 through July 4, 1989
- July 14 through July 20, 1989 *
- July 30 through August 5, 1989
- August 15 through August 21, 1989 *
- August 31 through September 6, 1989
- September 16 through September 22, 1989

* These are premium tours and include an upgraded selection of first class accommodation and dining at such world renowned places as Chateau Lake Louise and the Banff Spring Hotel. There is a surcharge of $300.

Trip Begins and Ends:	Calgary, Alberta

Highlights:
Head southwest out of Calgary on isolated roads unknown even to most locals. Climb ever higher in the rugged Canadian Rockies. Relax in the natural hot springs that emerge from fissures high above Banff. You'll see breathtaking peaks that tower over the icy Bow River on your way to beautiful British Columbia. After a short ferry ride to the secluded Kootenay Lake area, you'll sight the famous Bugaboo Mountains. Follow the deep mountain lakes to the Washington border. Experience some of the most diverse geography in North America on your ride to Winthrop, a western town complete with wild west saloons and boardwalks. Climb the mountains on rugged roads then descend to agricultural lands of lovely Okanagan Valley. The lakes are never-ending as you push north toward the Monashee Pass. Follow the trail of early prospectors over the Selkirk Mountains. Emerge from the foothills of the Rocky Mountains. Sweep

through the unfolding prairie to Calgary. You'll capture the rugged and remote mountains of western Canada at their best on this tour.

Price (includes motorcycle rental):
- Normal tour, double occupancy, per person .... $1,875 CAN
- Normal tour, single occupancy, per person .... $2,235 CAN
- Premium tour, double occupancy, per person .... $2,175 CAN
- Premium tour, single occupancy, per person .... $2,735 CAN

Notes:
Because of the type of riding and somewhat isolated accommodations on this tour, double room occupancy is encouraged. These tours are for single riders only, due to the kind of bikes used and the somewhat rugged roads traveled.

Price Includes:
Pickup at designated hotels on first morning of tour; use of fully insured 600cc or 650cc motorcycle; all gas and oil; six nights deluxe and, if possible, unique accommodations (double occupancy); all breakfasts and lunches; two special interest excursions; and the services of an experienced tour guide.

Motorcycle Provisions:
Use of a Honda XL 600 or Kawasaki KLR 650 dual-purpose motorcycle equipped for touring.

Luggage Provisions:
Tour van for luggage and other needs accompanies the riders.

Special Notes:
Spend three nights either on remote guest ranches in Alberta and British Columbia or in western style towns with boardwalks. About one-third of this tour is on isolated gravel routes. Due to vast uninhabited areas, you'll travel together for company and safety. Maximum tour size is six. Riding pace is moderate with some daily mileages higher because of remote destinations.

SOUTHWEST CANADA **Canada**

Tour Operator:

mhs Motorradtouren GmbH
Hans-Urmiller-Ring 59
D-8190 Wolfratshausen
WEST GERMANY

Contact: Mr. Herbert Schellhorn
Phone: (49) 81 71 12 38

Length of Tour: 14 days, approximately 3,800 km

Dates:
- July 8 through July 21, 1989
- August 5 through August 18, 1989
- August 19 through September 1, 1989
- September 2 through September 15, 1989

Trip Begins and Ends: Calgary, Alberta

Highlights:

This is a tour of one of the most beautiful sections of Canada, the southwest. Its variety is often astonishing. Riders on the July tour will have the rare opportunity to visit the world's biggest outdoor show, the Calgary Stampede.

After visiting the city and its Olympic park you start toward the solitude of the Rocky Mountains. You'll pass Fort Steele, a reconstructed frontier city, and the Okanagan Valley, where peaches and other fruits are grown. Finally, you reach the Pacific Ocean and Vancouver, a beautiful city famous for its architecture and its aquarium.

Continue your ride to the northeast, back into the mountains, arriving next at Jasper National Park. Exceptional features of the park include Lake Maligne and the Columbia ice fields. After leaving the mountains you descend to the prairie with its enormous stretches of wheat fields and oil pumps. At Edmonton you may view the Capitol building or Fort Edmonton, a legacy of the city's frontier days, or take in the fabulous West Edmonton Mall, a building of 400,000 square meters which encloses about 750 shops, a perfect replica of one of Christopher Columbus' ships, the world's largest swimming pool, and even a roller coaster. You can spend a full day just exploring this amazing center.

Then onward to Yoho National Park, where you can enjoy horseback riding, white-water rafting on the Kicking Horse River, or just lying in the sun to watch the wildlife. The next day you return to Calgary, and then home — or perhaps to further adventures in Canada.

GUIDED TOURS – CANADA & ALASKA

Price (does not include motorcycle rental):
- Single rider, double occupancy .... 3,995 DM
- Motorcycle passenger, double occupancy .... 3,545 DM
- Supplement for single room occupancy .... 750 DM

Price Includes:
Full board; hotel stays in middle class or better hotels, in double bed rooms; table drinks to all meals; entrance fees; one day riding on horseback; gas; good food.

Not Included in Price:
Flight and rental bikes are not included, but will be provided at minimum rates.

Motorcycle Provisions:
Suzuki rental bikes available from and to Calgary. Depending on the model motorcycle, the price is 1,700 DM, or higher.

Luggage Provisions:
Bikes are equipped with luggage holders and panniers.

Special Notes:
- Languages spoken: German, English, and French (if needed).

Reader Discount:
A discount of $50 applies to this tour when you send in the Reader Discount Coupon.

CANADA and U.S.A.	**Fairbanks to Vancouver**
Tour Operator:	Bike Tours Einsiedeleiweg 16 5942 Kirchhundem 4 WEST GERMANY Contact: Ms. Eveline Veenkamp Phone: (49) 2764-7824 FAX: Not available Telex: Not available
Length of Tour:	21 days

Dates:
- July 30 through August 19, 1989
- July 29 through August 18, 1990 *

* Note: 1990 dates may vary slightly.

Trip Begins: Fairbanks, Alaska

Trip Ends: Vancouver, British Columbia

Highlights:
Watch eagles soar 20,320 feet to the snowcapped peak of Mount McKinley, North America's highest mountain. Look for grizzly bear and other spectacular wildlife in the frozen northwest wilderness. Spin through heavily glaciated mountains toward Anchorage on the Kenai Peninsula. Journey farther north across the Alcan Highway. Enter the Klondike, heart of gold rush country. From here, you'll loop southeast through Hazelton and Prince George. Pass Spatsizi Plateau and glimpse snowcapped Mount Edziza in the distance. Head down the Caribou Highway toward Vancouver.

Price (includes motorcycle rental):
- Single rider .... 3,650 DM
- Motorcycle passenger .... 950 DM
- Luggage van passenger .... 1,850 DM
- Combination trip, Vancouver to Fairbanks to Vancouver ..... 6,500 DM

Price Includes:
Camping equipment (except sleeping bag); transfer from airport to camp; campground fees; tents; maintenance and repairs.

Not Included in Price:
Food, fuel, insurance. Cost approximately $165 weekly.

Motorcycle Provisions:
Yamaha XT 600

Luggage Provisions:
A luggage van accompanies this tour.

Special Notes:
The principal language of this tour is German. English can be spoken if necessary. This trip is timed to start just as the reverse trip ends; it takes a completely different route from Vancouver. For those travelers who want more of this beautiful countryside, plan to combine this tour and the reverse tour for a complete Vancouver-Fairbanks-Vancouver loop. May also be combined with Vancouver-San Francisco trips.

CANADA	**Fly 'N' Bike – Canada – 1989**
Tour Operator:	Tee Mill Tours Ltd. 56 Tooting High Street London SW17 0RN ENGLAND Contact: Mr. Reg Thomas Phone: (44) 01-767-8737 (24 hours) FAX: (44) 01-682-0138 Telex: 945307 (TEEMIL G)
Length of Tour:	Rider's choice. This tour is tailored to individual requirements.
Dates:	May through October.
Trip Begins and Ends:	United Kingdom

Highlights:
Rider's choice. This is not a guided tour but is an arrangement for U.K. travelers who wish to tour Canada, usually through Toronto. Tee Mill Tours can offer suggestions about routing, suggested sights, and other attractions.

Price:
Varies according to the particular trip requirements.

Price Includes:
Transportation for rider and motorcycle round trip from the U.K.

Motorcycle Provisions:
Rider provides his own motorcycle.

Luggage Provisions:
Rider is responsible for carrying his own luggage.

GUIDED TOURS – CANADA & ALASKA 53

CANADA	**Vancouver Coach Road Rider**
Tour Operator:	TransCyclist International CPO Box 2064 Tokyo, 100-91 JAPAN Contact: Mr. Volker Lenzner Phone: (81) 3-402-5385 FAX: (81) 3-402-5358
Length of Tour:	7 days, approximately 1,200 km

Dates:
1989 (the following dates are approximate):
- July 1 through July 7, 1989 (Three Coast)
- July 8 through July 14, 1989 (Kettle Valley)
- July 29 through August 4, 1989 (Three Coast)
- August 5 through August 11, 1989 (Kettle Valley)
- September 2 through September 8, 1989 (Three Coast)
- September 9 through September 15, 1989 (Kettle Valley)
- September 23 through September 29, 1989 (Three Coast)
- October 7 through October 13, 1989 (Three Coast)

1990 (the following dates are approximate):
- June 30 through July 16, 1990 (Three Coast)
- July 7 through July 13, 1990 (Kettle Valley)
- July 28 through August 3, 1990 (Three Coast)
- August 4 through August 10, 1990 (Kettle Valley)
- September 1 through September 7, 1990 (Three Coast)
- September 8 through September 14, 1990 (Kettle Valley)
- September 22 through September 28, 1990 (Three Coast)
- October 6 through October 12, 1990 (Three Coast)

Trip Begins and Ends:	Vancouver, British Columbia

Highlights:
The legend of the Canadian west coast comes to life as you ferry across to Vancouver Island. This is a land of soaring eagles where ancient Douglas fir trees tower in the landscape. Navigate along the old coach road down the Saanich Peninsula to Victoria, port town of old castles and gardens, totems, and old English tradition. Take a one-day coastal adventure galley cruise complete with fishing and diving adventures. Next, head up-island to Nanaimo, the Harbour City, and nearby Gabriola Island. The landscape shows evidence of island coal mines, native petroglyphs, and centuries of

wind and waves. After leaving Nanaimo you will head toward the rugged coast with Tofino as an overnight stop. On your final day, journey to Comox and board another British Columbia ferry for a cruise to the town of Powell River on the Sunshine Coast.

Take the Kettle Valley Tour leaving early in the morning for the Seymour Mountains. See Vancouver at its scenic best. Visit Fort Langley Museum at Manning Lodge; take a ferry ride; stop at Kelona and Merritt. Travel along the mighty Fraser River through spectacular Fraser Canyon. Switch from motorcycle touring to exhilarating river rafting. Ride a famous tram across the river at Hell's Gate and return to Vancouver.

Price (includes motorcycle rental):
- Single rider, double occupancy $1,250
- Passenger (bike, van) double occupancy .... $ 850

Note: A $250 refundable insurance bond is required.

Price Includes:
Six nights accommodations; breakfasts and dinners; motorcycle rental; fuel and oil; Third Party Insurance; ferries; camps; guide; route maps; tour briefings; one day free sightseeing in Vancouver; half-day shopping trip; airport transfers can be arranged; support van for larger groups. Not included: lunch snacks, travel/accident insurance.

Motorcycle Provisions:
Choice of:
- Honda: Nighthawk 650/750, Shadow 500
- Yamaha: Maxim 650/750, Virago 650/750, Seca 550/650, Special 400
- Suzuki: GS 400
- Kawasaki: KZ 650/750

Luggage Provisions:
A support van for luggage and spares for larger groups. Travel lightly if member of a small group.

Special Notes:
International driver's license valid for motorcycle operation required by participants. Tour price is for a minimum of six participants. You are advised to book well in advance (45-day booking deadline, full payment 30 days before tour departure). Cost adjustment will be made if you bring your own bike. In addition to these tours, a variation of short/long duration North American Stage Coach Rider Tours are offered. Send a self-addressed, stamped envelope and one international reply coupon (available from the post office) when inquiring about the tours.

CANADA and ALASKA

Vancouver to Fairbanks

Canadian fauna on the road to Fairbanks

Tour Operator:
Bike Tours
Einsiedeleiweg 16
5942 Kirchhundem 4
WEST GERMANY

Contact: Ms. Eveline Veenkamp
Phone: (49) 2764-7824
FAX: Not available
Telex: Not available

Length of Tour:	21 days

Dates:
- July 9 through July 29, 1989
- July 8 through July 28, 1990 *
* Note: 1990 dates may vary slightly.

Trip Begins:	Vancouver, British Columbia
Trip Ends:	Fairbanks, Alaska

Highlights:
Follow the sunrise toward spectacular Banff and Jasper National Parks in the rugged Canadian Rockies. Cruise through Dawson Creek where civilization ends and the wilderness begins. Head north on the famous Alcan Highway. At Whitehorse, Jack London's hometown, visit the pioneer museum. Pan for gold in northern streams. Enjoy the unspoiled pleasure of America's largest state.

Price (includes motorcycle rental):
- Single rider .... 3,650 DM
- Motorcycle passenger .... 950 DM
- Luggage van passenger .... 1,850 DM
- Combination trip, Vancouver to Fairbanks to Vancouver ..... 6,500 DM

Price Includes:
Camping equipment (except sleeping bag); transfer from airport to camp; campground fees; tents; maintenance and repairs.

Not included in Price:
Food, fuel, insurance. Cost approximately $165 weekly.

Motorcycle Provisions:
Yamaha XT 600

Luggage Provisions:
A luggage van accompanies this tour.

Special Notes:
The principal language of this tour is German. English can be spoken if necessary. The reverse direction of this trip is timed to start just as this trip ends; it takes a completely different route back to Vancouver. For those travelers who want more of this beautiful countryside, plan to keep on going for another three weeks and take advantage of the combined Vancouver-Fairbanks-Vancouver loop.

GUIDED TOURS - U.S.A.

U.S.A. — Best of the West

"Did someone get the moneybag?"

Tour Operator:
California MotoTours
2170 Avenida de la Playa #B
La Jolla, CA 92037

Booking Agent:
Ms. Izabella Miram, Terra Tours
Phone: 800-444-9554 or
619-454-9551
FAX: 619-454-3549
Telex: 495-0609

Length of Tour:	16 days, approximately 2,000 miles

Dates:
- Tour #1: May 7 through May 22, 1989
- Tour #3: October 9 through October 24, 1989

There will be tours scheduled for 1990. Contact California MotoTours for current information.

Trip Begins and Ends:	San Diego, California

Highlights:
Thrill to some of the best motorcycling in the U.S. in the high desert country of the Old West and the white beaches of San Felipe in Baja California. Sweep through the fantastic rock formations of three national parks — Bryce Canyon, Zion, and the splendor of the Grand Canyon, where you have time for a mule ride into the chasm. Buy turquoise and treasured Navajo rugs from Indian craftsmen. From forests of saguaro cactus, you'll climb the mountain road to the copper mining town of Jerome. In Sedona, the most beautiful area of the red rock country, you'll tour the back country by jeep. Ride through the desert floor of the canyons with cliffs towering 1,500 feet above. Play the gambling tables of glittering Las Vegas.

Price (does not include motorcycle rental):
- Single rider, double occupancy $1,875
- Supplement for single room occupancy .... $ 350

Price Includes:

Twelve nights luxury hotels; three nights luxury camping in Baja California; 11 gourmet dinners; 11 full breakfasts; picnic lunches; all tips and taxes on lodging and meals paid; jeep and boat trips; national park fees; Las Vegas Follies show; airport transfers; two guides; maps; tour gift. Does not include airfare to/from San Diego.

Motorcycle Provisions:

The 16-day tour rental ranges from $650 to $925 (liability insurance included), depending upon the motorcycle you choose. Models available include cruiser style bikes (e.g., Yamaha Virago, Suzuki Intruder), sport bikes (Kawasaki EX 500) and larger touring bikes (e.g., Honda Gold Wing, Honda V65 Sabre, and BMW R80RT).

Luggage Provisions:

A van with motorcycle trailer accompanies each tour to carry luggage and transport motorcycles, if needed.

U.S.A.	**California Grand Tour**
Tour Operator:	California MotoTours 2170 Avenida de la Playa #B La Jolla, CA 92037
Booking Agent:	Ms. Izabella Miram, Terra Tours Phone: 800-444-9554 or 619-454-9551 FAX: 619-454-3549 Telex: 495-0609
Length of Tour:	17 days, approximately 2,000 miles

Dates:
- July 8 through July 24, 1989
- September 4 through September 20, 1989

There will be tours scheduled for 1990. Contact California MotoTours for current information.

Trip Begins and Ends:	Los Angeles, California

Highlights:

Immerse yourself in the wonder of California's natural beauty on the Grand Tour. In Sequoia National Park, you'll stand in awe of the giant sequoias, nature's largest living things. Speed through redwood groves high in the Sierra Nevadas to Lake Tahoe, one of the grandest of deep blue mountain lakes. Raft down the Trukee River. Take Tioga Pass through the Alpine region of Yosemite National Park to your dream of open roads and open skies in cattle country. Climb on challenging roads that curve to astonishing views. Dip inland for wine tasting tours in the lush vineyards of Napa Valley. Tour cosmopolitan San Francisco and charming Carmel by the Sea. Cruise the twists of the Big Sur coast with its sheer rocky cliffs and sheltered coves.

Price (does not include motorcycle rental):
- Single rider, double occupancy $1,975
- Supplement for single room occupancy .... $ 375

Price Includes:
Sixteen nights luxury hotels; 11 gourmet dinners; 12 full breakfasts; some picnic lunches; all tips and taxes on lodging and meals paid; river rafting trip; Hearst Castle tour; ferry to San Francisco; national park fees; airport transfers; two guides; maps; tour gift.

Motorcycle Provisions:
The 16-day tour rental ranges from $650 to $925 (liability insurance included), depending upon the motorcycle you choose. Models available include cruiser style bikes (e.g., Yamaha Virago, Suzuki Intruder), sport bikes (Kawasaki EX 500) and larger touring bikes (e.g., Honda Gold Wing, Honda V65 Sabre, and BMW R80RT).

Luggage Provisions:
A luggage van accompanies each tour to carry luggage.

U.S.A. **California "Left Bank" Tour**

Tour Operator: California MotoTours
2170 Avenida de la Playa #B
La Jolla, CA 92037

Booking Agent:	Ms. Izabella Miram, Terra Tours Phone: 800-444-9554 or 619-454-9551 FAX: 619-454-3549 Telex: 495-0609
Length of Tour:	14 days, covering approximately 1,500 miles

Dates:
- June 5 through June 18, 1989

There will be tours scheduled for 1990. Contact California MotoTours for current information.

Trip Begins and Ends:	Los Angeles, California

Highlights:
Explore California's Pacific coastline at a leisurely pace. Drive over the famed Golden Gate Bridge into romantic San Francisco. Visit the improbable castle built by newspaper magnate William Randolph Hearst. Stroll the elegant village of Carmel by the Sea with its cozy artists' cottages and shops set among pine and cypress woods. Wind through the spectacle of the Big Sur coast. You'll cover extraordinary motorcycle routes that include inland mountains and the vineyards of Napa Valley with coastal rides. This is a tour to satisfy the soul of an artist and the spirit of a motorcyclist.

Price (does not include motorcycle rental):
- Single rider, double occupancy $1,700
- Supplement for single room occupancy .... $ 375

Price Includes:
Thirteen nights luxury hotels; eight gourmet dinners; eight full breakfasts; picnic lunches; all tips and taxes on lodging and meals paid; Hearst Castle tour; airport transfers; two guides; maps; tour gift.

Motorcycle Provisions:
The 14-day tour rental ranges from $600 to $850 (liability insurance included), depending upon the motorcycle you choose. Models available include cruiser style bikes (e.g., Yamaha Virago, Suzuki Intruder), sport bikes (Kawasaki EX 500) and larger touring bikes (e.g., Honda Gold Wing, Honda V65 Sabre, and BMW R80RT).

Luggage Provisions:
A van with motorcycle trailer accompanies each tour to carry luggage and transport motorcycles, if needed.

GUIDED TOURS – U.S.A.

U.S.A.	**Colorado and the Best of the West**
Tour Operator:	California MotoTours 2170 Avenida de la Playa #B La Jolla, CA 92037
Booking Agent:	Ms. Izabella Miram, Terra Tours Phone: 800-444-9554 or 619-454-9551 FAX: 619-454-3549 Telex: 495-0609
Length of Tour:	17 days, covering approximately 2,500 miles

Dates:
- Tour #2: August 8 through August 24, 1989

There will be tours scheduled for 1990. Contact California MotoTours for current information.

Trip Begins and Ends:	San Diego, California

Highlights:
This trip combines the incomparable touring of the "Best of the West" high desert country with red rock canyons and the majesty of the Colorado mountains. Climb steep mountain passes and soar above the timberline of the San Juan Mountains. Travel past rustic ranches to the isolated mining town of Telluride where Butch Cassidy staged his first robbery in 1889. Venture on a day of white-water rafting at Arches National Park, known for the world's largest concentration of sandstone arches. Add this to the excitement of red rock country and the awe-inspiring Grand Canyon, Bryce Canyon, and Zion National Park.

Price (does not include motorcycle rental):
- Single rider, double occupancy $2,050
- Supplement for single room occupancy .... $ 375

Price Includes:
Sixteen nights luxury hotels; 11 gourmet dinners; 10 full breakfasts; picnic lunches; all tips and taxes on lodging and meals paid; jeep and boat trips; national park fees; Las Vegas Follies show; airport transfers; two guides; maps; tour gift.

Motorcycle Provisions:

The 17-day tour rental ranges from $650 to $925 (liability insurance included), depending upon the motorcycle you choose. Models available include cruiser style bikes (e.g., Yamaha Virago, Suzuki Intruder), sport bikes (Kawasaki EX 500) and larger touring bikes (e.g., Honda Gold Wing, Honda V65 Sabre, and BMW R80RT).

Luggage Provisions:

A van with motorcycle trailer accompanies each tour to carry luggage and transport motorcycles, if needed.

U.S.A. / SOUTHWEST	**The Indian Badlands Rider**
Tour Operator:	TransCyclist International CPO Box 2064 Tokyo, 100-91 JAPAN Contact: Mr. Volker Lenzner Phone: (81) 3-402-5385 FAX: (81) 3-402-5358 Telex: Not available
Length of Tour:	Five days, six nights; on- and off-road; covering approximately 2,000 km

Dates:
- Monthly during 1989 and 1990 (specific dates subject to booking requests).

Trip Begins and Ends:	Albuquerque, New Mexico

Highlights:
On this unique adventure you will relive the old Wild West and explore the lifestyles, history, and culture of the first citizens of the United States, the American Indians. Ride through magical New Mexico and South Colorado mountains; take part for a day in the life of Farmington, New Mexico; Durango, Colorado; Chama, New Mexico; Taos, New Mexico — all rich in the cultural heritage of the old west, and still alive today. Stunning canyons, towering peaks, wildly rushing rivers. This is the homeland of the Apache, the Aztecs, Navajo, and others.

Browse through the remains of Victorian splendor in frontier towns, all in a storybook setting straight out of Butch Cassidy and the Sundance Kid! Pull up at the roadside and soak up the spectacular scenery, all the way up to the high Rocky Mountains and down to the wide open desert.

Your dual-purpose bike comes in handy as you climb 400 feet above the desert floor to the 1000-year-old Indian community of the Acoma Puelo tribe. This was the site of the great battle in 1599 when the Spaniards faced a rebellion by the Indians, also known for their beautiful pottery.

Visit the Mesa Verde National Park, with the nation's first apartment dwellings, carved about 2,000 years ago into the hanging cliffs. Study the unique art and colorful culture mix at Taos, with its Mexican, Spanish, and Indian flavor. Journey on through the spectacular Rio Grande River gorge, site of the Carson National Forest and Fort Sumner, built by Colonel Kit Carson in 1864 as a military reservation for Navajo and Apache Indians. Expect every single day, every mile to be filled with adventure and excitement.

Price (includes motorcycle rental):
- Single rider, double occupancy $1,650
- Passenger (van), double occupancy .... $ 950

Note: A $400 insurance bond is requested when renting the motorcycle; it is refundable when the motorcycle is returned free of damage.

Price Includes:
Deluxe accommodation for six nights; breakfasts and dinners (13 meals, in all); rental of motorcycle with unlimited mileage and insurance; support vehicle for additional passengers and luggage; tour escort-guide; tour briefings and information folder with maps, etc.; Albuquerque airport transfers; admissions to national parks, Indian reservations, museums, etc.

Not Included in Price:
Lunch snacks; fuel; travel/accident insurance.

Motorcycle Provisions:
Kawasaki KLR 650 dual purpose (no pillion riding)

Luggage Provisions:
A support van will accompany the tour to carry luggage.

Special Notes:
International driver's license valid for motorcycle operation required by participants other than U.S. residents. Prices are subject to change. Youced to book well in advance. The tour requires a minimum of six participants. Five passengers can be accommodated in the support van. Key events, such as the Albuquerque Balloon Festival and Indian Festival can offer additional value to tours if timed properly. This would result in slight increase to cover additional costs. Send a self-addressed, stamped en-

velope and one international reply coupon (available from the post office) when inquiring about the tours.

U.S.A.	**Motorail™ Tour: New Orleans and Daytona Beach**
Tour Operator:	Bike Tours Unlimited P.O. Box 1965 San Pedro, CA 90733 Contact: Mr. Vic Perniciaro Phone: 213-833-2671 FAX: Not available Telex: Not available
Length of Tour:	17 days

Dates:
- March 1 through March 17, 1989 (for reference)
(1990 dates not yet established)

Trip Begins and Ends:	Los Angeles, California

Highlights:
Board Amtrak's Sunset Limited with your own motorcycle, bound for Daytona Bike Week — first stop New Orleans, birthplace of jazz. Meander down Bourbon Street with the sounds of Dixieland echoing through the festival of the steamy French Quarter. New Orleans food ranges from fabulous high-style French to peppery Cajun cooking. As you tour this gracious southern city of iron lace balconies, be sure to take time out for chicory coffee and sugary fried cakes known as crullers in the French Market. Then, cruise down the coast of the Gulf of Mexico heading for Florida's east coast and on to the fabulous *Daytona International Bike Week*. After *Bike Week*, you'll hop aboard the Sunset Limited to travel back to Los Angeles (or another destination of your choice).

Price:
- Single rider, double occupancy, coach $1,006
- Two riders, double occupancy, coach $1,406
- Single rider, double occupancy, economy bedroom $1,758
- Two riders, double occupancy, economy bedroom $1,358
- Cost to ship additional motorcycle, one way .... $ 612

66 GUIDED TOURS – U.S.A.

Price Includes:
Transportation of rider(s) and motorcycle round trip Los Angeles/New Orleans/Los Angeles; loading and unloading charges; taxes and gratuities; use of lounge car and deck dome. "Economy bedroom" also includes meals while en route.

Motorcycle Provisions:
Riders are expected to furnish their own motorcycle; round trip shipping from Los Angeles is included in the price.

Luggage Provisions:
A motorcycle trailer is brought along on this tour to carry reasonable overflow luggage. Travelers are expected to carry the bulk of their own luggage.

NORTHERN CALIFORNIA — Ride America

Tour Operator:	Tee Mill Tours Ltd. 56 Tooting High Street London SW17 0RN ENGLAND Contact: Mr. Reg Thomas Phone: (44) 01-767-8737 FAX: (44) 01-682-0138 Telex: 945307
Length of Tour:	7 days
Dates:	Weekly, beginning June, 1989
Trip Begins and Ends:	San Francisco, California

Highlights:
Sample the American experience with a seven-day jaunt through northern California. Start in cosmopolitan San Francisco and take to the open road on your Harley for a week of adventure. Use this as an addition to a longer holiday.

Price:
Contact Tee Mill

Motorcycle Provisions:
Harley-Davidson motorcycles

Reader Discount:
A discount of $25 applies to this tour when you send in the Reader Discount Coupon.

U.S.A. and CANADA

San Francisco to Vancouver & Vancouver to San Francisco

Tour Operator:
Bike Tours
Einsiedeleiweg 16
5942 Kirchhundem 4
WEST GERMANY

Contact: Ms. Eveline Veenkamp
Phone: (49) 2764-7824
FAX: Not available
Telex: Not available

Dining with the locals

Length of Tour:
21 days

Dates:
San Francisco to Vancouver:
- June 11 through July 1, 1989
- June 10 through June 30, 1990 *

Vancouver to San Francisco:
- August 27 through September 16, 1989
- August 26 through September 15, 1990 *

* Note: 1990 dates may vary slightly

Trip Begins and Ends:
San Francisco to Vancouver or Vancouver to San Francisco

Highlights:
Sweep from beautiful San Francisco Bay up to Tioga Pass on into Death Valley. Capture the full flavor of the American West. Visit the high-stake

gambling tables of Las Vegas. See the red sandstone miracle of the Grand Canyon. Cross Wyoming and head toward Yellowstone National Park through the rugged Rocky Mountains and the continental divide. Ride hard and fast across the dry plateaus of east Washington, over the heavily forested Cascade Range, toward the Pacific Ocean and your final stop in Vancouver.

Price (includes motorcycle rental):
- Single rider .... 3,650 DM
- Motorcycle passenger .... 950 DM
- Luggage van passenger .... 1,850 DM

Price Includes:
Camping equipment (except sleeping bag); transfer from airport to camp; campground fees; tents; maintenance and repairs.

Not Included in Price:
Food, fuel, insurance. Cost approximately $112 weekly.

Motorcycle Provisions:
Yamaha XT 600

Luggage Provisions:
A luggage van accompanies this tour.

Special Notes:
The principal language of this tour is German. English can be spoken if necessary.

USA – Southeast   Smoky Mountains

Tour Operator: Smoky Mountain Motorcycle
                          Vacations
                          200 Upper Herron Cove Road
                          Weaverville, NC 28787

                          Contact: Mr. Gary Dagiel
                          Phone: 704-658-0239
                          FAX: Not available
                          Telex: Not available

Length of Tour:
Seven days, covering between 700 and 1,000 miles

Dates:
- June 11 through June 17, 1989
- September 24 through September 30, 1989
- June 3 through June 9, 1990
- July 8 through July 14, 1990
- August 5 through August 11, 1990
- September 23 through September 29, 1990

Trip Begins and Ends:
Asheville, North Carolina

Highlights:
Cruise through 600 miles of the sweetest riding you'll ever experience, as you wind through the spectacular Blue Ridge and Great Smoky Mountains. Follow the Blue Ridge Parkway over mountains wrapped in blue mists and covered with virgin forests — nature at her best. Greet an Appalachian spring with rhododendrons and mountain laurel or run through the dappled golden splendor of autumn in the Smokies. Travel at your own pace. Explore what interests you most. Ride horseback. Try white-water rafting. See a preserved 1850s farming community. Visit the fabulous Biltmore House and Gardens. Stay in country inns and hotels nestled in some of the world's oldest mountains. Your guide, Gary Dagiel, has one goal and that is to emulate the service of a fine restaurant: all the courses arrive at the proper time; your wine glass is never empty and you hardly notice he's around. He is a friendly source of information who lives in the Smoky Mountains and knows where to be and when to be there.

Price (does not include motorcycle rental):
- Single rider, double occupancy $569
- Passenger, double occupancy $519
- Supplement for single room occupancy $150

Price Includes:
Six nights accommodations; most breakfasts; six dinners; and a well-informed tour guide.

Motorcycle Provisions:
Travelers are expected to bring their own motorcycle. Storage is available for trailers and tow vehicles.

Luggage Provisions:
You must carry your own luggage.

GUIDED TOURS – U.S.A.

Reader Discount:
A discount of $25 applies to this tour when you send in the Reader Discount Coupon.

U.S.A.

Southwest U.S.A.

Tour Operator:	Von Thielmann Tours P.O. Box 87764 San Diego, CA 92138 Contact: Ms. Gina Guzzardo Phone: 619-463-7788 or 619-291-7057 FAX: 619-291-4630 Telex: 910 335 1607 MESA SERV SDG
Length of Tour:	21 days

Dates:
- October 15 through November 4, 1989

Trip Begins and Ends:	Frankfurt, Germany and San Diego, California

Highlights:
See California, Arizona, Nevada, Utah. Very scenic ride from San Diego via Palms Springs, Grand Canyon, Bryce Canyon, Las Vegas, Goldfield, Yosemite National Park, Lake Tahoe, Tahoe National Forest, Muir Woods, San Francisco. Ride California's most scenic road along the Pacific coast from Monterey to Santa Barbara.

Price (does not include motorcycle rental):
- Single rider, double occupancy $2,626
- Two people, double occupancy $5,252
- Single passenger, double occupancy $2,626
- Supplement for single room occupancy .... $ 580

Price Includes:
Round trip airfare Frankfurt/Los Angeles/San Diego; hotel accommodations; transfers; several meals; tour guide; road maps; luggage van with motorcycle trailer.

Motorcycle Provisions:
Rentals available (foreigners must have international driver's license).

Luggage Provisions:
Luggage van with motorcycle trailer.

Options:
Tour members may join the group in San Diego. In this case, the tour prices are reduced by the transatlantic and domestic airfares.

U.S.A.	**U.S.A. The Great American Dream: The New World**
Tour Operator:	Motorrad-Reisen Postfach 44 01 48 D-8000 Munich 44 WEST GERMANY Contact: Mr. Hermann Weil Phone: (49) 89 39 57 68 FAX: (49) 89 34 48 32 Telex: 5218511
U.S. Agent:	Motorrad-Reisen P.O. Box 591 Oconomowoc, WI 53066 Contact: Jean Fish Phone: 414-567-7548
Length of Tour:	15 days, approximately 995 miles

Dates:
- April 29 through May 13, 1989
- May 21 through June 4, 1989
- June 11 through June 25, 1989
- September 10 through September 24, 1989

Trip Begins and Ends:	Los Angeles, California

Highlights:

Enjoy almost 1,000 miles of American road. Drive from the freeways of Los Angeles to the glittering strip in Las Vegas. Bet your fortune on a roll of the dice in the casinos. Enjoy a dinner show. Hit the road again and head for the sands of Death Valley. See the vast beauty of Yosemite National Park. Thrill to the Grand Canyon, one of the natural wonders of the world. Ride over the Golden Gate to cosmopolitan San Francisco. Cruise down the Pacific coast to charming Monterey. Eat at truck stops and steak houses on the way. Try sophisticated restaurants and San Francisco's Chinatown specialties. You'll sample the variety that is America.

Price (includes motorcycle rental):

- Two riders, double occupancy $5,200
- Single rider, double occupancy $3,200
- Supplement for single room occupancy .... $ 400

Price Includes:

All land arrangements; bilingual (German and English) tour guide on motorcycle; board and lodging in twin bed rooms at familiar American hotels such as Sheraton, Holiday Inn, etc.

Motorcycle Provisions:

Rental of a BMW R80RT for $58 per day and Yamaha 750 for $42 per day. Price includes 100 miles per day. Extra mileage is $.18 (BMW) and $.14 (Yamaha); insurance is $10 per day (BMW) and $8 per day (Yamaha).

Luggage Provisions:

Van may accompany tour.

Special Notes:

This tour is designed for European motorcyclists.

U.S.A.   **USA Four Corners Motorcycle Tour**

Tour Operator: Southern California Motorcycling Association
c/o Mr. Dennis Carlberg
12555 Piñon Court
Garden Grove, CA 92643
Contact: Mr. Dennis Carlberg
Phone: 714-554-4575 (leave message)

Length of Tour:	21 days
Dates:	Start anytime in 1989.
Trip Begins and Ends:	Any of: Madawaska, Maine; Key West, Florida; Blaine, Washington; or San Ysidro, California.

Highlights:

Sing the praise of this vast country as you tour America "from the redwood forest to the Gulf Stream waters . . ." From San Ysidro, California to Key West, Florida, then head north to the rocky Atlantic Coast and touch base in Madawaska, Maine. Take to the road across the breadth of this varied land, past the lake region and over the majestic Rocky Mountains. Finish in Blaine, Washington. Instead, you might start in Maine and finish in Florida. Grant yourself ultimate independence. Run back roads or major highways, whatever suits your fancy. Layover in National Parks. Visit small town U.S.A. See the bright lights of the big cities.

Your challenge in the USA Four Corners Tour is to touch base in the four cities mentioned above within 21 days. Earn awards and join the special group of 222 who have finished this tour. Attend the annual banquet to celebrate those riders who have completed this unique trip.

Entry Fee: $65 per person

Special Notes:

If you are unable to start the event and return the complete package within 90 days, the club offers a full refund on the starter package. Awards for finishers include an embroidered back patch, a cloisonné pin or necklace, an album for your photos, an embossed cap, and a personalized certificate of completion.

U.S.A.	**USA Motorcycle Tour**
Tour Operator:	Tee Mill Tours Ltd. 56 Tooting High Street London SW17 0RN ENGLAND Contact: Mr. Reg Thomas Phone: (44) 01-767-8737 (24 hours) or (44) 051-632-5532 (M. Wolff) FAX: (44) 01-682-0138 Telex: 945307 (TEEMIL G)

74 GUIDED TOURS – U.S.A.

Length of Tour: 30 days, covering over 7,000 miles

Dates:
Tours start on the first of each month, from May through September. All tours include the Rocky Mountains, except the tour in August; the August departure will visit Sturgis, South Dakota for the huge annual motorcycle rally held there. Note: 21-day tours can also be arranged.

Trip Begins and Ends: Toronto, Ontario

Highlights:
Experienced riders, load your touring machines and head for 30 days of hard riding across a 7,000-mile sweep of open road. Join the search for the real America outside of the cities. Discover monumental U.S.A. where presidents' faces are carved into the rock of Mount Rushmore. Journey from Yellowstone National Park to the wonder of the Grand Canyon, carved by the Colorado River into a marvel of vivid red and ochre sandstone. Buy traditional turquoise jewelry from native Americans, Indians who still live on their forefathers' land within magnificent Grand Canyon. Leave cowboy territory and the pungent smell of sagebrush to speed along the banks of the mighty Mississippi River. Visit the home of Elvis Presley, king of rock 'n' roll. Wind through the Appalachian Mountains on switchback roads. Rush to Niagara Falls and the roaring, tumbling splendor of its waters. You'll earn the spacious skies.

Price (does not include motorcycle rental):
- Single rider, double occupancy £2,125
- Passenger, double occupancy .... £ 650

Price Includes:
Round trip airfare from London to Toronto; airfreight for motorcycle; and guide.

Motorcycle Provisions:
Bring your own or rent a motorcycle through Tee Mill. Their closest available rental location is New York City.

Luggage Provisions:
Riders are expected to carry all their own luggage throughout the trip.

Reader Discount:
A discount of $25 applies to this tour when you send in the Reader Discount Coupon.

GUIDED TOURS – MEXICO & CARIBBEAN

MEXICO — "Best of Baja" Tour

Tour Operator:	Pancho Villa Moto-Tours 9437 E.B. Taulbee El Paso, TX 79924 Contact: Mr. Skip Mascorro Phone: 915-757-3032 FAX: 915-562-1505
Length of Tour:	20 days

Dates:
- January 15 through February 3, 1990
- March 12 through March 31, 1990

Trip Begins:	San Diego, California
Trip Ends:	Nogales (Mexico-Arizona)

Highlights:
Even with the completion of the paved Highway 1 in the early 1970s, this thousand-mile stretch of peninsula remains one of the last frontiers of the Americas. Heading south from San Diego this tour covers some of the most fascinating terrain in Mexico. Shortly after crossing into Mexico through Tijuana, you'll see Pacific waves crashing against rocky cliffs a thousand feet below Highway 1. Every day the sights will change, with rugged mountains, desert forests, and the ever present ocean views of the Pacific or the Sea of Cortez. You'll also experience the electric night life of Mazatlan, and enjoy the spectacular train journey to the Copper Canyon region of the High Sierra Madres. In this remote mountain region, you'll see the lifestyle of the primitive Tarahumara Indian, an indigenous group known for their natural prowess and long distance runners. The train trip itself is exciting; you pass through a maze of tunnels, over, through, and across the most forbidding region of the Sierras. It took nearly 100 years to complete construction of the railroad and you will see why!

Price (does not include motorcycle rental):
- Single rider, double occupancy $1,295
- Two people (one bike) $2,495
- Surcharge, second bike .... $ 50
- Supplement for single room occupancy .... $ 479

Price Includes:
Deluxe hotel accommodations for 18 nights (double occupancy); at least 12 meals; a bilingual tour escort; road logs, maps, and information; fiesta

at the Playa Mazatlan Hotel; ferry cabin and transport for your motorcycle across the Sea of Cortez to the Mexico mainland; train tickets and transfers for the train ride to the Copper Canyon; Pancho Villa T-shirt; and processing of all visas and vehicle permits. If there are eight or more motorcycles, a followup vehicle will travel with the group to assist in the event of mechanical failures.

Motorcycle Provisions:
Travelers are invited to bring their own motorcycle or they may rent one from Pancho Villa Moto-Tours (PVMT). Rental machines must be picked up and delivered at El Paso, Texas; delivery to Laredo and pickup from McAllen, Texas can be arranged by PVMT.

Luggage Provisions:
Travelers should be prepared to carry their own luggage with them. Excess luggage and purchases may be stored in followup vehicle on a space-available basis.

Reader Discount:
A discount of $25 applies to this tour when you send in the Reader Discount Coupon.

MEXICO — Colonial 10-Day Tour

Tour Operator:	Pancho Villa Moto-Tours 9437 E.B. Taulbee El Paso, TX 79924 Contact: Mr. Skip Mascorro Phone: 915-757-3032 FAX: 915-562-1505
Length of Tour:	10 days; covers approximately 1,400 miles (longest day is 325 miles; shortest is 120 miles)

Dates:
- April 10 through April 19, 1989
- October 9 through October 18, 1989
- November 6 through November 15, 1989
- December 19 through December 28, 1989 (Christmas Tour)
- March 19 through March 28, 1990
- April 9 through April 18, 1990

Trip Begins:	McAllen, Texas
Trip Ends:	Laredo, Texas

Highlights:
This has become one of the most popular trips offered by Pancho Villa Moto-Tours (PVMT). Combining a rich blend of history, scenic riding, culture diversities, and special activities, this tour offers you a chance to see Mexico as few Americans do. You will ride through the heart of the Bajio region, a territory so influenced by the Spanish and French that you'll think you're in Europe. Sharp Gothic lines blend with Moorish domes; walled fortresses give way to cobblestone walkways and sidewalk cafes. Out in the country, you're likely to see men working a field with a wooden plow pulled by a team of oxen. Add to this the flavor of native markets, the fiesta, the sights, sounds, and smells that are Mexico, and you'll have an unforgettable trip.

Price (does not include motorcycle rental):
- Single rider, double occupancy .... $ 695
- Two people (one or two bikes) $1,329
- Supplement for single room occupancy .... $ 265

Price Includes:
Ten overnight stays (double occupancy); 10 meals; a bilingual tour escort; road logs, maps, and information; guided tour of Guanajuato; boat excursions to Patzcuaro Lake Island of Janitzo; Pancho Villa T-shirt; and processing of all visas and vehicle permits. If there are eight or more motorcycles, a followup vehicle will travel with the group to assist in the event of mechanical failures.

Motorcycle Provisions:
Travelers are invited to bring their own motorcycle or they may rent one from Pancho Villa Moto-Tours. Rental machines must be picked up and delivered at El Paso, Texas; delivery to McAllen and pickup from Laredo can be arranged by PVMT.

Luggage Provisions:
Travelers should be prepared to carry their own luggage with them. Excess luggage and purchases may be stored in followup vehicle on a space-available basis.

Reader Discount:
A discount of $25 applies to this tour when you send in the Reader Discount Coupon.

MEXICO

Copper Canyon Trail Ride

Tour Operator:
Great Motorcycle Adventures
8241 Heartfield Lane
Beaumont, TX 77706

Contact: Mr. Les "Gringo" French
Phone: 800-642-3933 (within Texas: 409-866-7891)
FAX: 409-832-1474

Rest stop in Copper Canyon

Length of Tour:	7 days, 6 nights

Dates:
- June 18 through June 24, 1989
- August 6 through August 12, 1989
- December 24 through December 30, 1989
- February 11 through February 17, 1990
- April 8 through April 14, 1990
- June 17 through June 23, 1990
- August 12 through August 18, 1990
- November 18 through November 24, 1990
- December 23 through December 29, 1990

Trip Begins and Ends:	El Paso, Texas

Highlights:
Explore the heights of the fabulous Sierra Madre Mountains and the depths of the great Copper Canyon. Discover incomparable scenery with mile-high sheer cliffs and tumbling waterfalls. Climb to mountain peaks at a height of 12,000 feet. Wind down the trail in Copper Canyon on a magnificent seven-mile descent to the historical mining town of Batopilas. Turn back the clock for your two-day stay in this Spanish colonial town. In the belly of this magnificent canyon, you'll find primitive yet still inhabited Indian cave dwellings and abandoned gold and silver mines. Ride through pine groves in cool mountain air. Wind your way through palm and banana trees in the tropical heat of the Canyon. Run improved dirt trails or challenging two-tracks, if it suits your fancy.

Price (does not include motorcycle rental):
- Rider, double occupancy $758
- Non-riding guest, double occupancy $758

Price Includes:
Six nights first class hotel accommodation (or best available in the more remote regions); all meals while in Mexico; bilingual tour guide; support vehicle; motorcycle fuel while in Mexico; and a souvenir shirt.

Motorcycle Provisions:
Motorcycle rentals are $354 for the entire trip. Great Motorcycle Adventures (GMA) requires a $100 damage deposit. This is refundable at the end of the trip provided the motorcycle is returned in good condition. GMA has a good selection of late model, well maintained, four-stroke motorcycles available in sizes from 200cc to 650cc. When you rent a bike from GMA they will perform all adjustments and repairs, including flats. Rental includes transportation for you and your rental motorcycle from the border to the trailhead in Mexico via one of their staff passenger vans.

Luggage Provisions:
A van accompanies this trip to carry luggage.

Special Notes:
Surcharge to transport non-riding guest from border departure point to trailhead hotel in Mexico, round trip, is $35. This fee is included in the price if you rent a motorcycle from Great Motorcycle Adventures.

Reader Discount:
A discount of $50 applies to this tour when you send in the Reader Discount Coupon.

MEXICO	**Cyclecruise™ to Mexico's Riviera**
Tour Operator:	Bike Tours Unlimited P.O. Box 1965 San Pedro, CA 90733 Contact: Mr. Vic Perniciaro Phone: 213-833-2671
Length of Tour:	15 days

GUIDED TOURS – MEXICO & CARIBBEAN 81

Dates:
- January 8 through January 22, 1989 (for reference)
- February 9 through February 19, 1989 (for reference)
- March 18 through April 1, 1989 (for reference)
- April 8 through April 22, 1989

[1990 dates not yet established]

Trip Begins and Ends:
Los Angeles, (Port San Pedro), California

Highlights:
On this combined sailing/motorcycling trip you'll start out with a luxurious three-day ocean cruise complete with fabulous food and floating casino as you journey from Los Angeles to Puerto Vallarta, Mexico. There, you'll mount your motorcycle and sample the resort area of Old Mexico for eight days of relaxed touring. Marvel at the serene beauty of historic Guadalajara and the majestic Indian pyramids outside Mexico City. View daring cliff divers in sparkling Acapulco. Shop for silver jewelry and Indian pottery. Delight in the fiery Mexican cuisine, a blend of Spanish and Indian influence. Finally, you will reboard the cruise ship for four days of pampered sailing back to the States, with stops at Mazatlan and Cabo San Lucas.

Price:
- Inside cabin, double occupancy $2,117
- Outside cabin, double occupancy $2,259
- Cost to ship additional motorcycle, round trip .... $ 165

Price Includes:
Round trip cruise on the M/V Stardancer; round trip for one motorcycle per couple or single; welcome and farewell lunches in Mexico; all hotel accommodations; all breakfasts and dinners in Mexico; guided tours in English.

Motorcycle Provisions:
Riders are expected to use their own motorcycle; shipping to and from Mexico is included in the price.

Luggage Provisions:
A motorcycle trailer is brought along on this tour to carry reasonable overflow luggage. Travelers are expected to carry the bulk of their own luggage.

MEXICO

"Dual Purpose" Expedition to the Sierra Madres

Tour Operator:	Pancho Villa Moto-Tours 9437 E.B. Taulbee El Paso, TX 79924 Contact: Mr. Skip Mascorro Phone: 915-757-3032 FAX: 915-562-1505
Length of Tour:	9 days

Dates:
- April 24 through May 2, 1989
- May 26 through June 3, 1989
- September 18 through September 26, 1989
- October 2 through October 10, 1989
- November 6 through November 14, 1989

Trip Begins and Ends:	El Paso, Texas

Highlights:
This tour is for adventurers only — the "dual purpose" touring enthusiast. This term refers to the highway and off-road paths taken by this tour as you explore parts of Mexico well beyond the interstates. You'll need an appropriate motorcycle to enjoy this trip: one like the BMW G/S, the Kawasaki KLR 650, or the Cagiva Elefant, with extended fuel capacity, lighter weight and longer suspension travel. Your extra effort on this trip will be rewarded by thrilling rides through breathtaking canyons with waterfalls cascading from shear cliffs, to remote villages accessible only by unpaved surfaces. You'll cross old wooden bridges and ford an occasional stream to reach the back country village of Batopilas, where you will see the Tarahumara Indian, a primitive group of people, many of whom still live in caves. Here, the men wear loin cloths, undaunted by modern custom. The Sierra Madres were long ago abandoned by Spanish explorers, but you'll see remnants of their influence in 17th century churches and follow their original trails. Here's an unusual chance to break away in a challenging and rewarding tour.

Price (does not include motorcycle rental):
- Single rider, double occupancy $695

Price Includes:
Hotel accommodations for eight nights (double occupancy); at least 10 meals; a bilingual tour escort; road logs, maps, and information; city tour of Chihuahua; Pancho Villa T-shirt; and processing of all visas and vehicle permits. A followup vehicle will travel with the group to assist with emergency motorcycle repairs.

Non-riders: Limited space may be available in the followup vehicle for non-riding tour participants. Tour price is the same for vehicle passengers as for riding participants. Call for space availability.

Motorcycle Provisions:
Travelers are invited to bring their own dual-purpose motorcycle or they may rent one from Pancho Villa Moto-Tours.

Luggage Provisions:
Travelers should be prepared to carry their own luggage with them. Excess luggage and purchases may be stored in followup vehicle on a space-available basis.

Special Notes:
No open pipes are allowed. This is a motorcycle tour not a motocross race or trials competition. Riders are expected to display respect for the tranquility and environment of the Sierra Madres and the primitive inhabitants.

Reader Discount:
A discount of $25 applies to this tour when you send in the Reader Discount Coupon.

JAMAICA — Jamaica

Tour Operator:	Von Thielmann Tours P.O. Box 87764 San Diego, CA 92138 Contact: Ms. Gina Guzzardo Phone: 619-463-7788 or 619-291-7057 FAX: 619-291-4630 Telex: 910 335 1607 MESA SERV SDG
Length of Tour:	9 days

84 GUIDED TOURS – MEXICO & CARIBBEAN

Dates:	Every Saturday
Trip Begins and Ends:	Los Angeles, California or Miami, Florida

Highlights:
Fly and ride arrangements include all necessary reservations for this motorcycle tour for individuals. Circle trip of a beautiful Caribbean Island with the finest beaches and many things to see and to do.

Price (includes motorcycle rental):
- Single rider, double occupancy $1,255
- Two people, double occupancy $2,170
- Single passenger, double occupancy $1,085
- Supplement for single room occupancy .... $ 260

Price Includes:
Airfare from Los Angeles, round trip; hotel accommodations; breakfast daily; transfers; rental motorcycles and third party liability insurance.

Motorcycle Provisions:
Rental motorcycle, approximately 200cc to 450cc, included.

Luggage Provisions:
Suitcases may be stored at first hotel. Riders should bring their own tank bag, and travel light (warm weather). For groups of at least 15 passengers, a luggage bus with driver can be provided at approximately $75 per person.

MEXICO — Los Pancho Rider

Tour Operator:	TransCyclist International CPO Box 2064 Tokyo, 100-91 JAPAN Contact: Mr. Volker Lenzner Phone: (81) 3-402-5385 FAX: (81) 3-402-5358
Length of Tour:	8 days on- and off-road, covering approximately 1,500 km

GUIDED TOURS – MEXICO & CARIBBEAN

Dates:
- 1989/1990, monthly (dates subject to booking requests)

Trip Begins and Ends: El Paso, Texas

Highlights:
This adventurous bike tour into rugged, rustic Old Mexico covers exhilarating climbs through the timeless Sierra Madre Mountains. Visit the Tarahumara Indians — the most primitive people north of Panama. See the spectacular Casa Grandes cave apartments in an archaeological side expedition to Madera, Creel, Batopilas, the Rancho Estancia, and the town of Chihuahua, home of the legendary bandit-revolutionary Pancho Villa, a brilliant guerrilla fighter with dozens of wives and even more offspring. The spirit of Pancho still lives in Old Mexico and the group will visit his home as part of a comprehensive tour of Chihuahua. The emphasis of this tour is to experience the lifestyles, history, and culture of Mexico and things Mexican while enjoying some superb and challenging riding. The trip will include some adventurous off-road spins into cactus-studded Macaroni Western scenery. Daily mileage not more than 450 km.

Price (does include motorcycle rental):
- Single rider, double occupancy $1,550
- Passenger (van), double occupancy ....$ 950

Note: A $400 U.S. insurance bond is required when renting the motorcycle; refundable when the motorcycle is returned free of damage.

Price Includes:
Seven nights accommodations; breakfasts and dinners; Mexican visa arrangements; El Paso airport transfers; guiding; support van for accompanying family/friends and your gear; motorcycle rental; fuel; tour briefings and information packet; souvenir; vehicle insurance; tour excursions. Not included: lunch snacks, travel/accident insurance.

Motorcycle Provisions:
Kawasaki KLR 650 dual purpose (no pillion riding).

Luggage Provisions:
A support van will carry luggage.

Special Notes:
International driver's license valid for motorcycle operation required by participants. Prices are subject to change. You are advised to book well in advance. The tour requires a minimum of six participants. Five passengers can be accommodated in the support van. Send a self-addressed, stamped envelope and one international reply coupon (available from the post office) when inquiring about the tour.

GUIDED TOURS – MEXICO & CARIBBEAN

MEXICO, WEST COAST	**Mardigras 1990 in Mazatlan**
Tour Operator:	Pancho Villa Moto-Tours 9437 E.B. Taulbee El Paso, TX 79924 Contact: Mr. Skip Mascorro Phone: 915-757-3032 FAX: 915-562-1505
Length of Tour:	13 days and 13 nights, covering approximately 1,600 miles (longest day is 300 miles; shortest is 130 miles).
Dates:	February 19 through March 4, 1990
Trip Begins and Ends:	Nogales, Arizona

Highlights:
This is a tour with fiesta as the principle highlight. Destination: the Pacific Pearl of Mexico, Mazatlan! Every year, Mardigras (or Carnival) is a weeklong celebration with entertainment, parades, music, and a night life that is nothing short of electric. The Mardigras tour is designed for those who want to party and enjoy watching others in the spirit of this pre-Lent celebration. To add balance to the tour, you will take in all of the activities included in the popular West Coast 10-day tour, notably the excursion on the Chihuahua al Pacifico Railroad to the remote Sierra Madre region known as the Copper Canyon. The stay in colonial Alamos and along the Rio Fuerte will be your chance to see native towns founded and occupied by the Spanish during the 18th century, still maintaining that Old World charm. With four nights at the Mexican Riviera where the beaches are some of the best in Mexico, and you are far from the cold of winter, this is truly a vacation tour. Book early as reservations for accommodations right on the playa require early notice and deposit. Come fiesta with Pancho Villa Moto-Tours!

Price (does not include motorcycle rental):
- Double occupancy, per person .... $ 969
- Per couple $1,879
- Supplement for single room occupancy .... $ 425

Price Includes:
Deluxe lodging for 13 nights; no fewer than ten meals; various Mardigras activities; admission to the famous fiesta at the Playa Mazatlan Hotel; train tickets and transfers for the overnight Copper Canyon excursion; guided

walking tour of old colonial Alamos; processing of vehicle permits and visas; bilingual tour escort; information packet, maps, printed materials, etc. Insurance is arranged but not included in the price.

Motorcycle Provisions:
Motorcycle rental available starting at $45 per day plus insurance and any transport fees to and from El Paso, Texas. Contact Pancho Villa Moto-Tours for updated inventory and details.

Luggage Provisions:
Travelers are expected to handle their own luggage. Purchases and excess gear can be kept in the followup vehicle on a space-availability basis. Followup vehicle and additional support staff require a minimum of 10 tour participants.

Special Notes:
Early reservations are a must for this tour. Mardigras dates are extremely popular and groups are limited to no more than 22 persons. Mexico insurance normally runs from four to six dollars per day on this and all Mexico tours and is based on vehicle value. Mazatlan hosts the fourth largest Mardigras celebration in the world.

Reader Discount:
A discount of $25 applies to this tour when you send in the Reader Discount Coupon.

MEXICO	**Mexico**
Tour Operator:	Von Thielmann Tours P.O. Box 87764 San Diego, CA 92138 Contact: Ms. Gina Guzzardo Phone: 619-463-7788 or 619-291-7057 FAX: 619-291-4630 Telex: 910 335 1607 MESA SERV SDG
Length of Tour:	15 days
Dates:	May 6 through May 20, 1989
Trip Begins and Ends:	San Diego or Los Angeles, California

88 GUIDED TOURS – MEXICO & CARIBBEAN

Highlights:
Sail from Los Angeles for four sparkling days aboard the glamorous Stardancer. Watch porpoise and flying fish from the deck or sun by the pool. Dock at Puerto Vallarta, one of Mexico's premier resorts, where your Guadalajara guide welcomes you with a zesty Mariachi band. You'll speed from international resorts to fishing villages and colonial towns. Sample the Mexican Riviera. From historic Puerto Vallarta with red-tiled roofs and cobblestone streets to the coral pools and pelicans of Mazatlan, you'll delight in the splendor of this coast's white beaches and sapphire seas. Visit El Fuerte, a colonial landmark from the 1600s. Remember, this is the land where Spanish conquistadors intermingled with native Indians.

Price (does not include motorcycle rental):
- Single rider, double occupancy $1,483
- Two people, double occupancy $2,966
- Single passenger, double occupancy $1,483
- Supplement for single room occupancy .... $ 388

Price Includes:
Hotel accommodations; cruise cabin accommodation; many meals; tour guide; maps; luggage transportation.

Motorcycle Provisions:
Bring your own motorcycle. (Rentals available in San Diego.)

Luggage Provisions:
Support vehicle (with motorcycle trailer) will carry luggage.

NORTHERN MEXICO **"'Mini-Chihuahua" Tour**

Tour Operator:	Pancho Villa Moto-Tours 9437 E.B. Taulbee El Paso, TX 79924 Contact: Mr. Skip Mascorro Phone: 915-757-3032 FAX: 915-562-1505
Length of Tour:	4 days and 4 nights, covering approx. 775 miles (longest day is 245 miles; shortest is 120 miles)

Dates:
1989:
- May 29 through June 2, 1989
- June 19 through June 23, 1989
- July 3 through July 7, 1989
- September 18 through September 22, 1989

1990:
- April 23 through April 27, 1990

Trip Begins and Ends: El Paso, Texas

Highlights:
If you are limited on time, and wish to sample Mexico before committing to a more extended excursion, then the Mini-Chihuahua Tour is the ideal opportunity. In most cases, to really experience Mexico requires the enthusiast to venture well beyond the border lands. However, the Mexican state of Chihuahua offers diverse cultural highlights such as the primitive Tarahumara Indian, the largest community of the religious Mennonites in the Americas, and of course the lifestyle of the urban Mexican in Chihuahua City.

New and improved roads permit travelers to see the beautiful Sierra Madres, once the remote refuge of Pancho Villa and his band of revolutionary Dorados. In the early 1600s the Spaniards occupied Chihuahua where, even today, colonial influences are evident. The Mini-Chihuahua Tour provides value, convenience, and just enough exposure to Old Mexico to have you wanting to come back for more. This is also a great tour for touring clubs who wish to sponsor a group event. Special group rates and exclusive dates will be arranged upon request.

Price (does not include motorcycle rental):
- Single rider, double occupancy $389
- Two riders, double occupancy $695
- Supplement for single room occupancy $100

Price Includes:
No fewer than six quality meals; tour of Pancho Villas' home, now the museum to the Mexican Revolution; guided tour of the Tarahumara Indian region outside of Creel; a visit to the Mennonite Colony; Mexican vehicle insurance (liability and theft only); four nights deluxe lodging; processing of vehicle documents and visas; bilingual tour escort; currency exchange service.

Motorcycle Provisions:
A variety of touring class and sport motorcycles are available for rent at rates starting from $45 per day. Contact PVMT for current inventory.

Luggage Provisions:
No followup vehicle is included in this tour due to the close proximity to the U.S. and in order to maintain economy in the tour package.

Special Notes:
Rendezvous to begin this tour is 5 p.m. on Mondays. The Mini-Chihuahua tour originates on Monday and exits Mexico by approximately 4 p.m. on Friday of the same week, allowing for weekend travel to and from the rendezvous point. Former customer discounts do not apply to the Mini-Chihuahua Tour.

Reader Discount:
A discount of $25 applies to this tour when you send in the Reader Discount Coupon.

MEXICO	Monterreys' Cascade Cola de Caballo Trail Ride
Tour Operator:	Great Motorcycle Adventures 8241 Heartfield Lane Beaumont, TX 77706 Contact: Mr. Les "Gringo" French Phone: 800-642-3933 (within Texas: 409-866-7891) FAX: 409-832-1474
Length of Tour:	7 days, 6 nights

Dates:
- May 28 through June 3, 1989
- September 3 through September 9, 1989
- November 19 through November 25, 1989
- January 14 through January 20, 1990
- May 27 through June 2, 1990
- September 2 through September 8, 1990

Trip Begins and Ends:	Laredo, Texas

Highlights:
South of the Mexican-American border, you'll caravan to an old hacienda high in the Sierra Madre Oriental Mountains. Use this as your base for a

week of exploration on the challenging trails of the eastern Sierra Madres. Explore fabulous Huasteca Canyon. Also, you'll pack out for a two-day trip to a ghost town high in the Sierras. Drive over 24 kilometers of cobblestone and through 2,000 meters of mine shaft tunnel to an abandoned mining town, once a boom town with 40,000 miners and its own mint. You'll find sun, adventure, and Latin hospitality in the rugged Mexican mountains.

Price (does not include motorcycle rental):
- Rider, double occupancy $758
- Non-riding guest, double occupancy $758

Price Includes:
Six nights first class hotel accommodation (or best available in the more remote regions); all meals while in Mexico; bilingual tour guide; support vehicle; motorcycle fuel while in Mexico; and a souvenir shirt.

Motorcycle Provisions:
Motorcycle rentals are $354 for the entire trip. Great Motorcycle Adventures (GMA) requires a $100 damage deposit. This is refundable at the end of the trip provided the motorcycle is returned in good condition. GMA has a good selection of late model, well maintained, four-stroke motorcycles available in sizes from 200cc to 650cc. When you rent a bike from GMA they will perform all adjustments and repairs, including flats. Rental includes transportation for you and your rental motorcycle from the border to the trailhead in Mexico via one of their staff passenger vans.

Luggage Provisions:
A van accompanies this trip to carry luggage.

Special notes:
Surcharge to transport non-riding guest from border departure point to trailhead hotel in Mexico, round trip, is $35. This fee is included in the price if you rent a motorcycle from Great Motorcycle Adventures.

Reader Discount:
A discount of $50 applies to this tour when you send in the Reader Discount Coupon.

MEXICO, WEST COAST — West Coast of Mexico with Copper Canyon Excursion

Tour Operator:	Pancho Villa Moto-Tours 9437 E.B. Taulbee El Paso, TX 79924 Contact: Mr. Skip Mascorro Phone: 915-757-3032 FAX: 915-562-1505
Length of Tour:	9 days and 9 nights, covering approx. 1,100 miles (longest day is 275 miles; shortest is 120 miles)

Dates:
1989:
- October 23 through November 1, 1989
- December 17 through December 26, 1989 (Christmas)

1990:
- March 5 through March 14, 1990
- April 16 through April 25, 1990
- May 14 through May 23, 1990

Trip Begins and Ends:	Nogales, Arizona

Highlights:
Touring enthusiasts from the western U.S. will find this trip particularly convenient. The itinerary was designed to offer different accommodations and points of interest on each leg of the trip. Some of those highlights include two nights at Kino Bay, home of the Seri Indians who are noted for their handmade iron wood figures. At Kino you can wander through a beach-side pueblo and see artisans crafting beautiful figures of eagles, dolphin, shark, turtle, seals, and quail from a dense hard wood. Iron wood is an expensive item in North American gift shops, but the price is definitely right when purchasing it from the artisan himself.

You will reach the Copper Canyon region in the high Sierra Madres via the Chihuahua al Pacifico Railway, the only way to get to this remote region. Here the Tarahumara live in caves clinging along the high cliffs of the barranca country. Stay overnight in a rustic lodge in the mountains, far from modern society.

Stop at colonial Alamos and the old Spanish village of El Fuerte, where you will spend the night in an 18th century converted hacienda. On your return, there will be two nights at the Sea of Cortez in San Carlos, today a popular wintering spot for North Americans escaping the cold of winter.

Price (does not include motorcycle rental):
- Single rider, double occupancy ....$ 795
- Couple, double occupancy $1,495
- Supplement for single room occupancy ....$ 350

Price Includes:
Deluxe lodging for nine nights; no fewer than eight meals; guided walking tour of colonial Alamos; train tickets and transfers to the Copper Canyon region of the Sierra Madres; processing of vehicle documents and visas; bilingual tour escort; currency exchange service; complete info packet, maps, and preparation materials. Insurance is arranged but not included in the price.

Motorcycle Provisions:
Motorcycles available for rent starting from $45 per day, plus any transport fees to and from El Paso, Texas. Does not include insurance. Call Pancho Villa Moto-Tours for inventory and details.

Luggage Provisions:
Riders are to handle their own luggage. Space in followup vehicle for excessive luggage on a space-availability basis. Information is provided concerning storage of trailers or other vehicles in Nogales while on tour.

Special Notes:
You will rendezvous at 5 p.m. the first day to begin the tour, crossing the following morning into Mexico. This schedule allows tour participants a full day of travel to the origination point at Nogales.

Reader Discount:
A discount of $25 applies to this tour when you send in the Reader Discount Coupon.

MEXICO	**Yucatan Peninsula Dual Sport/Road Trip**
Tour Operator:	Great Motorcycle Adventures 8241 Heartfield Lane Beaumont, TX 77706 Contact: Les "Gringo" French Phone: 800-642-3933 (within Texas: 409-866-7891) FAX: 409-832-1474
Length of Tour:	14 days

Dates:
- October 14 through October 27, 1989
- March 4 through March 17, 1990
- October 13 through October 26, 1990

Trip Begins and Ends:	Laredo, Texas

Highlights:

The Yucatan Peninsula has some of the most incredible sights this hemisphere has to offer. This 3,000-mile, two-week trip encompasses just about every kind of scenery, including winding mountain roads, ancient Mayan ruin sites with towering pyramids jutting high above lush tropical canopies, colonial cities, quaint Mayan villages, and the beautiful Caribbean beaches along the primitive coast of Quintana Roo.

You'll meet your riding companions in Laredo, Texas for this adventure and then ride down the east coast of Mexico to the Yucatan. There you'll do a 600-mile route to circumnavigate the Mayan pyramids. You'll visit the major ruin sites as well as some remote, little-known spots Les French has discovered in his many years of travel in this area. You'll travel from pine forested mountains to tropical jungles complete with fascinating wildlife, waterfalls, and bromiliads. Southern Mexico has some of the most spectacular flora and fauna in the world.

You'll spend a couple of days on the Caribbean beaches at the Hotel Akumal Club-Caribe. This is a great hotel right on the beach, that has all the amenities travelers have come to expect. Scuba diving is available; you'll be next to the clearest water in the world, according to Jacques Cousteau.

You'll stay in first class hotels during the entire trip, some of which are Club Meds at the major ruin sites. The Yucatan cuisine is wonderful and is a culinary adventure in itself.

The first few days of this trip will be 300-mile days. After that, the pace will slow down to give you time to really experience the Yucatan.

Price (does not include motorcycle rental):
- Rider, double occupancy $1,679
- Riding or non-riding passenger, double occupancy $1,456

Price Includes:
All deluxe hotel accommodation (or best available in the more remote regions); all meals south of the border; insurance for your motorcycle; support vehicle; all motorcycle fuel while in Mexico; experienced bilingual tour guide (including "Gringo" himself).

Motorcycle Provisions:
Large displacement touring motorcycles and 600cc or larger dual sport bikes are recommended for this trip. You may bring your own motorcycle to the trail head, or rent a late model dual purpose bike, 600cc and larger from Great Motorcycle Adventures. Rental rates are $775 for the 14-day tour; includes all maintenance, repairs (provided they are not caused by negligence or abuse), insurance, and fuel. Great Motorcycle Adventures has a limited number of dual purpose motorcycles available for this trip, so make your reservation early.

Luggage Provisions:
A van accompanies this trip to carry luggage and spares. Non-riding guests are welcome and can ride in the van if they wish.

Reader Discount:
A discount of $50 applies to this tour when you send in the Reader Discount Coupon.

MEXICO — Yucatan Tour

Tour Operator:	Pancho Villa Moto-Tours 9437 E.B. Taulbee El Paso, TX 79924 Contact: Mr. Skip Mascorro Phone: 915-757-3032 FAX: 915-562-1505
Length of Tour:	29 days; covers approx. 4,200 miles
Dates:	February 12 through March 12, 1990

Trip Begins:	Laredo, Texas
Trip Ends:	McAllen, Texas

Highlights:
This is probably the ultimate motorcycle excursion to Mexico. You'll travel far south to the Yucatan Peninsula, through rain forests, jungle, high mountains, and low deserts. You'll see remnants from the lost Mayan civilization: ceremonial ball courts, advanced astronomical observatories, sacrificial wells, and fascinating temples rivaling the pyramids of Egypt. In addition to exploring the history and archaeology of the Mayans, you will also have plenty of time to enjoy the sunny beaches and blue waters of the Caribbean, the Gulf of Mexico, the Gulf of Campeche, and the Pacific on this tour. Perhaps the greatest reward though will be to get acquainted with the tribal peoples of Mexico, far from the influence of tourists. You will experience the lifestyle of Mexico's original native inhabitants. Here, you'll be called upon to adapt, so put on your explorer's hat.

Price (does not include motorcycle rental):
- Single rider, double occupancy $1,849
- Two people (one or two bikes) $3,595
- Supplement for single room occupancy .... $ 450

Price Includes:
Deluxe hotel accommodations for 28 nights (double occupancy); at least 14 meals; a bilingual tour escort; road logs, maps, and information; guided tours of archaeological sites at Monte Alaban, Palenque, Chichen Itza, Tulum, and others; Light and Sound show at the temples of Uxmal; walking tour of the Spanish fortress of Ulula in Veracruz; excursion to Isla Mujeres in Cancun; city tour of colonial Oaxaca; Pancho Villa T-shirt; and processing of all visas and vehicle permits.

Motorcycle Provisions:
Travelers are invited to bring their own motorcycle or they may rent one from Pancho Villa Moto-Tours. Rental machines must be picked up and delivered at El Paso, Texas; delivery to Laredo and pickup from McAllen can be arranged by PVMT.

Luggage Provisions:
Travelers should be prepared to carry their own luggage with them. Excess luggage and purchases may be stored in followup vehicle on a space-available basis.

Reader Discount:
A discount of $25 applies to this tour when you send in the Reader Discount Coupon.

GUIDED TOURS - SOUTH AMERICA

ARGENTINA | Argentina

Tour Operator:	Von Thielmann Tours P.O. Box 87764 San Diego, CA 92138 Contact: Ms. Gina Guzzardo Phone: 619-463-7788 or 619-291-7057 FAX: 619-291-4630 Telex: 910 335 1607 MESA SERV SDG
Length of Tour:	20 days
Dates:	November 1989; February 1990
Trip Begins and Ends:	Los Angeles, California

Highlights:
Changing scenery: dense forests, lakes and beaches, Los Cantaros Waterfalls, Pueblo National Park, Los Alercos National Park, Peninsula de Valdez, "Bird Island," Bariloche, Buenos Aires.

Price (does not include motorcycle rental):
- Single rider, double occupancy $2,750
- Two people, double occupancy $5,500
- Single passenger, double occupancy $2,750
- Supplement for single room occupancy .... $ 680

Price Includes:
Round trip airfare from Los Angeles; transfers; hotel accommodations; breakfast daily; plus many other meals; excursions and sightseeing; tour guide; luggage transportation; and maps.

Motorcycle Provisions:
Rentals available.

Luggage Provisions:
Luggage will be carried in support vehicle.

GUIDED TOURS – SOUTH AMERICA

VENEZUELA	The Inca Rider
Tour Operator:	TransCyclist International CPO Box 2064 Tokyo, 100-91 JAPAN Contact: Mr. Volker Lenzner Phone: (81) 3-402-5385 FAX: (81) 3-402-5358

Length of Tour:
- Six-day tour of Central Venezuela, covering approximately 1,200 km
- Nine-day tour of Western Venezuela and the Andes, covering approximately 2,000 km
- 13-day tour of Northeast Venezuela, covering approximately 2,500 km
- 20-day tour combining West and the Andes and Northeast Venezuela, covering approximately 4,500 km

Dates:
1989 (the following dates are approximate):
- April 2 through April 21, 1989 (20-day tour)
- October 15 through October 27, 1989 (13-day tour)
- October 28 through November 5, 1989 (9-day tour)
- November 15 through November 27, 1989 (13-day tour)
- November 29 through December 11, 1989 (13-day tour)

1990 (the following dates are approximate):
- January 17 through January 29, 1990 (13-day tour)
- February 10 through February 18, 1990 (9-day tour)
- February 28 through March 12, 1990 (13-day tour)
- April 1 through April 20, 1990 (20-day tour)
- October 14 through October 26, 1990 (13-day tour)
- October 27 through November 4, 1990 (9-day tour)
- November 14 through November 26, 1990 (13-day tour)
- November 28 through December 10, 1990 (13-day tour)

Six-day tours are operational with a minimum of four bookings at any time between May and September.

Trip Begins and Ends:	Caracas, Venezuela airport

Highlights:
Enjoy TransCyclist's (TC) unique motorcycle tour of exotic Venezuela, the safe and unspoiled South America. A country of breathtaking scenic contrasts with no modern traffic hassles. Ride along palm fringed Carib-

bean beaches, over dusty desert, and shady jungle road up into Inca territory; the majestic Andes towering 13,000 feet above the ocean. Taste delicious jungle fruit and Caribbean fish. Make lifelong friendships with other tour participants in a paradise where the sun always shines.

Price (includes motorcycle rental):
Six-Day Tour:
- Single rider, double occupancy .... $ 800
- Passenger, double occupancy .... $ 420

Nine-Day Tour:
- Single rider, double occupancy $1,200
- Passenger, double occupancy .... $ 620

13-Day Tour:
- Single rider, double occupancy $1,700
- Passenger, double occupancy .... $ 900
- Surcharge for Honda or BMW: six-day $125; nine-day $135; 13-day $200.
- Supplement for single-occupancy hotel room: six-day $100; nine-day $175; 13-day $270.

Note: A $500 U.S. insurance bond is required when renting the motorcycle; refundable when motorcycle is returned free of damage.

Price Includes:
Caracas airport reception/farewell; welcome party; first day route and traffic orientation; all hotels (double occupancy); one major meal per day; Yamaha motorcycle rental and insurance; and tour guide. Does not include gasoline, breakfasts or lunches. Add about $20 per day for gasoline, meals, etc.

Motorcycle Provisions:
Choice of BMW R100S/RS, Honda GL, or Yamaha RD350LC. Yamaha motorcycle rental is included with the tour price.

Luggage Provisions:
A van accompanies the tour to carry luggage.

Special Notes:
International driver's license valid for motorcycle operation required by participants. Tour price based on minimum of six participants. You are advised to book well in advance. Only male/female couples are allowed to ride double by Venezuelan regulations. Send a self-addressed, stamped envelope and one international reply coupon (available from the post office) when inquiring about the tour.

SOUTH AMERICA	**Peru**
Tour Operator:	Team Aventura Karlsebene 2 8924 Steingaden WEST GERMANY Contact: Mr. Christoph del Bondio Phone: (49) 08862-6161 or (49) 08807-8360
Length of Tour:	14 days, about 1,200 miles

Dates:
- Tour One: June 17 through July 1, 1989
- Tour Two: July 8 through July 22, 1989

Trip Begins and Ends:	Lima, Peru airport

Highlights:

The trip passes along the most interesting and spectacular parts of Peru. You'll start in Arequipa (the white town) and travel to Lake Titicaca to an altitude of 3,800 meters. You'll see Cuzco and, of course, Machu Picchu. Cross the mountains and come down to the coast near Nazca. View from a small airplane the famous Nazca lines, huge geometric and animal patterns, some more than two kilometers (1.25 miles) long, etched into the surrounding stony desert. Spend your last day on the beach near Ica.

Price (includes motorcycle rental):

With round trip airfare between Milan, Italy and Lima, Peru:
- Single rider, double occupancy $4,000
- Passenger, double occupancy $3,400

Without airfare:
- Single rider, double occupancy $2,800
- Passenger, double occupancy $2,200

Price Includes:

Eleven evenings in the best hotels; three organized camp nights; breakfast and dinner each day; luggage transport on a four-wheel drive vehicle; motorcycle rental; airfare from Lima to Arequipa/Ica to Lima; round trip flight of Nazca; boat ride on Lake Titicaca; entrance fees; an English-French, Spanish, and German speaking tour guide (who spent over two years traveling on a motorcycle in South America); insurance; farewell party.

Motorcycle Provisions:
KTM 350 or Honda XL 600 R

Luggage Provisions:
A four-wheel drive vehicle will transport your luggage.

Special Notes:
You must be a very good motorcyclist with experience on dirt roads to participate in this tour. The roads in Peru are very, very bad; on three days you will reach altitudes of about 5,000 meters on the motorcycles.

You can stay one additional week (without bike) and go with Team Aventura to the jungle, or to the mountains.

SOUTH AMERICA

Venezuela: East, West and the Andes

Tour Operator:	Tours, S.R.L. Edif. Res. Los Sauces Entrada A, Piso 8, Apto. 1 Valencia VENEZUELA Contact: Mr. Werner Glode or Mr. Martin Glode Phone: (58) 41-213007 (office) or (58) 41-213752 (home) FAX: (58) 41-342950 Telex: (58) 41-45116
Length of Tour:	20 days, covering approx. 2,700 miles

Dates:
• Tour Seven: March 7 through March 26, 1990

Trip Begins and Ends:	Valencia, Venezuela

Highlights:
This tour covers essentially the Northeast and the West-Andes routes. It extends to the south, visiting Puerto Ordaz and Ciudad Bolivar, with a side trip to the second largest water-driven electrical power plant, Raul Leoni. Return through the Llanos states, Guarico and Apure, and afterward into the Andes. On this tour you'll get a fairly complete round trip of the country.

Price (includes motorcycle rental):
- Single rider, double occupancy, with Yamaha RD 350 LC $2,600
- Passenger, double occupancy $1,370
- Surcharge for Honda GL 1000 or BMW R100 .... $ 300
- Surcharge for single room occupancy ....$ 400

Price Includes:
Insured motorcycle; overnight stays (double occupancy) in the best hotels; a midday or evening meal each day; transport of luggage throughout the trip; an English- and German-speaking tour guide; welcome and farewell parties; transport to and from the Caracas airport.

Motorcycle Provisions:
Yamaha RD 350 LC included with the tour price; BMW R100 or Honda GL 1000 also available at extra cost.

Luggage Provisions:
A van accompanies each tour to carry luggage, except if only one guest motorcycle is on tour.

SOUTH AMERICA

Venezuela: The Northeast

A breezy Caribbean beach

Tour Operator:
Tours, S.R.L.
Edif. Res. Los Sauces
Entrada A, Piso 8, Apto. 1
Valencia
VENEZUELA

Contact: Mr. Werner Glode or Mr. Martin Glode
Phone: (58) 41-213007 (office) or (58) 41-213752 (home)
FAX: (58) 41-342950
Telex: (58) 41-45116

Length of Tour:
13 days, covering approx. 1,500 miles

Dates:
- Tour One: October 15 through October 27, 1989
- Tour Three: November 15 through November 27, 1989

Trip Begins and Ends:
Valencia, Venezuela

Highlights:
If you want to experience the blue waters of the Caribbean, sleepy fishing villages, and unusual sights, then this is the tour for you. You'll ride along the coast through tropical vegetation rich with bananas and papayas, eat fresh fish with the locals and, of course, have plenty of time to relax and swim. Also on the program are the world famous Guacharo caves, with their strange birds; Colonia Tovar, a village high in the Cordilleras founded by German settlers in 1843; and the National Park of Morrocoy, where exceptional bird watching is possible. You'll ride mostly on paved roads in good condition and mix hilly, winding, and flat roads, avoiding highways wherever possible. To take advantage of the short days in Venezuela (it gets dark about 6:30 p.m.) you'll get up early. The daily itinerary is tightly packed. Groups are limited to six motorcycles.

Price (includes motorcycle rental):
- Single rider, double occupancy, with Yamaha RD 350 LC $1,700
- Passenger, double occupancy .... $ 900
- Surcharge for Honda GL1000 or BMW R100 .... $ 200
- Supplement for single room occupancy .... $ 270

Price Includes:
Insured motorcycle; overnight stays (double occupancy) in the best hotels; a midday or evening meal each day; transport of luggage throughout the trip; an English- and German-speaking tour guide; welcome and farewell parties; transport to and from the Caracas airport.

Motorcycle Provisions:
Yamaha RD 350 LC included with the tour price; BMW R100 or Honda GL 1000 also available at extra cost.

Luggage Provisions:
A van accompanies each tour to carry luggage, except if only one guest motorcycle is on tour.

Special Notes:
You can combine Tour One with Tour Two for a three-week trip, or Tour Three with Tour Four for an exceptional four-week trip. See "Venezuela: The West and the Andes." The combined tours (One plus Two, or Three plus Four will have a 10% discount for both).

SOUTH AMERICA

Venezuela:
The West and the Andes

Atop Eagle Pass, the highest in South America (4,116 meters)

Tour Operator:	Tours, S.R.L. Edif. Res. Los Sauces Entrada A, Piso 8, Apto. 1 Valencia ,VENEZUELA Contact: Mr. Werner Glode or Mr. Martin Glode Phone: (58) 41-213007 (office) or (58) 41-213752 (home) FAX: (58) 41-342950 Telex: (58) 41-45116
Length of Tour:	9 days, covering approx. 1,350 miles; 13 days, covering approx. 1,500 miles

Dates:

Nine-day tour:
- Tour Two: October 28 through November 5, 1989
- Tour Six: February 10 through February 18, 1990

13-day tour:
- Tour Four: November 29 through December 12, 1989
- Tour Five: January 17 through January 29, 1990

Trip Begins and Ends:	Valencia, Venezuela

Highlights:

Start this tour visiting the National Park of Morrocoy, where exceptional bird watching is possible, together with snorkeling and swimming in crystal clear water. You'll ride along the dunes of National Park Medanos de Coro, and walk around the old colonial town of Coro. Ride then to Maracaibo (the second most important city of the country) over the largest bridge in South America (eight kilometers). Down south as far as San Cristobal, the road runs through the most fertile part of Venezuela, center of Venezuela's important milk and beef production. In Merida, you have the opportunity to use the world's highest funicular and afterward, pass the highest paved road of all South America. Drive through the Llanos (flat lands) with their vast cattle herds and return to Valencia.

This tour is great for riders who like curves; you'll get 300 miles of them.

Price (includes motorcycle rental):

Nine-day tour:
- Single rider, double occupancy, with Yamaha RD 350 LC $1,200
- Passenger, double occupancy .... $ 620
- Surcharge for Honda GL 1000 or BMW R100 .... $ 135
- Supplement for single room occupancy .... $ 175

13-day tour:
- Single rider, double occupancy, with Yamaha RD 350 LC $1,700
- Passenger, double occupancy .... $ 900
- Surcharge for Honda GL 1000 or BMW R100 .... $ 200
- Supplement for single room occupancy .... $ 270

Price Includes:

Insured motorcycle; overnight stays (double occupancy) in the best hotels; a midday or evening meal each day; transport of luggage throughout the trip; an English- and German-speaking tour guide; welcome and farewell parties; transport to and from the Caracas airport.

Motorcycle Provisions:

Yamaha RD 350 LC included with the tour price; BMW R100 or Honda GL 1000 also available at extra cost.

Luggage Provisions:

A van accompanies each tour to carry luggage, except if only one guest motorcycle is on tour.

Special Notes:

You can combine Tour One with Tour Two for a three-week trip, or Tour Three with Tour Four for an exceptional four-week trip. See "Venezuela: The Northeast." The combined tours (One plus Two, or Three plus Four will have a 10% discount for both).

GUIDED TOURS – GREAT BRITAIN

British Isles

Running through the Scottish Highlands

AMA's EuroTour

Tour Operator:
American Motorcyclist Association
P.O. Box 6114
Westerville, OH 43081

Contact: Mr. Greg Harrison
Phone: 614-891-2425
FAX: 614-891-5012

Length of Tour:
22 days

Dates:
- May 18 through June 8, 1989 (for reference) *
* Note: This trip may be filled by press time. Contact American Motorcyclist Association (AMA) for information about their 1990 tour, as well as other tours that may become available.

Trip Begins and Ends: Any of the following cities: New York, Chicago, Los Angeles, San Francisco.

Highlights:
Join AMA members on their annual motorcycle adventure, covering England, Scotland, Wales, and of course the Isle of Man TT races. Explore the quaint villages and quiet country back roads of the English Cotswolds. Join 25,000 motorcyclists for exhibitions and contests at the Peterborough Rally, Europe's largest one-day motorcycling event. Wind along the edge of infamous and scenic Loch Ness. Travel to the remote, wind-swept Isle of Skye for some of the most spectacular settings in the British Isles. You'll roll through deep green forest, past stunning blue lakes near Loch Lomond and the southern uplands of Scotland. With all this panoramic scenery, you'll still spend five days on the Isle of Man. This is a motorcycle enthusiast's heaven for three weeks in May and June with all the events associated with the incredible TT race.

Price (does not include motorcycle rental):
Single rider, double occupancy:
- New York departure $3,150
- Chicago $3,250

GUIDED TOURS – GREAT BRITAIN   109

- Los Angeles $3,350
- San Francisco $3,350
- Supplement for single room occupancy ....$ 375

Price Includes:
Round trip airfare, all hotels, full board, daily maps and routing, all ferries, plus admission to several attractions and discounts on others.

Motorcycle Provisions:
A variety of mid-sized motorcycles are available for rent. They are usually shaft-driven, water-cooled twins or fours fitted with a small fairing and luggage rack. Price depends upon exchange rate at the time of trip. AMA will arrange motorcycle or car rental and recommends that you rent a motorcycle rather than ship your own.

UNITED KINGDOM — British Bat

Tour Operator:	Beach's Motorcycle Adventures, Ltd. 2763 West River Parkway P.O. Box 36 Grand Island, NY 14072-0036 Contact: Mr. Robert D. Beach Mrs. Elizabeth L. Beach Mr. Rob Beach Phone: 716-773-4960 FAX: 716-773-0783 Telex: 6854139 GIBCO UW
Length of Tour:	22 days

Dates:
- August 5 through August 26, 1989
- August 4 through August 25, 1990
- August 3 through August 24, 1991
- August 2 through August 23, 1992

Trip Begins and Ends:	Boston, Massachusetts

Highlights:
The British Bat is truly a trip through history. Start with a free day in London, and rest from the long flight or see some of that great city's famous

attractions: Trafalgar Square, the National Gallery, the Houses of Parliament, Big Ben, Buckingham Palace, and so much more.

Head west, through Winchester and past Stonehenge. Visit the Welsh Folk Museum in St. Fagan's; meander through the Brecon Beacons, the Black Mountains, and on to the scenic luxury of Snowdonia Forest. Visit Chester, a city right out of the Middle Ages, with its enclosing ramparts still intact. Then it's on to the Lakes District, an area of picturesque villages and hamlets surrounding a variety of azure blue lakes.

Get a taste of Scotland riding through the emptiness of the Scottish highlands on your way to Glasgow, a center of industry and population. Overnight on the islands of Harris and Lewis in the Outer Hebrides. These islands are so isolated they are rarely on an American's itinerary. All Beach tours strive to visit such locations, allowing an in-depth look at the culture and timbre of the area.

The morning ferry returns to the mainland and the day's delightful ride may result in a glimpse of Nessie, the Loch Ness monster, as you travel by the mysterious body of water whose name she bears. Then it's on to Edinburgh to enjoy the fascinating contrast between the Georgian architecture of New Town and the medieval buildings around the Royal Mile. Push on to Tan Hill, the highest pub in Britain, and sample the local pub lunch.

The trip terminates in London, with a free day to take in more of that wonderful city.

Price (does not include motorcycle rental):
- Tour, per person $3,275
- Supplement for single room occupancy . . . . $ 225

Price Includes:
Airfare Boston/London/Boston; hotel accommodation for entire trip; all breakfasts; 16 evening meals; all airport/hotel bus transfers; casual tour jacket, and special tour gifts.

Motorcycle Provisions:
Autos or motorcycles are available for rent on the British Bat. Motorcycles are all current BMW models and have the required liability insurance coverage. In the event of damage to the motorcycle the rider is responsible for the first $350 of repair costs. Rental rates: R80 – $950; R80RT – $1,100; K75C – $1,200. Value Added Tax is included in rental prices. Motorcycles must be reserved 30 days prior to the tour departure date.

Luggage Provisions:
A van accompanies each tour to carry luggage.

Reader Discount:
A discount of $50 applies to this tour when you send in the Reader Discount Coupon.

BRITISH ISLES

British Isles	
Tour Operator:	Von Thielmann Tours P.O. Box 87764 San Diego, CA 92138 Contact: Ms. Gina Guzzardo Phone: 619-463-7788 or 619-291-7057 FAX: 619-291-4630 Telex: 910 335 1607 MESA SERV SDG
Length of Tour:	21 days
Dates:	August 10 through August 30, 1989
Trip Begins and Ends:	New York, New York

Highlights:
Trip includes visit to London, and visits to many historical sites en route. England, Scotland, and the Republic of Ireland.

Price (does not include motorcycle rental):
- Single rider, double occupancy $2,985
- Two people, double occupancy $5,970
- Single passenger, double occupancy $2,985
- Supplement for single room occupancy .... $ 680

Price Includes:
Round trip airfare from New York; hotel accommodations; transfers; breakfast daily; and many other meals; tour guide; maps; luggage transportation.

Motorcycle Provisions:
Rentals available.

Luggage Provisions:
Luggage will be carried in support van.

GUIDED TOURS – GREAT BRITAIN

UNITED KINGDOM	**England and Wales**
Tour Operator:	mhs Motorradtouren GmbH Hans-Urmiller-Ring 59 D-8190 Wolfratshausen WEST GERMANY Contact: Mr. Herbert Schellhorn Phone: (49) 81 71 12 38
Length of Tour:	Eight days, covering approximately 1,750 km
Dates:	June 25 through July 2, 1989
Trip Begins and Ends:	Ostend, Belgium

Highlights:
This tour begins on the ferry at Ostend. You'll pass the White Cliffs of Dover, through Hastings, Stonehenge, Dartmoor, Land's End, the picturesque coastal villages, and the lonely ways through the hills of Cornwall to the relics of the Stone Ages, and onward in the direction of Wales. There are marvelous biking roads with lots of curves, a gold mine which was active in Roman times, a trip on one of the narrow dirt roads, and a visit to Llanfairpwllgwyngyll, the place with the longest name in Great Britain, on the northwest coast of Wales. Snowdonia National Park and many other sights are on the program. You'll go past Stratford-on-Avon, birthplace of Shakespeare, Oxford, and Canterbury and then back to Dover.

Price (does not include motorcycle rental):
- Single rider, double occupancy .... 1,995 DM
- Motorcycle passenger, double occupancy .... 1,675 DM
- Supplement for single room occupancy .... 300 DM

Price Includes:
Ferry from Ostend to Dover and back; accommodation in middle class and better hotels in double bed rooms; full board, including table drinks; gas; entry fees and tolls; typical British food.

Motorcycle Provisions:
No rental bikes available.

Luggage Provisions:
Travelers are responsible for their luggage (no minibus).

GUIDED TOURS – GREAT BRITAIN   113

Special Notes:
The primary languages for this tour are German and English.

Reader Discount:
A discount of $50 applies to this tour when you send in the Reader Discount Coupon.

BRITAIN / ISLE OF MAN   **Isle of Man "Insiders" Tour**

Tour Operator:
Coach House Tours
70 Coolidge Street
Ashland, OR 97520

Contact: Mr. Jack Evans
Phone: 503-482-2257

Riders getting airborne: Isle of Man, 1988

Length of Tour:	12 days
Dates:	May 30 through June 11, 1989
Trip Begins and Ends:	West Coast or East Coast, U.S.A.

Highlights:
Join Jack Evans for 12 days in Britain and the Isle of Man. Visit motorcycle museums. See Norton and Matchless in production on tours of the factories. You'll have time to shop for spare parts and time to buy a new or vintage motorcycle to bring home. Low cost shipping can be arranged. Jack knows where the bargains are on leathers, helmets, rain gear, manuals, etc. Note, this is not a tour *on* a motorcycle but a tour *about* motorcycles.

Price (does not include motorcycle rental):
• Tour, double occupancy, per person $1,745

Price Includes:
Round trip airfare from east or west coast of U.S.; all transportation; hotels; tour guide; all breakfasts and dinners; several pub nights hosted by tour guide.

Motorcycle Provisions:
This is a motorcoach tour; however, tour guide will assist with the purchase of motorcycles. Those riding their bikes will have their luggage transported and can rendezvous with the group at the nightly stop.

Luggage Provisions:
Tour participants are expected to handle their own luggage.

Reader Discount:
A discount of $25 applies to this tour when you send in the Reader Discount Coupon.

EUROPE	**Isle of Man TT Races**
	Tour Operator: Von Thielmann Tours P.O. Box 87764 San Diego, CA 92138 Contact: Ms. Gina Guzzardo Phone: 619-463-7788 or 619-291-7057 FAX: 619-291-4630 Telex: 910 335 1607 MESA SERV SDG
Length of Tour:	17 days
Dates:	May 29 through June 14, 1989
Trip Begins and Ends:	New York, New York

Highlights:
European tour including the Isle of Man TT Races

Price (does not include motorcycle rental):
- Single rider, double occupancy $2,985
- Two people, double occupancy $5,970

- Single passenger, double occupancy $2,985
- Supplement for single room occupancy ....$ 680

Price Includes:
Round trip airfare; hotel accommodations; most meals; arrangements to visit the TT races; tour guide.

Motorcycle Provisions:
Bring your own motorcycle, or rentals available.

Luggage Provisions:
Bring tank bag, saddle bags, bags, back pack. (No luggage van on this tour.)

UNITED KINGDOM	Scotland
Tour Operator:	mhs Motorradtouren GmbH Hans-Urmiller-Ring 59 D-8190 Wolfratshausen WEST GERMANY Contact: Mr. Herbert Schellhorn Phone: (49) 81 71 12 38
Length of Tour:	14 days, approximately 2,500 km
Dates:	August 20 thru September 2, 1989
Trip Begins and Ends:	Rotterdam, The Netherlands

Highlights:
Once you've left the ferry from Rotterdam to Hull you'll go past the cathedral town of York, to the place where Count Dracula was said to have landed when he left the Carpathian mountains. At Gretna Green, the former honeymoon paradise, you'll cross the border, and your path will lead further west on the coast. If you have clear weather you can see as far as Northern Ireland, the Isle of Man, and England.

Your main direction from here on is north. You go past sculptures of Henry Moore, through Glasgow and Sterling into the highlands. Your companions for the coming days will be the heather, the highlands, whiskey breweries, lochs, stories of sprites and fairies, feuds of the clans, fortresses, castles, and ruins. You'll go around Loch Ness and Calloden, the holy battlefields of the Scots.

Next, you'll turn back to the south and toward civilization. It's back toward Perth, the former capital of Scotland; St. Andrews, the home of golf (mentioned for the first time in the year 1547), with the oldest university in the country; and the bridge at the Firth of Forth. These are all stations on your trip back to Edinburgh, the capital of Scotland. Pass Edinburgh, Newcastle, and perhaps Leeds. If time allows, then you go back to Hull and the ferry to Rotterdam.

Price (does not include motorcycle rental):
- Single rider, double occupancy . . . . 3,675 DM
- Motorcycle passenger, double occupancy . . . . 2,975 DM
- Supplement for single room occupancy . . . . 600 DM

Price Includes:
Accommodation in good hotels, partly former castles; full board with typical Scottish food; table drinks; ferry from Rotterdam to Hull and back (no single room possible); gas; tolls; and entry fees, e.g. to the Highland Games.

Motorcycle Provisions:
No rental bikes available.

Luggage Provisions:
No minibus.

Special Notes:
The primary languages for this tour are German and English.

Reader Discount:
A discount of $50 applies to this tour when you send in the Reader Discount Coupon.

GUIDED TOURS – WESTERN EUROPE

EUROPE

AlpenTour™ East

A rest stop high in the Alps

Tour Operator:	Desmond Adventures, Inc. 1280 South Williams Street Denver, CO 80210 Contact: Mr. Thomas E. Desmond Phone: 303-733-9248
Length of Tour:	16 days

Dates:
1989:
- June 16 through July 2, 1989
- July 28 through August 13, 1989
- September 8 through September 24, 1989

1990:
- June 15 through July 1, 1990
- July 27 through August 12, 1990
- September 7 through September 23, 1990

Trip Begins and Ends:	New York – JFK Airport

Highlights:

On this spectacular trip, you'll soar through the breathtaking European Alps and the Italian Dolomites, the most jagged, stunning mountains available for motorcycling. Explore the palaces and castles of King Ludwig of Bavaria. These opulent strongholds were the inspiration for Walt Disney's Fantasyland. Visit Mozart's birthplace in Salzburg, Austria, a city popularized in the movie *The Sound of Music*. Near Europe's highest waterfall, you'll curl through a mountain pass that is so narrow and winding that it only accommodates one-way traffic, changing direction every half-hour. You'll spend a charming night in an operating Austrian hunting lodge and then dash on to Italy to the picturesque village of Cortina D'-Ampezzo. Then you'll see the chic chalets and commanding ski slopes of St. Moritz and Interlaken. From dramatic mountain passes to dense mossy forests, you'll sample the rich flavor of the Eastern Alps and some thrilling motorcycling.

Price (includes motorcycle rental):
- Driver, double occupancy $3,795
- Passenger, double occupancy $3,195
- High season surcharge (July trip, per person) ....$ 100
- Supplement for single room occupancy ....$ 280

Price Includes:

Round trip airfare New York/Zurich/New York; all required insurance; motorcycle rental (additional surcharge applies to some motorcycle models); all accommodations; airport/hotel transfers; all breakfasts; dinner is provided every evening except when the tour spends more than one night in a particular town. On the second night guests are free to make their own arrangements. When dinner is provided it is a group setting enabling riders to share their experiences and plan for the next day's travel.

Motorcycle Provisions:

A wide variety of motorcycles are available, averaging less than one year old, from BMW (K75S, K75C, K100RT, K100RS); Honda (Hawk 650, TransAlp 600 Dominator, VT-750, Interceptor 750, Hurricane 600, Hurricane 1000); Suzuki (GS-550V, Katana 600, Katana 1100); Yamaha (Maxim 750, FZX 750, XJ 600); and Kawasaki (ZL 600, Concours 1000). On specific bikes there is sometimes a surcharge; contact Desmond Adventures for complete information.

Luggage Provisions:

A van accompanies each tour to carry luggage. Luggage is picked up from your hotel room as you leave a hotel, and delivered to your room at the destination. This service saves a lot of trips up and down stairs.

Special Notes:
- By the end of 1988, this tour had been run 31 times and is debugged.
- A complimentary laundry service is offered midway through the trip.
- Single room occupancy available only on the first and last trip of each season.
- People wishing to arrange their own transatlantic transportation to Zurich can deduct $600 from the prices above.

EUROPE — AlpenTour™ West

Tour Operator:
Desmond Adventures, Inc.
1280 South Williams Street
Denver, CO 80210

Contact: Mr. Thomas E. Desmond
Phone: 303-733-9248

Length of Tour:
16 days

It doesn't get any better than this . . .

Dates:
1989:
- May 26 through June 11, 1989
- July 7 through July 23, 1989
- August 18 through September 3, 1989
- September 29 through October 15, 1989

1990:
- May 25 through June 10, 1990
- July 6 through July 22, 1990
- August 17 through September 2, 1990
- September 28 through October 14, 1990

Trip Begins and Ends:	New York – JFK Airport

Highlights:

You'll meet challenge on every turn in this thrilling and romantic tour. Conquer the mighty Matterhorn, charging past postcard-perfect villages improbably perched on those forbidding slopes. Near San Vittorio, Italy, you run the best road in motorcycle touring. After hours of full-throttle driving on the Autostrada, you'll sweep onto a deserted but well-paved two-lane road that cries to be ridden hard. Winding through endless curves, the tree-lined mountain road forces you to deep-leaning turns. Another day of spectacular riding ends at Monte Carlo, glamour capital of the world.

Resist the temptation to compete with Italian bikers on their favorite sport, riding. Instead, delight in the landscape of vineyards and walled medieval villages. The narrow road delivers you right through the ancient gates of Ceriana, a small olive processing village dated five hundred years before Christ. When you finally tear yourself away from the topless beaches of the French Riviera, you discover the true grandeur of the Alps, following roads used by the conquerors Napoleon and Hannibal. From the massive granite cliffs of Canyon de Verdon to a route in Sestriere, Italy that includes six magnificent passes in one day, the panoramic scenery found on this trip is unequaled.

Price (includes motorcycle rental):
- Driver, double occupancy $3,795
- Passenger, double occupancy $3,195
- High season surcharge (July trip, per person) ....$ 100
- Supplement for single room occupancy ....$ 280

Price Includes:

Round trip airfare New York/Zurich/New York; all required insurance; motorcycle rental (additional surcharge applies to some motorcycle models); hotel accommodations; airport/hotel transfers; laundry service; all breakfasts; dinner is provided every evening except when the tour spends more than one night in a particular town. On the second night guests are free to make their own arrangements. When dinner is provided it is a group setting enabling riders to share their experiences and plan for the next day's travel.

Motorcycle Provisions:

A wide variety of motorcycles are available, averaging less than one year old, from BMW (K75S, K75C, K100RT, K100RS); Honda (Hawk 650, TransAlp 600 Dominator, VT-750, Interceptor 750, Hurricane 600, Hurricane 1000); Suzuki (GS-550V, Katana 600, Katana 1100); Yamaha (Maxim 750, FZX 750, XJ 600); and Kawasaki (ZL 600, Concours 1000). On specific bikes there is sometimes a surcharge; contact Desmond Adventures for complete information.

Luggage Provisions:

A van accompanies each tour to carry luggage. Luggage is picked up from your hotel room as you leave a hotel, and delivered to your room at the destination. This service saves a lot of trips up and down stairs.

Special Notes:
- By the end of 1988, this tour had been run 31 times and is very well debugged.
- A complimentary laundry service is offered midway through the trip.
- Single room occupancy available only on the first and last trip of each season.
- People wishing to arrange their own transatlantic transportation to Zurich can deduct $600 from the prices above.

EUROPEAN ALPS   Alpine Adventures

Lots of castles along the way

Tour Operator:

Beach's Motorcycle Adventures, Ltd.
2763 West River Parkway
P.O. Box 36
Grand Island, NY 14072-0036

Contact: Mr. Robert D. Beach
Mrs. Elizabeth L. Beach
Mr. Rob Beach
Phone: 716-773-4960
FAX: 716-773-0783
Telex: 6854139 GIBCO UW

GUIDED TOURS – WESTERN EUROPE

Length of Tour: 16- and 22-day tours, covering approximately 1,900 miles

Dates:
1989:
- June 10 through July 1, 1989
- July 8 through July 29, 1989
- August 5 through August 20, 1989
- September 2 through September 23, 1989

1990:
- June 9 through June 30, 1990
- July 7 through July 28, 1990
- August 4 through August 19, 1990
- September 1 through September 22, 1990

1991:
- June 8 through June 29, 1991
- July 6 through July 27, 1991
- August 3 through August 18, 1991
- September 7 through September 28, 1991

1992:
- June 6 through June 27, 1992
- July 4 through July 25, 1992
- August 1 through August 16, 1992
- September 5 through September 26, 1992

Trip Begins and Ends: Boston, Massachusetts

Highlights:
Is your dream about magnificent mountain riding on the finest roads in the world; breathtaking scenery; diet-shattering food; unique shopping opportunities and enough cultural overload to last a lifetime? Then your choice has to be the European Alps. It's all there — and all in a small area, providing a motorcyclist's paradise.

The Beach family has combined the best of Germany, Austria, Northern Italy, Switzerland, a bit of France, and even tiny Liechtenstein into exciting two- and three-week motorcycling adventures.

After a pleasant flight across the Atlantic on Swiss Air, catch a glimpse of the modern airport at Zurich before boarding a flight to your jumping-off point, Munich. This location provides a glimpse of the friendly Bavarian capital with its magnificent museums, famous beer halls and German efficiency. The September tour permits a visit to the Oktoberfest. With so much to do, see, and experience, many tour members choose to arrive a few days early or stay a few days beyond the tour.

Austria offers beautiful scenery and the world famous Grossglockner mountain pass. The area around Salzburg was the setting for the famous movie, *The Sound of Music*. Rugged Dolomite Mountains, beautiful lakes, and formidable castles are part of the scenery of northern Italy.

Sample French cuisine on a short side trip into the French Alps, an area with a romance all its own. See mighty Mt. Blanc, the highest mountain in the Alps, towering over the French/Swiss border. In Switzerland the mountains, high meadows with ringing cowbells, and superb roads create memories that never fade.

Beach's Alpine Adventures are structured to avoid the big cities and places where tourists usually gather. Riding in large groups is discouraged so everyone has the opportunity to schedule his own daily activities.

So, if you dream of motorcycling with mountains, glaciers, gorges, vineyards, waterfalls, picnics, gentle curves, switchbacks, tunnels and bridges, castles, palaces, lakes and mountain streams, hiking trails and resting vistas, join the Beaches for the adventure of a lifetime!

Price (does not include motorcycle rental):
- 16-day tour, per person $2,750
- Supplement for single room occupancy .... $ 170
- 22-day tour, per person $3,550
- Supplement for single room occupancy .... $ 250

Price Includes:
Airfare Boston/Munich/Boston; all hotels; all breakfasts; 17 evening meals included on 22-day tours (13 evening meals included on 16-day tours); all airport/hotel bus transfers; casual tour jacket; tour book; tour map; and special tour gifts.

Motorcycle Provisions:
Automobiles or motorcycles are available for rent on the Alpine Tour. The motorcycles are all late model BMWs and have the required liability insurance coverage. The rider is responsible for the first $500 damage to the motorcycle in the event of an accident. Rental rates are as follows: 16-day tour – $785; 22-day tour – $1,100.

Luggage Provisions:
A van accompanies each tour to carry luggage.

Special Notes:
Drivers must have state driver's license as well as an international driver's license, both valid for motorcycle operation. Drivers must be at least 25 years of age to qualify for insurance.

Reader Discount:
A discount of $50 applies to this tour when you send in the Reader Discount Coupon.

EUROPEAN ALPS

Alpine and Dolomites Excursion

Rugged Alps dominate the lush meadows

Tour Operator:	Bosenberg Motorcycle Excursions Mainzer Straße 54 D-6550 Bad Kreuznach WEST GERMANY Contact: Mr. Leon A. Heindel Phone: (49) 671-67580
U.S. Agent:	Around the Globe Travel, Ltd. 1417 North Wauwatosa Avenue Milwaukee, WI 53213 Contact: Mr. Walt Weber Phone: 800-234-4037 or 414-257-0199 (in Wisconsin or Canada)
Length of Tour:	18 days, covering approximately 1,750 miles

Dates:
- June 13 through June 30, 1989
- August 29 through September 15, 1989
- September 26 through October 13, 1989

Trip Begins and Ends:	Bad Kreuznach, West Germany

Highlights:
Enjoy the best of group travel and individual discovery in the Alpine paradise of majestic mountains and fantasy castles. Ride with a group of seven or eight motorcycles and a multilingual guide. With three-day stopovers at St. Ulrich and Saalbach, you'll have time to visit castles and museums as well as meet the challenge of fabulous Alpine motorcycling. Swing through switchbacks. Dare the high mountain passes. Storm the incomparable Italian Dolomites, Europe's most rugged Alps. Take an excursion to Salzburg or visit Neuschwanstein Castle, King Ludwig's pleasure palace that inspired Walt Disney's Fantasyland. Cap off your excursion with a final day in Bad Kreuznach and a relaxing river cruise on the Rhine.

Price (does not include motorcycle rental, air transport of motorcycle, or airfare):
- Single rider, double occupancy $1,785
- Passenger, double occupancy $1,535
- Supplement for single room occupancy .... $ 185

Price Includes:
Transportation to/from Frankfurt Airport; 17 nights in select hotels/inns; all meals including mealtime beverages; excursion information package; multilingual tour leader on a motorcycle; daily route briefings; traffic laws and safety slide show; gas and oil for motorcycle; entrance fees for attractions and events (Rhine river cruise, wine tastings, castles, museums, etc.); toll-road and ferry fees; excursion gift.

Motorcycle Provisions:
Ship your own motorcycle or rent a BMW at a 15-day rate with unlimited mileage.

Luggage Provisions:
Luggage van accompanies tour, depending on number of participants.

Special Note:
Options include a longer stay at no additional airfare and rental of a car for friends and family members. Call U.S. agent for details.

Reader Discount:
A discount of $35 applies to this tour when you send in the Reader Discount Coupon.

GUIDED TOURS – WESTERN EUROPE

EUROPEAN ALPS | Alpine Countries

Churches, churches everywhere...

Tour Operator:
World Motorcycle Tours
14 Forest Avenue
Caldwell, NJ 07006

Contact: Mr. Warren Goodman
Phone: 201-226-9107 or 800-443-7519

Length of Tour:
21 days

Dates:
• July 6 through July 27, 1989

Trip Begins and Ends: New York; Chicago; Los Angeles

Highlights:
Begin your Alpine adventure in the luxurious resort area of Northern Yugoslavia. Step from the door of your first-class hotel to fine beaches on the beautiful Adriatic Sea. Enjoy fantastic restaurants and the casino of this Yugoslavian resort. Sweep around the curves of Europe's most spectacular highway to snowcapped Grossglockner, Austria's highest peak. Conquer Europe's most magnificent pass. Scale The Stelvio on twisted roads quarried from the sheer mountain face on each side of the pass. Average five hours of Alpine touring most days. Arrive in time to appreciate your destination. Stay in the lap of luxury with four- and five-star hotels at every stop.

Price (does not include motorcycle rental or shipping):
• Single rider, double occupancy, from New York City $3,195
• From Chicago $3,295
• From Los Angeles $3,395

Price Includes:
Round trip airfare; luxury hotels with two meals daily.

Motorcycle Provisions:
Mr. Goodman specializes in shipping the client's motorcycle. The motorcycle is shipped uncrated. Cost is about $.80 per pound from New York City, higher in other cities. Liability insurance in Europe will cost $101.

Luggage Provisions:
Luggage van will accompany tour.

GERMANY	**Alpine Wandervogel Rider**
Tour Operator:	TransCyclist International CPO Box 2064 Tokyo, 100-91 JAPAN Contact: Mr. Volker Lenzner Phone: (81) 3-402-5385 FAX: (81) 3-402-5358
Length of Tour:	7 days, covering approx. 1,300 km

Dates:
1989 (following dates are approximate):
- May 31 through June 4, 1989
- June 4 through June 8, 1989
- July 5 through July 9, 1989
- July 9 through July 13, 1989
- September 6 through September 10, 1989
- September 10 through September 14, 1989
- September 20 through September 24, 1989
- September 24 through September 28, 1989

1990 (following dates are approximate):
- May 30 through June 3, 1990
- June 3 through June 7, 1990
- July 4 through July 8, 1990
- July 8 through July 12, 1990
- September 5 through September 9, 1990
- September 9 through September 13, 1990
- September 19 through September 23, 1990
- September 23 through September 27, 1990

Trip Begins and Ends: Munich, West Germany

Highlights:
Exhilarating tour of European Alps including visits to the famous Hofbräuhaus in Munich and Hofburg in Innsbruck. Small mountain roads turn into wide sweeping turns as you navigate down into breathtaking Alpine valleys with awesome mountain peaks above. Hundreds upon hundreds of kilometers of fantastic mountain scenery almost as if seen from a birds-eye view. Enjoy those rustic but homey feelings created by Alpine farms, churches, and colorful village pubs where friendly and warm people invite you to rest in preparation for mountain peaks and passes, creeks and rivers, Alpine meadows and glaciers. This is a spectacular ride you will never forget. The spicy-red Alpine wine and Tyrolean dumplings you will enjoy at night in the cozy Gasthaus after a full day's ride add to your memories.

Price (includes motorcycle rental):
- Single rider, double occupancy $1,200
- Passenger (pillion), double occupancy ....$ 750

Note: A $500 U.S. refundable insurance bond is required when renting a motorcycle.

Price Includes:
Six nights in comfortable hotels; six breakfasts; six dinners; safety and traffic rule instruction; warm-up loop; welcome and farewell evenings; daily route briefing; various sightseeing tours (Hofbräuhaus, Hofburg, and others); tour gift; motorcycle rental; tour information packet; tour guide on motorcycle. Not included: fuel, lunch snacks, riding wear, insurance.

Motorcycle Provisions:
BMW K75, BMW K100

Luggage Provisions:
A van accompanies the tour to carry luggage, provided a 15-member group is booked.

Special Notes:
International driver's license valid for motorcycle operation is required for participants. Dates and prices are subject to change. You are advised to book at least two months ahead. In addition to this tour, a colorful choice of one week Wandervogel Rider Tours originating in various European and neighboring countries is offered from June 1 through September 30 each year. Prices range from $1,200 to $1,500, usually all-inclusive except for fuel, lunch snacks, and insurance. Also self-guided touring possible. Send a self-addressed, stamped envelope and one international reply coupon (available from the post office) when inquiring about the tours.

130 GUIDED TOURS – WESTERN EUROPE

ALPS AND SOUTHERN FRANCE

Alps and Southern France

"How about some skiing, guys?"

Tour Operator:	Motorrad-Reisen Postfach 44 01 48 D-8000 Munich 44 WEST GERMANY Contact: Mr. Hermann Weil Phone: (49) 89 39 57 68 FAX: (49) 89 34 48 32 Telex: 5218511
U.S. Agent:	Motorrad-Reisen P.O. Box 591 Oconomowoc, WI 53066 Contact: Ms. Jean Fish Phone: 414-567-7548
Length of Tour:	12 days, approximately 2,150 miles.

Dates:
- May 13 through May 24, 1989
- June 6 through June 17, 1989
- June 27 through July 8, 1989
- August 23 through September 3, 1989

Trip Begins and Ends:	Munich, West Germany

Highlights:

If you're a mountain enthusiast with joie de vivre and enjoy cultural pursuits, this is the perfect tour. Run the high mountain curves of the Alps. Then delight in the Mediterranean Sea and the sensual pleasures of food, sun, and scenery in an area that has attracted Roman nobles and artistic giants. Cross the Alps through the high Swiss and French passes to reach the Massif Central, steam toward Nice and Monte Carlo finally reaching Provence and the fabulous city of Arles. Van Gogh's home was also the farthest summer seat of Roman emperors. You'll see well-preserved arenas, amphitheaters, forums, and temples from Roman times. Marvel at the prehistoric caves. Visit historic Avignon, formerly the residence of Popes in exile. The fabulous Château-Noeuf-du-Pape is also located in Avignon. Live like a king in France. Return to Munich through the mountains along the Rhone Valley.

Price (does not include motorcycle rental):
- Two riders, double occupancy $3,325
- Single rider, double occupancy $1,900
- Motorcycle rental $1,470

Price Includes:
All land arrangements; bilingual (German and English) tour guide on motorcycle; board and lodging in twin bed rooms at comfortable inns; transportation to and from Munich airport; free transportation for you and/or your motorcycle to Munich in case of illness or accident; technical assistance from tour guide.

Motorcycle Provisions:
Purchase a BMW through Motorrad-Reisen, rent their motorcycles, or ship your own motorcycle to Munich. You can rent complete accessories and gear or purchase additional insurance from the agency. You must have an international driver's license valid for motorcycle operation. If you ship your motorcycle, bring the registration card and an international insurance card.

Luggage Provisions:
Contact agent.

Special note:
U.S. agent can make arrangement for air travel to Munich and additional land and air arrangements including shipping your own motorcycle.

GUIDED TOURS – WESTERN EUROPE

EUROPE	**Alps: East and West**
Tour Operator:	Edelweiss Bike Travel Steinreichweg 1 A-6414 Mieming AUSTRIA Contact: Mr. Werner Wachter Phone: (43) 05264/5690 FAX: (43) 05264/58533 Telex: 534158 (rkmiem)
U.S. Agent:	Armonk Travel 146 Bedford Road Armonk, NY 10504 Contact: Ms. Linda Rosenbaum Phone: 800-255-7451 or 914-273-8880
Length of Tour:	15 days, covering approximately 2,000 miles

Dates:
- June 17 through July 2, 1989
- July 8 through July 23, 1989
- August 19 through September 3, 1989
- September 9 through September 24, 1989

Trip Begins and Ends:	Munich, West Germany

Highlights:
Benefit from Edelweiss' decade of experience guiding motorcycle tours through the Alps. Thrill to the pinnacle of mountain motorcycling with experts. The Alps are the basis for comparing any other mountains in the world. Follow a guide who knows the Alps like his back yard: every curve, every cafe, and every cozy restaurant. Storm the majestic Italian Dolomites. Wind through vineyards and orchards on your way to romantic Lake Garda. Spirited riders test the mountain passes with exhilarating climbs as high as 8,000 feet. You'll experience heart stopping scenery at every turn of the switchback roads through these magnificent mountains covering France, Switzerland, Italy, Austria, and Germany.

Price (includes motorcycle rental):
- Single rider, double occupancy $3,595
- Motorcycle passenger, double occupancy $2,995

Price Includes:
Round trip airfare New York to Munich; 14 nights in comfortable hotels; breakfasts; dinners; two tour guides; tour information package; daily route briefing; safety and traffic rule instruction; welcome and farewell evenings; various sightseeing tours; tour gift.

Motorcycle Provisions:
Suzuki 500cc street bikes; 750cc Suzuki enduro bikes; 750cc BMW K75 (extra charge). You may bring your own motorcycle.

Luggage Provisions:
A luggage van accompanies this tour.

Special Notes:
It can rain in the Alps, although this is unusual; it is important to bring a rain suit. At high altitudes the air can be chilly even under sunny skies, so long underwear and a windbreaker are advised.

WESTERN EUROPE	**Ardennes (a gourmet tour)**
Tour Operator:	mhs Motorradtouren GmbH Hans-Urmiller-Ring 59 D-8190 Wolfratshausen WEST GERMANY Contact: Mr. Herbert Schellhorn Phone: (49) 81 71 12 38
Length of Tour:	Four days, approximately 1,200 km

Dates:
- May 4 through May 7, 1989
- May 25 through May 28, 1989
- June 22 through June 25, 1989
- September 2 through September 5, 1989
- September 28 through October 1, 1989

Trip Begins and Ends:	Echternach, directly at the border between Germany and Luxembourg.

Highlights:
Directly after leaving Echternach you will see valleys with rock formations like those in the Alps. Visit castles, churches with marvelous art treasures, and fortresses built for three different wars. At the border to Belgium there is no customs agent to check passports, no barriers to hinder your crossing, only a small sign beside the road to inform you of the frontier between two states. Visit Spa, the town with the oldest Casino in the world. Taste some racing atmosphere on the public road to Francorchamps, where the famous Ardennes Race takes place every year. In the afternoon you'll reach Durbuy, the smallest town in Belgium with only 320 inhabitants. The next day you reach the champagne region of France. Visit a cellar where this famous wine is produced. See historic graveyards and fortresses. Roads are windy and deserted. You'll eat French cuisine at its best and stay in well-equipped hotels.

Price (does not include motorcycle rental):
- Single rider, double occupancy .... 1,195 DM
- Motorcycle passenger, double occupancy .... 895 DM
- Supplement for single room occupancy .... 180 DM

Price Includes:
Three nights in well-equipped hotel rooms, in double bed rooms; full board with best French cuisine; drinks to all meals; gas for bike.

Motorcycle Provisions:
No rental bikes available for this trip.

Luggage Provisions:
Travelers are responsible for transporting their own luggage.

Special Notes:
German and French are the main languages on this trip. Additionally, in case of English-speaking customers, English will be spoken.

Reader Discount:
A discount of $25 applies to this tour when you send in the Reader Discount Coupon.

AUSTRIA | Austria – Suzuki Test Drives

Tour Operator:	mhs Motorradtouren GmbH Hans-Urmiller-Ring 59 D-8190 Wolfratshausen WEST GERMANY Contact: Mr. Herbert Schellhorn Phone: (49) 81 71 12 38
Length of Tour:	2 days or 4 days

Dates:
Two-day tour:
- Starting every Saturday from May 13 to June 10, 1989
- July 8 through July 9, 1989
- July 22 through July 23, 1989
- August 5 through August 6, 1989
- August 26 through August 27, 1989
- September 2 through September 3, 1989
- September 16 through September 17, 1989
- September 30 through October 1, 1989
- October 7 through October 8, 1989

Four-day tour:
- May 18 through May 21, 1989
- May 25 through May 28, 1989
- June 1 through June 4, 1989
- June 8 through June 11, 1989
- July 6 through 9, 1989
- August 3 through 6, 1989
- September 14 through 17, 1989

Trip Begins and Ends:	Wolfratshausen, West Germany

Highlights:
Do you have a little time? Then select one of these two- or four-day trips. You can either opt for a bit of Austria or a larger dream trip through the lowlands of the Alps with a lot of curves and a hearty portion of care and service. Both tours start at Wolfratshausen.

You'll see the highest brick building in the world, the longest castle in Europe (about 1 kilometer long) and the world's biggest church organ. Visit the marvelous city of Mühldorf (translated: Mill-village) with its typical houses, a never finished Second World War underground airport, and come to the border of Czechoslovakia. You will see the forest of Böhmen, where the famous poet Adalbert Stifter was born, and have a view of the lake Moldau in Czechoslovakia.

Your four-day tour leads you further to the East. Pass the medieval city of Freistadt and Kefermarkt with its beautiful carved altar from the Gothic era. You'll see the grapevines of the Wachau and taste the good wine produced there. On the way back to Wolfratshausen you'll pass the towns of Linz and Passau before you reach Landshut and the world's tallest brick building.

Price for two-day tour (does not include motorcycle rental):
- Single rider, double occupancy .... 245 DM
- Motorcycle passenger, double occupancy .... 175 DM
- Supplement for single room occupancy .... 20 DM

Price for four-day tour (does not include motorcycle rental):
- Single rider, double occupancy .... 595 DM
- Motorcycle passenger, double occupancy .... 395 DM
- Supplement for single room occupancy .... 60 DM

Price Includes:
One or three nights in a double-occupancy room, with shower and bath, in cozy inns or hotels; breakfast and evening meals; rented bike; entry fees; and tour guidance.

Motorcycle Provisions:
The following models are available:
- Suzuki GS 500 E
- Suzuki DR 750 BIG
- Suzuki GSX 600 F
- Suzuki GSX 750 F
- Suzuki GSX 1100 F

Minimum rental price starts at 120 DM for two days and 240 DM for four days.

Luggage Provisions:
There is no minibus on this trip, as all rental bikes are equipped with luggage holders and saddlebags.

Special Notes:
The primary languages for this tour are German and English.

Reader Discount:
A discount of $25 applies to this tour when you send in the Reader Discount Coupon.

GERMANY AND FRANCE — The Black Forest

Tour Operator:	Motorrad-Reisen Postfach 44 01 48 D-8000 Munich 44 WEST GERMANY Contact: Mr. Hermann Weil Phone: (49) 89 39 57 68 FAX: (49) 89 34 48 32 Telex: 5218511
U.S. Agent:	Motorrad-Reisen P.O. Box 591 Oconomowoc, WI 53066 Contact: Ms. Jean Fish Phone: 414-567-7548
Length of Tour:	6 days

Dates:
- May 16 through May 21, 1989
- June 19 through June 24, 1989
- October 1 through October 6, 1989

Trip Begins:	Freiburg, Germany
Trip Ends:	Baden-Baden, Germany

Highlights:
On both sides of the Rhine River, you'll find extraordinary landscape for motorcycling. Glide through the romantic scenery of the Black Forest and the Vosges Mountains; any road offers fine riding and beautiful scenery. Wind through the narrow roads of the Alsace. Taste the wine and enjoy French cuisine. You'll delight to the combination of nature, culture, and joie de vivre.

Price (does not include motorcycle rental):
- Two riders, double occupancy $1,650
- Single rider, double occupancy .... $ 950
- Supplement for single room occupancy .... $ 100

Price Includes:	Contact agent.
Motorcycle Provisions:	Contact agent.

GUIDED TOURS – WESTERN EUROPE

AUSTRIA	BMW Holiday Week
Tour Operator:	Bosenberg Motorcycle Excursions Mainzer Straße 54 D-6550 Bad Kreuznach WEST GERMANY Contact: Mr. Leon A. Heindel Phone: (49) 671-67580
U.S. Agent:	Around the Globe Travel, Ltd. 1417 North Wauwatosa Avenue Milwaukee, WI 53213 Contact: Mr. Walt Weber Phone: 800-234-4037 or 414-257-0199 (in Wisconsin or Canada)
Length of Tour:	18 days, covering approximately 1,850 miles.
Dates:	July 4 through July 21, 1989
Trip Begins and Ends:	Bad Kreuznach, West Germany

Highlights:
After four days excursion through the BlackForest, Unterschächen, Switzerland and St. Ulrich, Italy, you will reach your destination in Austria. Join members of the Vienna BMW club for a week of festivities in the charming Austrian village of Obervellach. Show off your riding skills at the BMW competition. Test your abilities in soccer and small arms firing rivalry. Dance at the Trabuschgen castle party. Watch fireworks break over snowcapped peaks of the Austrian Alps. Spend a day hiking. Visit the open air museum at Plöcken. Wind through picturesque Tyrol and Upper Carinthia regions on day trips. End this festive sixth annual summer celebration back in Bad Kreuznach with a leisurely cruise on the Rhine River.

Price (does not include motorcycle rental, air transport of motorcycle or airfare):
- Single rider, double occupancy $1,735
- Passenger, double occupancy $1,485
- Supplement for single room occupancy .... $ 185
- Discount for campers in Obervellach .... $ 125

Price Includes:
Transportation to/from Frankfurt airport; 17 nights in select hotels/inns; all meals including mealtime beverages; multilingual tour leader on a motorcycle; excursion information packet; daily route briefings; traffic laws and safety slide show; gas and oil for motorcycle; entrance fees for attractions and events (Rhine river cruise, wine tastings, castles, museums, etc.); toll-road and ferry fees; excursion gift; all costs at BMW events; arrival packet and gift.

Motorcycle Provisions:
Ship your own motorcycle or rent a BMW at a 15-day rate with unlimited mileage.

Luggage Provisions:
Luggage van accompanies tour, depending on number of participants.

Special Notes:
Options include a longer stay at no additional airfare and rental of car for friends or family members. Call U.S. agent for details.

Reader Discount:
A discount of $35 applies to this tour when you send in the Reader Discount Coupon.

Struedel stop at an Alpine cafe (photo by Beach's MC Adven.)

ALSACE AND MOSEL WINE REGIONS — Castles & Grapes Excursion

Tour Operator:	Bosenberg Motorcycle Excursions Mainzer Straße 54 D-6550 Bad Kreuznach WEST GERMANY Contact: Mr. Leon A. Heindel Phone: (49) 671-67580
U.S. Agent:	Around the Globe Travel, Ltd. 1417 North Wauwatosa Avenue Milwaukee, WI 53213 Contact: Mr. Walt Weber Phone: 800-234-4037 or 414-257-0199 (in Wisconsin or Canada)
Length of Tour:	12 days, covering approximately 1,050 miles

Dates:
- May 30 through June 10, 1989
- June 20 through July 1, 1989
- July 18 through July 29, 1989
- August 8 through August 19, 1989
- September 19 through September 30, 1989

Trip Begins and Ends:	Bad Kreuznach, West Germany

Highlights:
Learn about fine white wines and experience great motorcycling on the same tour. Test your skill on the loop of the Nurburgring race track, if you (as the Germans say) "have some gas in your blood." Run the daunting roads in the Vosges Mountains. Perhaps you'll crease the top speed limits as you fly past vineyards one day. Then on the next, savor the landscape from a leisurely boat ride on the Mosel River. Visit numerous castles; explore Roman ruins or indulge in military history with a visit to Patton's grave and the memorial to the soldiers of the Battle of the Bulge. With three-day layovers in the choice wine regions of the Alsace and Mosel, you'll have time to explore the region and sample its products.

Price (does not include motorcycle rental, air transport of motorcycle or airfare):
- Single rider, double occupancy $1,465
- Passenger, double occupancy $1,235
- Supplement for single room occupancy ....$ 145

Price Includes:
Transportation to/from Frankfurt airport; 11 nights in select hotels/inns; all meals including mealtime beverages; multilingual excursion leader; information packet; daily route briefings; traffic laws and safety slide show; gas and oil for motorcycle; entrance fees for attractions and events (Rhine river cruise, wine tastings, castles, Nurburgring loop, etc.); toll-road and ferry fees; excursion gift.

Motorcycle Provisions:
Ship own motorcycle or rent BMW at nine-day rate with unlimited mileage.

Luggage Provisions:
Luggage van accompanies tour, depending on number of participants.

Special Notes:
Options include a longer stay at no additional airfare and rental car for friends or family members. Contact U.S. agent for details.

Reader Discount:
A discount of $35 applies to this tour when you send in the Reader Discount Coupon.

EUROPE	**Destination Spain**
Tour Operator:	Von Thielmann Tours
P.O. Box 87764
San Diego, CA 92138

Contact: Ms. Gina Guzzardo
Phone: 619-463-7788 or
619-291-7057
FAX: 619-291-4630
Telex: 910 335 1607 MESA SERV SDG |
| Length of Tour: | 21 days |

Dates:
• September 5 through September 26, 1989

| Trip Begins and Ends: | New York (or other airports) |

Highlights:
Travel through the most scenic Alpine countries, including Bavaria, Austria, Switzerland, Italy, France, to Andorra and Spain. Return via the Riviera and the High Alps, to the original Oktoberfest in Munich.

Price (does not include motorcycle rental):
• Single rider, double occupancy $2,985
• Two people, double occupancy $5,970
• Single passenger, double occupancy $2,985
• Supplement for single room occupancy .... $ 680

Price Includes:
Round trip airfare from New York; hotels; many meals; transfers; Oktoberfest reservation with fried chicken and beer; tour guide.

Motorcycle Provisions:
Bring your own motorcycle or purchase a BMW tax-free. Or rent a motorcycle.

Luggage Provisions:
Luggage van with motorcycle trailer.

ITALY	**The Dolomites**
Tour Operator:	mhs Motorradtouren GmbH Hans-Urmiller-Ring 59 D-8190 Wolfratshausen WEST GERMANY Contact: Mr. Herbert Schellhorn Phone: (49) 81 71 12 38
Length of Tour:	5 days, approximately 1,200 km

Dates:
• June 28 through July 2, 1989
• July 19 through July 23, 1989

- August 23 through August 27, 1989
- September 13 through September 17, 1989

| Trip Begins and Ends: | Wolfratshausen, West Germany |

Highlights:
Southern Tyrolia is a beloved destination for a vacation, and with good reason. In the summer months the streets are filled with autos, buses, and trucks, but this trip has been planned for paths which are as unknown and untraveled as possible and which lead to the most beautiful points. You'll visit the lakes at Molveno, Tenno, and Valvestino, unknown Alpine crossings and passages like Manghen, Tremalzo or Giau, as well as some of the famous passes such as Sella, Pordol, and Falzarego. At times you'll spend the night on the tip of a mountain, sometimes in a sport hotel, and at other times in a small, homey pension. You'll have plenty of opportunity to try regional cuisine specialties, as well as the good wine.

Price (does not include motorcycle rental):
- Single rider, double occupancy .... 795 DM
- Motorcycle passenger, double occupancy .... 575 DM
- Supplement for single room occupancy .... 130 DM

Price Includes:
Accommodation in middle class hotels (one night on top of a mountain in a simple house); breakfast and evening meals with good, typical Southern Tyrolian food; tolls and entry fees; cable car ride to top of a mountain.

Motorcycle Provisions:
Rental bikes available: Suzuki middle class bikes, like DR 750 BIG, for 540 DM. Minimum rental price starts at 540 DM for five days.

Luggage Provisions:
No minibus available. Rental bikes have panniers.

Special Notes:
The primary languages for this tour are German, English, and Italian.

Reader Discount:
A discount of $25 applies to this tour when you send in the Reader Discount Coupon.

ALPS — Enduro High Alps Tour

Tour Operator:	mhs Motorradtouren GmbH Hans-Urmiller-Ring 59 D-8190 Wolfratshausen WEST GERMANY Contact: Herbert Schellhorn Phone: (49) 81 71 12 38
Length of Tour:	6 days, approximately 1,400 km and 14 days, approximately 2,800 km

Dates:

Six-day tours:
- June 25 through June 30, 1989
- July 24 through July 29, 1989
- September 5 through September 10, 1989

14-day tours:
- July 10 through July 23, 1989
- September 11 through September 24, 1989

Trip Begins and Ends: Wolfratshausen, West Germany

Highlights:

After their great success with off-road tours last year, two new trips have been organized for mountain-loving enduro riders. As the popularity of the mountains in Piedmont along the French-Italian border grew among German and Swiss bikers, many of the roads were closed to the public.

The new 14-day enduro trip offers everything for those who have always wanted a real enduro adventure: off-roading, swimming, relaxing, and good eating. The tour encompasses southern Tyrol, the Lake Garda region, Cinque Terre, the Riviera, and the Côte d'Azur of the Mediterranean, the mountains of Liguria and Piedmont, the Rhone Alps, the Aosta Valley, and Switzerland.

Even beginning off-roaders will find the trip to be great fun, while the more experienced riders will find plenty to test their skills. For those who desire a less expensive or shorter expedition a six-day trip to southern Tyrol is also available.

Price (does not include motorcycle rental):

Six-day Tour:
- Single rider, double occupancy .... 995 DM
- Motorcycle passenger, double occupancy .... 695 DM
- Vehicle passenger, double occupancy .... 695 DM
- Supplement for single room occupancy .... 160 DM

14-day Tour:
- Single rider, double occupancy .... 2,245 DM
- Motorcycle passenger, double occupancy .... 1,695 DM
- Vehicle passenger, double occupancy .... 1,695 DM
- Supplement for single room occupancy .... 500 DM

Price Includes:
Accommodation in middle class hotels, in double bed rooms; breakfast and evening meals; meals are typical southern Tyrolian food; club bus for luggage transportation; passenger service; return service for any broken down bikes back to Germany; entrance fees.

Motorcycle Provisions:
Suzuki TS 250; DR 600; or KTM 600 bikes are available. Prices range from 540 DM to 1,800 DM, depending on length of trip and the bike desired. Rental price: starts at 600 DM for six days and 1,350 DM for 14 days.

Luggage Provisions:
Club bus accompanies trip to transport luggage.

Special Notes:
The minimum number of participants is ten. When there are more than ten participants, there will be two tour guides.

A club bus will accompany the party to carry luggage and passengers and to provide transportation back to Germany for riders and bikes in the case of a breakdown. Languages spoken: German, Italian, English; or German, Italian, French, and English.

Reader Discount:
A discount of $25 applies to the six-day tour and $50 to the 14-day tour when you send in the Reader Discount Coupon.

Swiss Browns coming down from summer pastures (Linda Fritz)

EUROPE

Grand Alpine Tour

A bit of old Europe on this tour

Tour Operator:
Von Thielmann Tours
P.O. Box 87764
San Diego, CA 92138

Contact: Ms. Gina Guzzardo
Phone: 619-463-7788 or
619-291-7057
FAX: 619-291-4630
Telex: 910 335 1607 MESA SERV SDG

Length of Tour: 15 days

Dates:
• April 27 through May 11, 1989

Trip Begins and Ends: New York (or other airports)

Highlights:
Enjoy spring in the Alps! Austria, Bavaria, Switzerland, Italy, Yugoslavia, and Liechtenstein. Very comfortable mileage; most scenic area. A good tour at a budget price.

Price (does not include motorcycle rental):
• Single rider, double occupancy $1,850
• Two people, double occupancy $3,700
• Single passenger, double occupancy $1,850
• Supplement for single room occupancy .... $ 580

Price Includes:
Round trip airfare from New York; hotel accommodations; breakfast daily; welcome and farewell dinners; transfers; tour guide; luggage transportation in support van with motorcycle trailer.

Motorcycle Provisions:
Bring your own motorcycle or purchase a BMW tax-free. Or rent a motorcycle.

Luggage Provisions:
Support van with motorcycle trailer.

EUROPEAN ALPS — High Alpine Circular Trip

Tour Operator:
Motorrad-Reisen
Postfach 44 01 48
D-8000 Munich 44
WEST GERMANY

Contact: Mr. Hermann Weil
Phone: (49) 89 39 57 68
FAX: (49) 89 34 48 32
Telex: 5218511

U.S. Agent:
Motorrad-Reisen
P.O. Box 591
Oconomowoc, WI 53066

Contact: Ms. Jean Fish
Phone: 414-567-7548

Length of Tour:
- 5 days, covering approximately 620 miles
- 7 days, covering approximately 930 miles
- 10 days, covering approximately 1,490 miles

Dates:

Five-day Tour:
- May 30 through June 3, 1989
- June 20 through June 24, 1989
- July 18 through July 22, 1989
- August 23 through August 27, 1989
- September 19 through September 23, 1989

Seven-day Tour:
- June 25 through July 1, 1989
- July 29 through August 4, 1989
- September 25 through October 1, 1989

Ten-day Tour:
- June 30 through July 9, 1989
- August 18 through August 27, 1989
- September 15 through September 24, 1989

Trip Begins and Ends: Munich, West Germany

Highlights:
Accept the challenge of mile upon mile of hairpin turns and the ecstasy of Alpine motorcycling. You'll find rolling hills, sapphire lakes, and romantic

sunsets along with the thrill of endless serpentine curves. Steam through the Lower Alps to the more impenetrable highlands, a panorama of rugged rock walls and sheer cliffs. Run back roads through the most beautiful and impressive Alpine regions. Climb the bare rock face of the Dolomites, the pinnacle of Alpine touring. Claim the splendor of the great Dolomite passes such as Sella, Pordoi Joch, and Falzarego. Relax with a day on the banks of romantic Lake Garda, enjoying fabulous Chianti and Italian food. Crisscross countries as you travel twisty Alpine roads. You'll know the journey is ending when the roads become wider and the curves more gentle.

Price (does not include motorcycle rental):
Five-day Tour:
- Two riders, double occupancy $1,080
- Single rider, double occupancy .... $ 650
- Motorcycle rental .... $ 650
- Supplement for single room occupancy .... $ 70

Seven-day Tour:
- Two riders, double occupancy $1,680
- Single rider, double occupancy .... $ 975
- Motorcycle rental .... $ 910
- Supplement for single room occupancy .... $ 100

Ten-day Tour:
- Two riders, double occupancy $2,435
- Single rider, double occupancy $1,435
- Motorcycle rental $1,330
- Supplement for single room occupancy .... $ 170

Price Includes:
All land arrangements; bilingual (German and English) tour guide on motorcycle; board and lodging in twin bed rooms at comfortable inns; transportation to and from Munich airport; free transportation for you and/or your motorcycle to Munich in case of illness or accident; technical assistance from tour guide.

Motorcycle Provisions:
Purchase a BMW through Motorrad-Reisen, rent their motorcycles, or ship your own motorcycle to Munich. You can rent complete accessories and gear or purchase additional insurance from the agency. You must have an international driver's license valid for motorcycle operation. If you ship your motorcycle, bring the registration card and an international insurance card.

Luggage Provisions:
Contact agent.

Special Notes:
U.S. agent can make arrangement for air travel to Munich and additional land and air arrangements including shipping your own motorcycle.

AUSTRIA	**Magic Austria**
Tour Operator:	Motorrad-Reisen Postfach 44 01 48 D-8000 Munich 44 WEST GERMANY Contact: Mr. Hermann Weil Phone: (49) 89 39 57 68 FAX: (49) 89 34 48 32 Telex: 5218511
U.S. Agent:	Motorrad-Reisen P.O. Box 591 Oconomowoc, WI 53066 Contact: Ms. Jean Fish Phone: 414-567-7548

Length of Tour:
- 2 days, covering approximately 600 miles
- 4 days, covering approximately 589 miles
- 5 days, covering approximately 775 miles
- 7 days, covering approximately 1,055 miles

Dates:
Two-day Tour:
- Every weekend starting with April 15 to 16, 1989 and finishing October 28 to 29, 1989

Four-day Tour:
- May 12 through May 15, 1989
- June 21 through June 24, 1989
- July 19 through July 22, 1989
- August 12 through August 15, 1989
- September 7 through September 10, 1989
- October 5 through October 8, 1989

Five-day Tour:
- May 24 through May 28, 1989
- July 18 through July 22, 1989
- August 11 through August 15, 1989
- September 19 through September 23, 1989

Seven-day Tour:
- July 2 through July 8, 1989
- August 5 through August 11, 1989
- October 1 through October 7, 1989

Trip Begins and Ends: Munich, West Germany

Highlights:
From the Bavarian Mountains, venture to the remarkable massifs of Tennengebirge. Climb a hidden pass and push through the picturesque Dachstein range. Spend the night in a hidden mountain inn. Fish for trout. Laze around the campfire or warm your backside by the tiled stove in the parlor. At Admont, gateway to the Gesäuse, you'll visit the Stiftsbibliothek, one of the world's most famous libraries. Storm the high mountains and the deep clefts and chasms of the Gesäuse. Run the forgotten pathways of this famous as well as notorious region. Follow the current of the river Enns on roads that become narrower and narrower as they twist around the mountain. Stay at a quaint mountain inn perched at 4,920 ft. Taste homemade goat and sheep cheese. Wash it down with local beer. Descend through the mountains along the river Enns. You'll cross the border to Germany at a place so small you must ring a bell to call the border guard to the gate. Finish your tour with a farewell party at a local Bavarian restaurant. Extend your stay in charming Austria with the five-day tour that includes Maria Zell, Jogland, Graz Basin, and Pongau. Add another two days for a seven-day trip that adds Murtal, Carinthia, Gurktal Alps, Tyrol, and Großglockner to the itinerary.

Price (does not include motorcycle rental):
Four-day Tour:
- Two riders, double occupancy .... $ 815
- Single rider, double occupancy .... $ 475
- Motorcycle rental .... $ 520
- Supplement for single room occupancy .... $ 50

Five-day Tour:
- Two riders, double occupancy $1,055
- Single rider, double occupancy .... $ 595
- Motorcycle rental .... $ 650
- Supplement for single room occupancy .... $ 70

GUIDED TOURS – WESTERN EUROPE 151

Seven-day Tour:
- Two riders, double occupancy $1,645
- Single rider, double occupancy ....$ 930
- Motorcycle rental ....$ 910
- Supplement for single room occupancy ....$ 100

Price Includes:
All land arrangements; bilingual (German and English) tour guide on motorcycle; board and lodging in twin bed rooms at comfortable inns; transportation to and from Munich airport; free transportation for you and/or your motorcycle to Munich in case of illness or accident; technical assistance from tour guide.

Motorcycle Provisions:
Purchase a BMW through Motorrad-Reisen, rent their motorcycles, or ship your own motorcycle to Munich. You can rent complete accessories and gear or purchase additional insurance from agency. You must have driver's license valid for motorcycle operation and international driver's license. If you bring your own motorcycle, you'll need the motorcycle registration and an international insurance card.

Luggage Provisions:
Luggage van may accompany tour. Check with agent.

Special Notes:
Motorrad-Reisen's U.S. agent will arrange air travel to Munich and additional land and air arrangements including shipping your own motorcycle.

SCANDINAVIA	**Midsummer's Night Tour**
Tour Operator:	Edelweiss Bike Travel Steinreichweg 1 A-6414 Mieming AUSTRIA Contact: Mr. Werner Wachter Phone: (43) 05264/5690 FAX: (43) 05264/58533 Telex: 534158 (rkmiem)

GUIDED TOURS – WESTERN EUROPE

U.S. Agent:	Armonk Travel 146 Bedford Road Armonk, NY 10504 Contact: Ms. Linda Rosenbaum Phone: 800-255-7451 or 914-273-8880
Length of Tour:	20 days, covering approximately 3,000 miles
Dates:	June 13 through July 3, 1989
Trip Begins and Ends:	Munich, West Germany

Highlights:
Follow the midnight sun through the lakes and forests of southern Sweden to the Norwegian fjords. In Mora, join in the folklore Festival of the Midnight Sun, a place where the sun never sets on the festivities of the fun-loving Swedes. Push farther north for your first look at the steep granite walls and deep dark waters of the Norwegian fjords. Climb to the sky on the fabulously curvy road called the Troll Steps. Ride through a magical scene where rainbows sparkle in waterfalls on your right, and the deep blue light from the glacier on your left serves as a backlight. Surrounded by fjords and glaciers, you'll feel as if you're riding directly into the North Sea. Swim in crystalline rivers and lakes. Visit fish markets and picturesque fishing villages. Enjoy the bounty of a magnificent smorgasbord.

Price (includes motorcycle rental):
- Single rider, double occupancy $4,635
- Motorcycle passenger, double occupancy $3,835

Price Includes:
Round trip airfare New York, Munich; 20 nights accommodations with breakfast and dinner; round trip ferry crossing with twin berth cabin including rider, passenger, and motorcycle; daily route briefing; tour guide; tour information package; sightseeing program; welcome and farewell evenings; tour gift.

Motorcycle Provisions:
Suzuki DR BIG (750cc single enduro, great fun on small twisties) or Suzuki GS 500E (street bike recommended for short riders) are included in the tour price. Suzuki Katana GSX 1100 F, BMW K75, BMW K100 RS, and BMW K100 RT are all available at a surcharge.

Luggage Provisions:
Each driver is responsible for his own luggage.

Special Notes:
It can rain in Scandinavia, although this is unusual; it is important to bring a rain suit. Here, in the far north, the air can be chilly even under sunny skies, so long underwear and a windbreaker are advised.

DANUBE VALLEY, AUSTRIA	**Romantic Castles: Landscape and Wines of the Danube Valley**
Tour Operator:	Motorrad-Reisen Postfach 44 01 48 D-8000 Munich 44 WEST GERMANY Contact: Mr. Hermann Weil Phone: (49) 89 39 57 68 FAX: (49) 89 34 48 32 Telex: 5218511
U.S. Agent:	Motorrad-Reisen P.O. Box 591 Oconomowoc, WI 53066 Contact: Ms. Jean Fish Phone: 414-567-7548
Length of Tour:	6 days, approximately 860 miles

Dates:
- May 29 through June 3, 1989
- June 19 through June 24, 1989
- July 18 through July 23, 1989
- August 14 through August 19, 1989
- September 26 through October 1, 1989

Trip Begins and Ends:	Munich, West Germany

Highlights:
You'll find apricot trees blooming while the Alpine passes are still snow covered or else ride through the autumn glory of vintage time in this tour of the beautiful Danube Valley. Follow romance through the borderlands of Upper and Lower Austria; forget this century, and step back in history

to the days of chivalry. Feast in the robust spirit of robber knights, perhaps listening to the same songs that entertained the Round Table. You'll enjoy evening wine tastings in countless cellars. Follow small roads and lanes to mountain crests on both sides of the Danube. Cross the river on a venerable Danube ferry. Sweep through a landscape where castles, monasteries, chateaux, and ruins cling to the Austrian slopes. Enjoy the beauty and serenity of this marvelous landscape of vineyards and medieval monuments.

Price (does not include motorcycle rental):
- Two riders, double occupancy $1,250
- Single rider, double occupancy .... $ 725
- Motorcycle rental .... $ 780

Price Includes:
All land arrangements; bilingual (German and English) tour guide on motorcycle; board and lodging in twin bed rooms at comfortable inns; transportation to and from Munich airport; free transportation for you and/or your motorcycle to Munich in case of illness or accident; technical assistance from tour guide.

Motorcycle Provisions:
Purchase a BMW through Motorrad-Reisen, rent their motorcycles, or ship your own motorcycle to Munich. You can rent complete accessories and gear or purchase additional insurance from agency. You must have an international driver's license valid for motorcycle operation. If you ship your motorcycle, bring the registration card and an international insurance card.

Luggage Provisions:
Luggage van may accompany tour.

Special Notes:
U.S. agent can make arrangement for air travel to Munich and additional land and air arrangements including shipping your own motorcycle.

At the end of a long day . . . (a Linda Fritz photo)

WESTERN EUROPE	**Surprise Tours**
Tour Operator:	mhs Motorradtouren GmbH Hans-Urmiller-Ring 59 D-8190 Wolfratshausen WEST GERMANY Contact: Mr. Herbert Schellhorn Phone: (49) 81 71 12 38
Length of Tour:	6 days, approximately 1,800 km, average 300 to 350 km per day.

Dates:
- April 22 through April 27, 1989
- September 12 through September 17, 1989

Trip Begins and Ends:
April trip begins and ends in Wolfratshausen. September trip may begin and end in Frankfurt; not able to confirm at press time.

Highlights:
With Herbert Schellhorn as the group leader, this tour is especially for drivers who place high value on accommodations and service. The choice of the destination occurs shortly after weather conditions are determined. Each day's riding is a bit longer than other mhs Motorradtouren trips. You'll get lots of curves — curves, curves, curves.

Price (does not include motorcycle rental):
- Single rider, single occupancy, approx. 1,400 to 2,000 DM
- Couples, double occupancy, approx. 2,000 to 3,500 DM

Please register early, as the number of participants is limited. You will only receive information about the cost after they have chosen the destination. (This is a special trip for customers who know mhs Motorradtouren and therefore trust their ability to organize such a special trip, and who don't care where they are riding to.)

Price Includes:
Accommodations in hotels of higher class; full service with typical good cuisine; drinks at the table; fuel; tolls; entry fees.

Motorcycle Provisions:
Suzuki GSX 750 or DR 750 BIG. Rental price: 750 DM

Luggage Provisions:
Bikes are equipped with luggage carriers and panniers.

Special Notes:
The primary languages are German and English, plus either Italian or French.

Reader Discount:
A discount of $25 applies to this tour when you send in the Reader Discount Coupon.

LUXEMBOURG	**Weekend in Luxembourg (a gourmet tour)**
Tour Operator:	mhs Motorradtouren GmbH Hans-Urmiller-Ring 59 D-8190 Wolfratshausen WEST GERMANY Contact: Mr. Herbert Schellhorn Phone: (49) 81 71 12 38
Length of Tour:	Two days, approximately 550 km

Dates:
- May 13 through May 14, 1989
- June 10 through June 11, 1989
- June 17 through June 18, 1989
- July 8 through July 9, 1989
- July 22 through July 23, 1989
- August 5 through August 6, 1989
- August 26 through August 27, 1989
- September 16 through September 17, 1989
- October 14 through October 15, 1989

Trip Begins and Ends:	Echternach, Luxembourg

Highlights:
This trip starts and ends at Echternach on the border between Germany and Luxembourg. Proceed immediately to a road with lots of curves. Travel through ravines and gorges with rock formations similar to those in the Alps. The landscape is dotted with old fortresses and churches. Take a glance at the Meysemburg as well as the St. Remigius church in Koerich and the Sûre River. Further along the German border, travel on isolated roads on your way to Vianden with its beautiful fortress. See the beautiful

carved altar in Luxembourg. After countless more curves, your weekend tour will end back at Echternach.

Price (does not include motorcycle rental):
- Single rider, double occupancy .... 475 DM
- Motorcycle passenger, double occupancy .... 355 DM
- Supplement for single room occupancy .... 45 DM

Price Includes:
Accommodation in good hotel; full board with best cuisine; table drinks; gas; entry fees; and tolls.

Motorcycle Provisions:
No rental bikes available.

Luggage Provisions:
Travelers responsible for their own luggage.

Special Notes:
The primary languages for this tour are German, French, and English. This tour is good for newcomers to motorcycling, people who are rekindling their interest in riding, or who want to ride on the weekend.

Reader Discount:
A discount of $25 applies to this tour when you send in the Reader Discount Coupon.

ALPS	**Weekend in Southern Bavarian Alps and Austria**
Tour Operator:	mhs Motorradtouren GmbH Hans-Urmiller-Ring 59 D-8190 Wolfratshausen WEST GERMANY Contact: Mr. Herbert Schellhorn Phone: (49) 81 71 12 38
Length of Tour:	2 days, approximately 550 km

Dates:
- May 13 through May 14, 1989
- May 20 through May 21, 1989

GUIDED TOURS – WESTERN EUROPE

- May 27 through May 28, 1989
- June 3 through June 4, 1989
- June 10 through June 11, 1989
- July 8 through July 9, 1989
- July 22 through July 23, 1989
- August 5 through August 6, 1989
- August 26 through August 27, 1989
- September 2 through September 3, 1989
- September 16 through September 17, 1989
- September 30 through October 1, 1989
- October 7 through October 8, 1989

Trip Begins and Ends:
Wolfratshausen, West Germany

Highlights:
This tour has been organized for all those who think they know Bavaria and Austria. You will travel through the unknown eastern part of the Bavarian land near the Alps, the lower Alps; visit the market at Dorfen, the subterranean airport at Muhldorf, and the old city in the center of town. You will travel further via Burghausen, which has the longest and most extensive fortress in Germany. The trip will then lead you past Braunau and Ried im Innkreis. The roads will get more and more deserted as you approach the border of Czechoslovakia; cast your glance toward the Bohemian woods and the place where three rivers converge in Passau. You'll explore a number of higher passages in the Bavarian woods, traveling in the direction of Landshut. Perhaps you will visit the fortress at Trausnitz on your way back to Wolfratshausen, your point of departure.

Price (does not include motorcycle rental):
- Single rider, double occupancy .... 245 DM
- Motorcycle passenger, double occupancy .... 175 DM
- Supplement for single room occupancy .... 20 DM

Price Includes:
Breakfast; evening meal; entry fees; accommodation in middle class hotel. Food is hearty Austrian food.

Motorcycle Provisions:
The following models are available:
- Suzuki GS 500 E
- Suzuki DR 750 BIG
- Suzuki GSX 600 F
- Suzuki GSX 750 F
- Suzuki GSX 1100 F

Minimum rental price starts at 120 DM for two days.

Luggage Provisions:
There is no minibus on this trip, as all rental bikes are equipped with luggage holders and saddlebags.

Special Notes:
The primary languages for this tour are German and English. This tour is particularly good for newcomers to motorcycling, people who are rekindling their interest in riding, or those who simply want to ride occasionally on the weekend.

Reader Discount:
A discount of $25 applies to this tour when you send in the Reader Discount Coupon.

ALPS — Western Alps Tour

Tour Operator:	mhs Motorradtouren GmbH Hans-Urmiller-Ring 59 D-8190 Wolfratshausen WEST GERMANY Contact: Mr. Herbert Schellhorn Phone: (49) 81 71 12 38
Length of Tour:	12 days, approximately 2,800 km

Dates:
- July 10 through July 21, 1989
- September 4 through September 15, 1989

Trip Begins and Ends:	Wolfratshausen, West Germany

Highlights:
This trip explores the less traveled western Alps, which boast the highest passes in the middle European mountains, as well as the largest canyon, the Grand Cañon du Verdon. You'll pass through a small dukedom on your way to Switzerland.

    The mountains are higher here, with the roads often set adventurously into the steep slopes. You will cross such well-known passes as the Furka, the Iseran, the Izoard, the Vars, and the Restefond-La Bonette, the highest paved pass at an altitude of 2,802 meters. Shortly afterward you'll come to the breathtaking sights of the canyon dug 800 meters into the mountains by the Verdon River.

Finally, your journey takes you to the Côte d'Azur, with an opportunity to relax at the beach or visit such world famous cities as Nice, Monte Carlo, or Menton. Naturally, you'll want to ride a short distance on the route of the Monte Carlo Rally, and taste the fine French cuisine offered by some little known restaurants. After five days your trip winds through the high Alps of Italy and Switzerland and back to Germany.

Price (does not include motorcycle rental):
- Single rider, double occupancy .... 2,995 DM
- Motorcycle passenger, double occupancy .... 2,295 DM
- Supplement for single room occupancy .... 450 DM

Price Includes:
Accommodation in middle class hotels, or better (always with bath in the rooms); full board (often à la carte) with fine French or Italian food; table drinks to all meals; gas; tolls and entry fees.

Motorcycle Provisions:
Suzuki and other rental bikes available, starting at 1,350 DM.

Luggage Provisions:
Rental bikes are equipped with panniers.

Special Notes:
Languages spoken: German, Italian, French, and English.

Reader Discount:
A discount of $50 applies to this tour when you send in the Reader Discount Coupon.

The dangers of sunburn are everywhere (a Linda Fritz photo)

GUIDED TOURS - EASTERN EUROPE

162 GUIDED TOURS – EASTERN EUROPE

RUSSIA   **First Motorcycle Tour of the Caucasus**

Just an ordinary neighborhood castle in Armenia.

Tour Operator:	Edelweiss Bike Travel Steinreichweg 1 A-6414 Mieming AUSTRIA Contact: Mr. Werner Wachter Phone: (43) 05264/5690 FAX: (43) 05264/58533 Telex: 534158 (rkmiem)
U.S. Agent:	Armonk Travel 146 Bedford Road Armonk, NY 10504 Contact: Ms. Linda Rosenbaum Phone: 800-255-7451 or 914-273-8880
Length of Tour:	15 days, covering approximately 2,000 miles

Dates:
- May 25 through June 9, 1989
- June 8 through June 23, 1989
- June 22 through July 7, 1989
- July 6 through July 21, 1989
- August 3 through August 18, 1989
- August 17 through September 1, 1989
- August 31 through September 15, 1989

Trip Begins and Ends: East Coast, U.S.A.

Highlights:
Be one of the first western motorcyclists to ride the high mountains of the Caucasus. Swing along the Black Sea coast on twisty roads between the sparkling blue waters and the stately Caucasus. Capture the feeling of wide open country in the plains dotted with charming rural villages. Race through enchanting steep-sided valleys heading for the snowcapped peaks of Europe's highest mountain range. On the way to Itkol, you'll run one of the most fascinating routes in the U.S.S.R. Ride under towering rock formations of gray, amber, and orange with echoes of rushing water from the waterfall that plunges toward a stream in the canyon floor. Climb 8,000 feet on the switchbacks of the Georgian Military Highway. Cross the only pass that breaks the impenetrable Caucasus. In Tbilisi, enjoy an evening with the hospitable Georgians. Drink Georgian wine, champanski from the Krim, and brandy from Armenia. At Lake Seven, delight in turquoise water at an altitude of 6,000 feet then descend to Yerevan, a city built of yellow, amber, and pink volcanic rock. You'll love the variety from the seashores to the glaciers, from the plains of Krasnodar to the desert of Yerevan, from the Armenians to the Georgians.

Price (includes motorcycle rental):
- Single rider, double occupancy $3,975
- Motorcycle passenger, double occupancy $3,225

Price Includes:
Round trip airfare from East Coast, U.S.A. to Frankfurt or Vienna and from there to Sochi, U.S.S.R.

Motorcycle Provisions:
Suzuki DR BIG 750cc single-cylinder enduro cycle, with three large luggage cases, and an electric starter. Okay for two-up riding for tall riders. Suzuki GS 500E or 500cc Twin with two luggage cases is suggested for short riders, but not for two-up riding.

Luggage Provisions:
Each rider is responsible for his own luggage.

Special Notes:
Amenities in the Soviet Union are not equivalent to American standards. Riders expecting the same services and conveniences as they would find in America will be disappointed. The daily distances are sometimes long and therefore endurance is required.

SOVIET UNION

Soviet Union

The welcome sun after a long journey

Tour Operator:
Edelweiss Bike Travel
Steinreichweg 1
A-6414 Mieming
AUSTRIA

Contact: Mr. Werner Wachter
Phone: (43) 05264/5690
FAX: (43) 05264/58533
Telex: 534158 (rkmiem)

U.S. Agent:
Armonk Travel
146 Bedford Road
Armonk, NY 10504

Contact: Ms. Linda Rosenbaum
Phone: 800-255-7451 or 914-273-8880

Length of Tour:
22 days, covering approximately 3,500 miles

Dates:
- May 9 through May 30, 1989
- June 4 through June 25, 1989
- July 2 through July 23, 1989
- July 30 through August 20, 1989
- August 29 through September 19, 1989

Trip Begins and Ends: New York

Highlights:
Enter the Soviet Union in a motorcycle cavalcade. You'll ride from West Germany, stopping in Vienna and Budapest, over the Carpathian Mountains and cross the U.S.S.R. border at Chop. Throughout this groundbreaking tour, you'll make close contact and spontaneous friendships with Soviet citizens. Visit the splendid metropolitan capital of this superpower nation. In Moscow, don't miss the fabulous Russian circus, the Cosmonaut museum and, of course, the Kremlin. You'll learn about the history of czarist Russia in Leningrad. See the splendor of the Hermitage, formerly the winter palace of Czar Peter the Great, now one of the world's great art museums. You will need to tolerate differences in the Soviet system; Soviet roads can be boring and difficult for motorcyclists; consumer goods can be limited. Think of this trip as an adventure rather than a holiday.

Price (does not include motorcycle rental):
- Single rider, double occupancy $4,975
- Motorcycle passenger, double occupancy $4,275

Price Includes:
Tour information package; four tour guides (two on motorcycles); one translator; 19 nights hotel accommodations; one night on ferryboat; 20 breakfasts and dinners; sightseeing tours in Hungary and Soviet Union; detailed riding instructions; daily route briefing; tour gift.

Motorcycle Provisions:
Cyclists will have their choice of renting a BMW K75; BMW K100; BMW K100RS; BMW K100RT; and Honda 650cc. Rental fees will range from $80 to $110 daily.

Luggage Provisions:
A luggage van will accompany this tour.

Special Notes:
Amenities in the Soviet Union are not equivalent to American standards. Riders expecting the same services and conveniences as they would find in America will be disappointed. The daily distances are sometimes long and therefore endurance is required.

BALTIC COUNTRIES	**Tour of the Baltic Countries**
Tour Operator:	Edelweiss Bike Travel Steinreichweg 1 A-6414 Mieming AUSTRIA Contact: Mr. Werner Wachter Phone: (43) 05264/5690 FAX: (43) 05264/58533 Telex: 534158 (rkmiem)
U.S. Agent:	Armonk Travel 146 Bedford Road Armonk, NY 10504 Contact: Ms. Linda Rosenbaum Phone: 800-255-7451 or 914-273-8880
Length of Tour:	10 days, approximately 1,070 miles

Dates:
- June 26 through July 5, 1989
- July 10 through July 19, 1989
- July 24 through August 2, 1989
- August 7 through August 16, 1989
- August 21 through August 30, 1989

Trip Begins:	Warsaw, Poland
Trip Ends:	Leningrad – Finnish border

Highlights:

Journey along wide, lonely Baltic beaches. Drive through endless birch forest. Soak in the countryside of Lithuania, Latvia, and Estonia where ice-free ports and a scenic coastline give way to the untouched beauty of low wooded hills, lakes, and meandering rivers. You'll appreciate the 13th and 14th century elegance of formerly wealthy cities. In Riga and Tallinin, see strong Teutonic fortifications with much of the walled cities still intact. Enjoy the gaiety of Tallinin, bristling with over 30 towers. Follow narrow winding streets to innumerable coffee houses, boutiques, and second-hand shops. Look for signs of freedom fighters in these once independent nations of the Soviet Union. Signs are subtle; perhaps you'll see a group bearing silent vigilance in a town square. Visit the Hermitage, formerly the winter palace, now one of the world's greatest art museums. End your journey in the grand city of Leningrad, founded in 1703 by Czar Peter the Great.

Price (does not include motorcycle rental):
- Single rider, double occupancy $1,875
- Motorcycle passenger, double occupancy $1,875

Price Includes:
Nine nights hotel accommodations; nine breakfasts; nine dinners; four sightseeing tours (Vilnius, Riga, Tallinin, Leningrad); a cultural tour in Leningrad or Riga; welcome and farewell evenings; daily route briefing; three tour guides (one on motorcycle); tour gift.

Motorcycle Provisions:
BMW and Suzuki motorcycles are for rent.

Luggage Provisions:
A luggage van accompanies this tour.

Special Notes:
Amenities in the Soviet Union are not equivalent to American standards. Riders expecting the same services and conveniences as they would find in America will be disappointed. The daily distances are sometimes long and therefore endurance is required.

YUGOSLAVIA

Yugoslavia, Dalmatia — Suzuki Test Drives

Tour Operator:	mhs Motorradtouren GmbH Hans-Urmiller-Ring 59 D-8190 Wolfratshausen WEST GERMANY Contact: Mr. Herbert Schellhorn Phone: (49) 81 71 12 38
Length of Tour:	7 days, approximately 1,200 to 1,600 km; average 200 to 250 km per day.

Dates:
- February 26 through March 4, 1989 (for reference)
- March 5 through March 11, 1989 (for reference)
- March 12 through March 18, 1989 (for reference)
- April 22 through April 28, 1989
- April 29 through May 5, 1989

- March 4 through March 10, 1990
- March 11 through March 17, 1990
- March 18 through March 24, 1990

Later dates possible, depending on demand.

Trip Begins and Ends:	Munich, West Germany

Highlights:
Before the start of the season, test drive the new Suzuki motorcycles which were presented at the International Fahrrad and Motorrad Ausstellung (IFMA) show. Experience the beauty of springtime in Yugoslavia. For example, in Dalmatia, before the South Yugoslavian Adriatic coast opens its doors for the annual stream of tourists, you'll have an opportunity to try the brand new Suzuki models on practically empty roads. Fly from winter weather and arrive in Dubrovnik. There, on the Adriatic coast, awaits a comfortable hotel from which you will take your bike excursions for the next six days along the beautiful coast and into the interior. Highlights are the romantic fishing village of Sibenik, medieval Dubrovnik, and the Bridge of Mostar.

Price (includes motorcycle rental):
- Single rider, double occupancy .... 1,995 DM
- Motorcycle passenger, double occupancy .... 1,745 DM
- Supplement for single room occupancy .... 200 DM

Price Includes:
Flight from Munich (other airports are possible with a slight surcharge); six nights in a double occupancy room with shower and bathroom in a middle-class hotel; daily breakfast and dinner (in the evening); rented bike; fuel; group leader; entrance fees and transfers.

Motorcycle Provisions:
The following models are available:
- Suzuki GS 500 E
- Suzuki DR 750 BIG
- Suzuki GSX 600 F
- Suzuki GSX 750 F
- Suzuki GSX 1100 F

Luggage Provisions:
All bikes are equipped with luggage holders and panniers. Since you return to the hotel each evening, no minibus is necessary to transport luggage.

Special Notes:
The primary languages for this tour are German and English.

GUIDED TOURS – EASTERN EUROPE 169

Reader Discount:
A discount of $25 applies to this tour when you send in the Reader Discount Coupon.

YUGOSLAVIA

Yugoslavia, Istra — Suzuki Test Drives

Tour Operator:	mhs Motorradtouren GmbH Hans-Urmiller-Ring 59 D-8190 Wolfratshausen WEST GERMANY Contact: Mr. Herbert Schellhorn Phone: (49) 81 71 12 38
Length of Tour:	7 days, approximately 1,200 to 1,600 km; average 200 to 250 km per day

Dates:
- March 25 through March 31, 1989 (for reference)
- April 1 through April 7, 1989
- April 8 through April 14, 1989
- April 15 through April 21, 1989
- April 22 through April 28, 1989
- April 29 through May 5, 1989
- May 6 through May 12, 1989

Trip Begins and Ends:	Munich, West Germany

Highlights:
It is only a short hop from Munich to Istra, but the climatic difference is very large. In mhs Motorradtouren's own club bus you'll reach your hotel in this small town on the Mediterranean where the new Suzuki models are awaiting you. After the daily excursions you will enjoy the wonderful regional specialties of cuisine; you will relax in the heated swimming pool or in your comfortable room. During your bike excursions you will visit, among other things, the Coliseum at Pula, the fascinating natural park at Lake Plitvice, and the world-famous grottoes of Postojna.

Price (includes motorcycle rental):
- Single rider, double occupancy .... 1,595 DM
- Motorcycle passenger, double occupancy .... 1,245 DM
- Supplement for single room occupancy .... 200 DM

Price Includes:
Trip in the club bus from Munich to Istra; six nights in a double occupancy room with a shower and bathroom in a middle-class hotel; daily breakfast and evening meal; rented bike; fuel; entry fees; and tour guidance.

Motorcycle Provisions:
The following models are available:
- Suzuki GS 500 E
- Suzuki DR 750 BIG
- Suzuki GSX 600 F
- Suzuki GSX 750 F
- Suzuki GSX 1100 F

Luggage Provisions:
All bikes are equipped with luggage holders and panniers. As you return to the hotel each evening, no minibus is necessary to transport luggage.

Special Notes:
The primary languages for this tour are German and English.

Reader Discount:
A discount of $25 applies to this tour when you send in the Reader Discount Coupon.

GUIDED TOURS – MEDITERRANEAN AREA

MEDITERRANEAN — Corsica and Sardinia

Tour Operator:	mhs Motorradtouren GmbH Hans-Urmiller-Ring 59 D-8190 Wolfratshausen WEST GERMANY Contact: Mr. Herbert Schellhorn Phone: (49) 81 71 12 38
Length of Tour:	14 days, approximately 3,500 km

Dates:
- May 21 through June 3, 1989 (camping tour with a low price of 1,795 DM)
- June 11 through June 24, 1989
- September 10 through September 24, 1989
- October 1 through October 14, 1989

Trip Begins:	Lugano, Switzerland
Trip Ends:	Brenner (border between Italy and Austria)

Highlights:

As a motorcyclist, you'll be welcomed to Sardinia and Corsica. You will see lots of strange buildings on both islands called nurages, built like towers more than two thousand years ago. The narrow, windy roads are mostly gravelled. There is hardly any traffic, and the landscape is overwhelming. You will see the grotto of Neptune, the well-fortified city Su nuraxi, built in the nurage-style, and medieval fortresses dating from Genoan invaders.

After visiting Cagliari, the capitol of Sardinia, you proceed into the quiet wilderness of the Gennargentu Mountains. Here, you'll find lots of ancient political graffiti painted on the walls in beautiful colors, showing the protest against the government of Rome. The next day you will reach the Costa Smeralda, where the Aga Khan had beautiful houses built in the sixties. These houses are well integrated into nature.

You will have one day off for relaxing and swimming before you start to Corsica. Corsica is much wilder than Sardinia. The highest mountain is 8,400 feet. Napoleon, the French emperor of the early 19th century, was born here. You will visit his home, see artifacts from the stone age and have time for swimming in one of the lonely bays.

After six days riding on the island, you will leave Corsica for La Spezia, which is the major harbor for marines in Italy. A last night at the Italian coast in a nice medieval city gives you the real feeling for La Dolce Vita, the sweet life, before you start your last day, bringing you to the Austrian border.

Price (does not include motorcycle rental):
- Single rider, double occupancy .... 3,695 DM
- Motorcycle passenger, double occupancy .... 2,795 DM
- Supplement for single room occupancy .... 600 DM

Price Includes:
Normal trip: overnight stays in middle class hotels (double occupancy); full board with typical fine food (French and Italian cuisine); passage in first class cabins from Genoa to Sardinia; passage from Sardinia to Corsica; passage from Corsica to La Spezia; table drinks with all meals; gasoline for the bike during the trip; all entry fees and tolls.

Camping trips include camping fees; breakfast; passages as described above, but in second class cabins; entry fees; tolls; minibus if ten or more participants.

Motorcycle Provisions:
Motorcycle rental only to and from Wolfratshausen. Rental prices start at 1,500 DM.

Luggage Provisions:
Bikes are equipped with luggage holders and panniers. Bus will accompany the camping tour if ten or more customers are booked.

Special Notes:
Primary languages: German, Italian, French, and English, if American travelers are on the tour.

Reader Discount:
A discount of $50 applies to this tour when you send in the Reader Discount Coupon.

Time out for a picnic (photo by Prima Klima Reisen)

174 GUIDED TOURS – MEDITERRANEAN AREA

MEDITERRANEAN Cyprus

Exploring the far reaches in Cyprus

Tour Operator:	Prima Klima Reisen GmbH Hohenstaufenstraße 69 1000 Berlin 30 WEST GERMANY Contact: Mr. Peter Schmidt Phone: (49) 030 216 10 82/83 Telex: 186381 pkr d
Length of Tour:	14 days

Dates:
Twice a month from March through December. Contact Prima Klima Reisen (PKR) for specific dates.

Trip Begins and Ends:
Larnaca Airport, Cyprus. Home base on Cyprus is the romantic village of Polis, 200 miles from the airport. PKR provides the transfers between the airport and Polis.

Highlights:
Cyprus is a beautiful mountainous island with scenic areas to explore and beaches to sample. Legend says that Aphrodite, greek goddess of love, was born of the sea foam on these shores. The island has been inhabited since the Stone Age. Artifacts from Cyprus date back 8,000 years.

The island's winding mountain trails are perfect for enduro riders of any level experience. Mount Olympus, home of the gods of Greek mythology, is 1,995 meters high. You can zigzag up the mountain through olive groves and return to the beach on another road that descends past citrus groves. When you tire of the heights, there are always beautiful coastal towns and old fishing villages to explore.

Price (includes motorcycle rental):
- Driver, riding double, double occupancy .... 1,690 DM
- Passenger, riding double, double occupancys .... 1,090 DM
- Single rider, single occupancy .... 2,690 DM

Price Includes:
Round trip charter flight from Hamburg, Berlin, Frankfurt, and Dusseldorf (other cites cost a little more or less); 14 days accommodation and breakfasts. You should plan on at least 300 DM for other food for two weeks.

Motorcycle Provisions:
A wide variety of motorcycles are available. The enduro bikes include: Yamaha XT 350, Yamaha DT 175, Honda XL 600R. Others available are: Honda 650 and 750 (four-cylinder) soft-chopper style, Cagiva 350 two-stroke super sport, and other smaller machines.

Luggage Provisions:
During this trip, you will stay in Polis every night except for two nights in the mountains of Troodos. Each person is responsible for carrying his own luggage.

Special Notes:
Cyprus was a British Colony until 1960, so nearly everyone speaks and understands English. Most of the 350,000 tourists who go to Cyprus annually are British. PKR's German tour guides speak English fluently.

Reader Discount:
A discount between 50 DM and 150 DM applies to this tour when you send in the Reader Discount Coupon. Amount depends upon season, accommodation, and the motorcycle you book.

TURKEY	East Turkey
Tour Operator:	Motorrad Spaett, KG Rüdesheimerstraße, 9 8000 Munich 21 WEST GERMANY Contact: Mr. Paul Spaett or office Phone: (49) 089-57937-38 FAX: (49) 089-57017-69 Telex: 5216823 mosp
Length of Tour:	14 days

Dates:
- July 1 through July 15, 1989
- July 22 through August 5, 1989
- August 12 through August 26, 1989

Trip Begins and Ends:	Munich, West Germany. For overseas customers, Motorrad Spaett can arrange a combination one-week tour through the Alps and two weeks in Turkey. They can book flights from any other location to Munich.

Highlights:
This tour features fourteen days in the important border region of Turkey. This small group (ten or under) travels with their tour guide to the coast of the Black Sea, along the border of Russian Georgia to Mt. Ararat, which is 17,000 feet above sea level. Continue through the mountainous border region with Iraq and Iran along Lake Van, the largest soda lake, with picturesque views of abbies and oriental palaces; return to the city of Erzurum. Stop in Ancara or Istanbul and visit national museums and the Blue Mosque.

Price (includes motorcycle rental):
- Rider, double occupancy .... 3,850 DM
- Passenger, double occupancy .... 3,150 DM
- Supplement for single room occupancy .... 350 DM

Price Includes:
Round trip airfare from Munich to Izmir; hotels; half-board (hotel includes Turkish breakfast and dinner); gasoline; guide; and sightseeing expenses.

Motorcycle Provisions:
Yamaha XJ650 and Honda CM400T.

Luggage Provisions:
Luggage is transported by a van and is limited to two pieces per person and a maximum of 30 kilograms (66 lbs.; limit of the flight to Turkey).

Special Notes:
The principal language of this tour is German; the tour guide also speaks English. Temperatures in east Turkey are cool and rain is possible in the mountains; pack accordingly. Riding gear is not available in Turkey.

TURKEY **East Turkey**

Tour Operator:	Von Thielmann Tours P.O. Box 87764 San Diego, CA 92138 Contact: Ms. Gina Guzzardo Phone: 619-463-7788 or 619-291-7057 FAX: 619-291-4630 Telex: 910 335 1607 MESA SERV SDG
Length of Tour:	14 days
Dates:	

- April through October: biweekly departures

Trip Begins and Ends:	Munich, West Germany

Highlights:
This tour features fourteen days in the important border region of Turkey. This small group (ten or under) travels with their tour guide to the coast of the Black Sea, along the border of Russian Georgia to Mt. Ararat, which is 17,000 feet above sea level. They continue through the mountainous border region with Iraq and Iran and return to the city of Erzurum.

Price (includes motorcycle rental):
- Single rider, double occupancy .... 3,850 DM
- Passenger, double occupancy .... 3,150 DM

Price Includes:
Airfare from Munich to Erzurum; hotels; half-board (daily breakfast plus either lunch or dinner); gasoline; guide; and sightseeing expenses.

Motorcycle Provisions:
Enduro type motorcycles with dual seat.

Luggage Provisions:
Support vehicle carries luggage. Bring your own riding gear and helmet.

ITALY	**Piggybike™ Tour of Italy**
Tour Operator:	Bike Tours Unlimited P.O. Box 1965 San Pedro, CA 90733 Contact: Mr. Vic Perniciaro Phone: 213-833-2671
Length of Tour:	15 days, approximately 1,100 miles

Dates:
- June 8 through June 22, 1989
- July 6 through July 20, 1989
- August 10 through August 24, 1989
- September 7 through September 21, 1989
- October 5 through October 19, 1989

[1990 dates not yet established]

Trip Begins and Ends:

Los Angeles, California (or other U.S. cities)

Highlights:

On this tour, you'll have a chance to sample the history and excitement that are truly Italy. Enjoy the robust food and delight in the exuberant people. Join Italians on hairpin turns of the Amalfi Drive and twist along the contours of the beautiful Sorrento peninsula. Sail to the romantic Isle of Capri. Spend three unforgettable nights in the eternal, enduring, and thoroughly modern Rome. Savor the sights — from the ancient Colosseum and the Roman Forum to holy St. Peter's cathedral and the Vatican museums. Then rush on to some of the world's most extravagant shopping on the Via Veneto. Along the way, you'll visit Florence, birthplace of Michelangelo and art capital of the world, and roll through Tuscan hills to discover medieval Siena. Italy is a fascinating country to visit by any mode of transportation; on a motorcycle you can feel its special magic.

Price (does not include motorcycle rental):

- Couple with one motorcycle, double occupancy, per person $3,402
- Single with one motorcycle $3,795
- Cost to ship additional motorcycle $1,485

Price Includes:

Round trip airfare from Los Angeles (price adjustments can be made from other cities); air freight for one motorcycle; all hotels; breakfast and dinner daily; cruise to the Island of Capri; maps; daily briefings; tour pin, patch, cap, book, and decal.

Motorcycle Provisions:

Riders are expected to use their own motorcycle; shipping to and from Europe is included in the price.

Luggage Provisions:

A motorcycle trailer is brought along on this tour to carry reasonable overflow luggage. Travelers are expected to carry the bulk of their own luggage.

ITALY	**Sicily and Southern Italy (a gourmet tour)**
Tour Operator:	mhs Motorradtouren GmbH Hans-Urmiller-Ring 59 D-8190 Wolfratshausen WEST GERMANY Contact: Mr. Herbert Schellhorn Phone: (49) 81 71 12 38
Length of Tour:	13 days, approximately 3,800 km, average 350 km per day. Only for experienced riders.

Dates:
- May 5 through May 17, 1989
- June 11 through June 23, 1989
- September 10 through September 22, 1989
- October 1 through October 13, 1989

Trip Begins:	Lugano, Switzerland
Trip Ends:	Wolfratshausen, West Germany

Highlights:
This is a special trip for connoisseurs of Italy, whether you're interested in history, bathing, or the best Italian seafood.

Ride up to the Monte Pellegrino, which the great German poet Schiller called one of the most beautiful spots in the world. Visit the catacombs of Palermo and the cathedrals of the harbor city and Monreale. In Trápani, on the west coast of the island, you can even see the coast of northern Africa on a clear day. On the trip through the island you'll see Selinunte, formerly a Greek city; Licata with its marvelous lonely bay; Enna, the geographical and once political center of Sicily; the romantic fishing village of Cefalu; Mount Etna, Europe's largest active volcano; and Taormina or Siracusa. Frequently you'll encounter traces of the ancient Greek and Roman cultures. After this, you'll leave the island for the lovely coast of Southern Italy. Journey to the National Park of Calábria, a place of astonishing vistas reminiscent of the Canadian Rockies. In Puglia you will encounter the strange round houses called "trulli," built in natural stone without mortar. You'll stay one night in a very comfortable hotel with an absolutely beautiful park — a night you may never forget. Near Alberobello, the center of the trulli region, visit the grottoes of Castellana before starting north. See the forest umbra, a wild and romantic wood, the

Adriatic coastline, Lake Trasimeno, and a great many other sights on the way to Tuscany, and then to the trip's ending point at Wolfratshausen.

Each tour offers its own special flair: the blooms of springtime in Italy, where the sea is often warm enough for swimming even though 't is still quite cool in Germany; the fresh fruit of autumn and the chance to spend hours basking in the warm sun or in the sea.

Price (does not include motorcycle rental):
- Single rider, double occupancy . . . . 3,595 DM
- Motorcycle passenger, double occupancy . . . . 2,745 DM
- Supplement for single room occupancy . . . . 600 DM

Price Includes:
Accommodation in very good hotels (double occupancy); full board with best Italian food (often seafood); table drinks; ferry from Genoa to Palermo in first class cabins (no single rooms possible); gas; entry fees and tolls.

Motorcycle Provisions:
Rental bikes available from 1,400 DM upwards. Bike rentals available only from and to Wolfratshausen.

Luggage Provisions:
Rental bikes are equipped with panniers.

Special Notes:
The primary languages for this tour are German, English, and Italian. Also important, don't forget your swimming suit since some of the hotels lie directly on the sea.

Reader Discount:
A discount of $50 applies to this tour when you send in the Reader Discount Coupon.

SPAIN & PORTUGAL

Spain and Portugal

Tour Operator: World Motorcycle Tours
14 Forest Avenue
Caldwell, NJ 07006

Contact: Mr. Warren Goodman
Phone: 201-226-9107 or
800-443-7519

Length of Tour: 22 days

Dates:
• October 12 through November 2, 1989

Trip Begins and Ends: New York and Los Angeles

Highlights:
Follow the Goodmans through the sun-drenched Iberian Peninsula. Stay in magnificent villas throughout Portugal and Spain. Start in Lisbon, Portugal, a modern city with an ancient lifestyle. Storm the steep-sided valleys and mountains of Tras-os-Montes. Leave the fragrance of gorse and the Portuguese mountains for the beautiful scenery of the Sierra De Guadarrama near Madrid, Spain's capital city. Journey through the mystery and romance of Spain's heartland to Seville, a city where magnificence is commonplace. Visit Columbus' tomb surrounded by precious metals and jewels in the Moorish Tower. In the Andalusian city of Granada, you'll hear strains of Spanish guitar and the click of flamenco dancers' heels on tiled courtyards. In Portugal, you'll be staying mostly in Pousadas (magnificent villas).

Price (does not include motorcycle rental or shipping):
• Single rider, double occupancy, from New York City $2,600
• From Los Angeles $2,800

Price Includes:
Round trip airfare; luxury hotels with two meals daily.

Motorcycle Provisions:
Mr. Goodman specializes in shipping the client's motorcycle. The motorcycle is shipped uncrated. Cost is about $.80 per pound from New York City, higher in other cities. Liability insurance in Europe will cost $101.

Luggage Provisions:
Luggage van will accompany tour.

TURKEY

Turkey – 15 Day Tour

Tour Operator:	Motorrad-Reisen Postfach 44 01 48 D-8000 Munich 44 WEST GERMANY Contact: Mr. Hermann Weil Phone: (49) 89 39 57 68 FAX: (49) 89 34 48 32 Telex: 5218511
U.S. Agent:	Motorrad-Reisen P.O. Box 591 Oconomowoc, WI 53066 Contact: Ms. Jean Fish Phone: 414-567-7548
Length of Tour:	15 days

Dates:
- July 1 through July 15, 1989
- July 22 through August 5, 1989
- August 12 through August 26, 1989

Trip Begins and Ends:	Munich, West Germany

Highlights:
You'll see sections of the country that haven't been opened to mass tourism. Despite a change from the luxury style of touring, this journey will bring you to the more adventurous section of Turkey. You'll find a land of rugged and varied terrain for motorcycling with ancient historical roots. Start the tour with a visit to the Museum of Anatolian Cultures in Ankara. Then begin your motorcycle touring in Erzurum. You'll travel through the ancient cities of Of, Aydere, Yusufell, Kars, Dogubayazit, Van, and Ahlat. Meet with a concerned people who offer warm hospitality, fascinating landscape, and a culture that takes you back to the Middle Ages.

Price (includes motorcycle rental):
- Two riders, double occupancy $4,590
- Single rider, double occupancy $2,490
- Single occupancy is not available

Price Includes:
Flight from Munich; transfers; hotel; full board; motorcycle rentals; gas and oil; sightseeing; and tour guide on motorcycle.

Motorcycle Provisions:
Honda Transalp.

Special Notes:
This is not intended to be a luxury trip. The choice of hotels in Turkey is quite limited; gravel roads and roads in bad condition cannot be avoided. Contact agent if you would like to prolong your stay in Istanbul.

ITALY	Tuscany (a gourmet tour)
Tour Operator:	mhs Motorradtouren GmbH Hans-Urmiller-Ring 59 D-8190 Wolfratshausen WEST GERMANY Contact: Mr. Herbert Schellhorn Phone: (49) 81 71 12 38
Length of Tour:	10 days, approximately 2,400 km, average 300 km per day

Dates:
- May 25 through June 1, 1989
- June 16 through June 25, 1989
- July 7 through July 16, 1989
- September 1 through September 10, 1989
- September 22 through October 1, 1989

Trip Begins and Ends:	Wolfratshausen, West Germany

Highlights:
On your way to Tuscany you'll pass beautiful landscapes: the lakes of Molveno and Garda, the Cinque Terre, a small region on the Mediterranean, the five villages of which have been accessible by road for only a few decades. You'll pass along the beaches of the Riviera and reach Pisa, with its famous leaning tower. After climbing the tower you leave this center of tourism for the quietness of nature.

GUIDED TOURS – MEDITERRANEAN AREA

Volterra, the city of alabaster, and San Gimignano, with its popular skyline of palace and church towers from the Middle Ages are the next destinations. Close to the house where Arnbolfo di Cambio, the most important architect of the 13th century, was born, you'll take rooms in a cozy hotel. The chef de cuisine will present the delights of middle Italian fare.

The next stations are Montepulciano, the pearl of the Renaissance, Perugia, one of the centers of the Etruscan culture, and Assisi, the home town of St. Francis. There will be some time to relax, swim, or ride while you stay in an old but very good guest house, once a farmhouse. You will stay in a 16th century villa, from which you will journey to Florence by bus — a real adventure on these narrow, twisting roads.

On your way back to Germany you'll want to stop at the new Ferrari Museum, and the small town of Cutigliano in the heights of the Apennines. A night in a castle in southern Tyrol will conclude your stay in Italy.

Price (does not include motorcycle rental):
- Single rider, double occupancy .... 2,795 DM
- Motorcycle passenger, double occupancy .... 2,145 DM
- Supplement for single room occupancy .... 350 DM

Price Includes:
Accommodation in very good hotels, often in castles or other medieval houses; full board with finest Italian food; table drinks; gas; tolls and entry fees.

Motorcycle Provisions:
Rental bikes available from 1,200 DM upwards.

Luggage Provisions:
Rental bikes have panniers.

Special Notes:
The primary languages for this tour are German, English, and Italian.

Reader Discount:
A discount of $50 applies to this tour when you send in the Reader Discount Coupon.

TUSCANY REGION, ITALY

Tuscany: The Magic Spell of Italy

An afternoon stop to taste the sea breeze

Tour Operator:
Motorrad-Reisen
Postfach 44 01 48
D-8000 Munich 44
WEST GERMANY

Contact: Mr. Hermann Weil
Phone: (49) 89 39 57 68
FAX: (49) 89 34 48 32
Telex: 5218511

U.S. Agent:
Motorrad-Reisen
P.O. Box 591
Oconomowoc, WI 53066

Contact: Ms. Jean Fish
Phone: 414-567-7548

Length of Tour:	10 days

Dates:
- June 15 through June 24, 1989
- August 25 through September 3, 1989
- September 15 through September 24, 1989

Trip Begins and Ends:	Munich, West Germany

Highlights:
Journey to Tuscany through the Italian Dolomites, skirting beautiful Lake Garda, and arriving in Florence, art capital of the world. Roll through the gentle hills of Tuscany, a region that nurtured many famous creative spirits including Michelangelo, Dante, Galileo, Filippo Brunelleschi, Leonardo da Vinci, Puccini, and Boccaccio. See Etruscan design in Sienna, the gem of medieval architecture. Sweep through an ochre landscape dotted with cyprus and olive trees to visit Arezzo, Sorano, Savona, and other charming but less well-known villages. Luxuriate in the richness and variety of Italian cuisine. Don't forget, the Italians taught the French how to enjoy food. Drink a glass of robust Chianti wine at sunset, listen to the delicate evening bells, and feel the enchantment that has nourished the Italian spirit for ages.

Price (does not include motorcycle rental):
• Two riders, double occupancy $2,795
• Single rider, double occupancy $1,620
• Motorcycle rental $1,300

Price Includes:
All land arrangements; bilingual (German and English) tour guide on motorcycle; board and lodging in twin bed rooms at comfortable inns; transportation to and from Munich airport; free transportation for you and/or your motorcycle to Munich in case of illness or accident; technical assistance from tour guide.

Motorcycle Provisions:
Purchase a BMW through Motorrad-Reisen, rent their motorcycles, or ship your own motorcycle to Munich. You can rent complete accessories and gear or purchase additional insurance from agency. You must have an international driver's license valid for motorcycle operation. If you ship your motorcycle, bring the registration card and an international insurance card.

Luggage Provisions:
Van may accompany tour. Check with agent.

Special Notes:
U.S. agent can make arrangement for air travel to Munich and additional land and air arrangements including shipping your own motorcycle.

TURKEY   West Turkey

Tour Operator:	Motorrad Spaett, KG Rüdesheimerstraße, 9 8000 Munich 21 WEST GERMANY Contact: Mr. Paul Spaett or office Phone: (49) 089-57937-38 FAX: (49) 089-57017-69 Telex: 5216823 mosp
Length of Tour:	14 days

Dates:
- May 6 through May 20, 1989
- May 27 through June 10, 1989
- September 9 through September 23, 1989
- September 30 through October 14, 1989

Trip Begins and Ends:
Munich, West Germany. For overseas customers, Motorrad Spaett can arrange a combination one-week tour through the Alps and two weeks in Turkey. They can book flights from any location to Munich.

Highlights:
Intended principally for sightseeing, this guided tour leaves from the Aegean city of Izmir, along the scenic Aegean coast, with visits to the ancient Roman and Greek towns, on to the oriental city Antalya with its well-known bazaar. On your way to Antalya, you will have enough time to swim in the creek's crystal water along the coast. Antalya will also be the most southerly point on this journey and the impression of the immense cultures there will overwhelm you. Over Pamukkale with dreamlike "chalksinterterraces," the tour heads back to Izmir.

Price (includes motorcycle rental):
- Rider, double occupancy .... 3,850 DM
- Passenger, double occupancy .... 3,150 DM
- Supplement for single room occupancy .... 280 DM

Price Includes:
Round trip airfare from Munich to Izmir; hotels; half-board (hotel includes Turkish breakfast and dinner); gasoline; guide; and sightseeing expenses.

Motorcycle Provisions:
Yamaha XJ650 and Honda CM400T.

Luggage Provisions:
Luggage is transported by a van and is limited to two pieces per person and a maximum of 30 kilograms (66lbs.; limit of the flight to Turkey).

Special Notes:
The principal language of this tour is German; the tour guide also speaks English. Temperatures in Turkey are high; pack accordingly. Riding gear is not available in Turkey.

TURKEY — West Turkey

Tour Operator:	Von Thielmann Tours P.O. Box 87764 San Diego, CA 92138 Contact: Ms. Gina Guzzardo Phone: 619-463-7788 or 619-291-7057 FAX: 619-291-4630 Telex: 910 335 1607 MESA SERV SDG
Length of Tour:	14 days

Dates:
- April through October: biweekly departures

Trip Begins and Ends:	Munich, West Germany

Highlights:
Guided sightseeing tour leaves from the Aegean city of Bodrum. The fourteen-day trip visits the ancient cities of Ephesus and Pamukkal, the south of Turkey and the Aegean coast.

Price (includes motorcycle rental):
- Single rider, double occupancy .... 3,850 DM
- Passenger, double occupancy .... 3,150 DM

Price Includes:
Airfare from Munich to Bodrum; hotels; half-board (daily breakfast and either lunch or dinner); gasoline; guide; and sightseeing expenses.

Motorcycle Provisions:
Enduro type motorcycles with dual seat.

Luggage Provisions:
Support vehicle carries luggage. Bring your own riding gear and helmet.

EUROPE/ASIA	**West Turkey and East Turkey**
Tour Operator:	Team Aventura Karlsebene 2 8924 Steingaden WEST GERMANY Contact: Mr. Christoph del Bondio Phone: (49) 08862-6161 or (49) 08807-8360
Length of Tour:	14 days, about 1,400 miles

Dates:
West Turkey:
- May 6 through May 20, 1989
- May 27 through June 6, 1989

East Turkey:
- September 9 through September 23, 1989
- September 30 through October 14, 1989

Trip Begins and Ends:	Munich/Bavaria

Highlights:
On both tours you will see fantastic landscapes, enormous mountains, lovely lakes, the Mediterranean or the Black Sea, and you will meet very friendly people.

Price (includes motorcycle rental):
- Single rider, double occupancy $2,300
- Passenger, double occupancy $2,000

Price Includes:
All flights from Munich; insured motorcycle; overnight stays in the best hotels (they are usually not as good as in the States); all food; entrance fees; gasoline; luggage transportation; an English-French, Spanish, and German speaking tourguide; farewell party.

Motorcycle Provisions:
- West Turkey: Yamaha XJ 650 or Honda CM 400T
- East Turkey: Honda Transalp or Yamaha Tenere

Luggage Provisions:
A vehicle will transport your luggage.

GUIDED TOURS – AFRICA & NEAR EAST

192 GUIDED TOURS – AFRICA & NEAR EAST

AFRICA   **Abidjan to Agadez to Tunis (Explo-Tours #M3)**

Full power

Tour Operator:	Explo-Tours Arnulfstraße 134 8000 Munich 19 WEST GERMANY Contact: Mr. Josef Geltl Phone: (49) 089-16-07-89 Telex: 1631 btxd/089161716 1+
Length of Tour:	4 weeks, covering approximately 4,000 km (1,300 hard km)

Dates:
Dates not available at time of publication. Contact Explo-Tours for 1989/90 dates.

Trip Begins:	Munich, West Germany
Trip Ends:	Genoa, Italy

Highlights:
Cut a 6,000 kilometer enduro swathe across Africa from the Atlantic Ocean to the Mediterranean Sea. From Abidjan, capital of the Ivory Coast, head to the shores of Lake Bandama Blanc deep in the tropical rain forest. Safari in Komoe National Park. Push north past huge sugar plantations where the landscape is distinguished by the strange white Senoufu trees. Pass villages of round straw huts, home to the Bobo and

the Waga people who populate the Upper Volta. In Niamey, capital of Niger, you'll visit a colorful market and a folk art museum. Run the wadis (dry river beds) that course down the high barren desert. At Agadez, storm your first sand dunes and claim the horizon-to-horizon yellow sand of the vast Sahara. Follow the migration route of the nomadic Tuareg people north through beautiful moonlike landscapes of the Hoggar Mountains. Test your skills in 2,000 kilometers of sand, driving all the way across the Sahara to Tunis on the Mediterranean Sea.

Price (does not include motorcycle rental):
- Single rider, double occupancy .... 4,980 DM
- Motorcycle passenger, double occupancy .... 4,380 DM

Price Includes:
Flight from Munich to Abidjan; tour guide; vehicle for baggage, passengers, equipment, water; full meals in Africa; tents and campground fees; breakdown guarantee; ferry from Tunis to Genoa.

Not Included in Price:
Gasoline; food on ferry; drinks; or hotel accommodations.

Motorcycle Provisions:
Your own motorcycle will be containerized and shipped from Munich to your destination, round trip, for free. When Explo-Tours receives your 400 DM deposit for space, they will tell you whether you have been placed.

Rental available for 490 DM per week. New Yamaha XT 350, 27hp. Price includes mileage, insurance, fuel, and gas.

Luggage Provisions:
A van will accompany this tour to carry luggage.

Special Notes:
The common language of this tour is German. Guide also fluent in English and French. Clients come from throughout Europe. Physical and mental endurance, along with endurocycle experience is strongly suggested for this trip.

Reader Discount:
A discount of 100 DM applies to this tour when you send in the Reader Discount Coupon.

AFRICA

Best Winter in Africa (Explo-Tours #M6 + #M7)

Tour Operator:	Explo-Tours Arnulfstraße 134 8000 Munich 19 WEST GERMANY Contact: Mr. Josef Geltl Phone: (49) 089-16-07-89 Telex: 1631 btxd/089161716 1+
Length of Tour:	8 weeks covering approximately 11,000 km (4,500 rough km)

Dates:
- October 21 through December 17, 1989

Trip Begins:	Genoa, Italy
Trip Ends:	Munich, West Germany

Highlights:
See descriptions of Explo-Tours #M6 (Tunis to Douala) and #M7 (Douala to Mombasa).

Price (does not include motorcycle rental):
- Single rider, double occupancy .... 7,490 DM

Price Includes:
Round trip ferry Genoa to Tunis; tour guide; full meals in Africa; tents and camping fees. Flight from Nairobi to Munich and return transport of motorcycle.

Not Included in Price:
Gasoline; food on ferry; drinks; or hotel accommodations.

Motorcycle Provisions:
Your own motorcycle accompanies you round trip from Genoa to Tunis. Rental available for 490 DM per week. New Yamaha XT 350, 27hp. Price includes mileage, insurance, fuel, and gas.

Luggage Provisions:
A van will accompany this tour to carry luggage.

Special Notes:
The common language of this tour is German. Guide also fluent in English and French. Clients come from throughout Europe. Physical and mental endurance, along with endurocycle experience is strongly suggested for this trip.

Reader Discount:
A discount of 100 DM applies to this tour when you send in the Reader Discount Coupon.

AFRICA   Central Sahara

Tour Operator:	Wüstenfahrer Bahnhofstraße 7e 8011 Baldham WEST GERMANY Contact: Mr. Thomas Troßmann or Mrs. Antje Vogel Phone: (49) 81 06/77 99

Length of Tour:
- 4-week tours, approximately 5,000 km (of which 2,200 km is off-road)
- 5-week tours, approximately 6,000 km (of which 3,500 is off-road)

Dates:
Four-week tour:
- September 30 through October 28, 1989
- November 25 through December 23, 1989
- January 27 through February 24, 1990
- March 24 through April 21, 1990

Five-week tour:
- September 30 through November 4, 1989
- November 25 through December 30, 1989
- January 27 through March 3, 1990
- March 24 through April 28, 1990

Trip Begins and Ends: Genoa, Italy

Highlights:
Experienced enduro drivers conquer relentless sands of the Sahara, the world's greatest desert. Rejoice in this extremely challenging tour without extreme torture. From Tunis, speed into the desert, leaving asphalt behind for 3,000 kilometers of open exploration. Experience the variety of the Sahara including 100-meter high sand hills, impressive mountain ranges, picturesque wadis (dry river beds), and rocky passes. Perhaps you'll climb the high plateau to view the other-worldly landscape and neolithic rock paintings. As you travel south, obstacles become more challenging with deep sand and tight passes. Scale the 2,700-meter-high Assekrem Mountain where sunrise casts shadows of rose gold. Thrust into the ever more daunting and difficult part of your tour inside the dunes of Amguid Erg and Issaouane Erg.

Price (does not include motorcycle rental):
Four-week tour:
- Single rider, double occupancy .... 3,950 DM
- Passenger, pillion or jeep, double occupancy .... 3,600 DM

Five-week tour:
- Single rider, double occupancy .... 4,520 DM
- Passenger, pillion or jeep, double occupancy .... 4,050 DM

Price Includes:
Round trip Genoa/Tunis/Genoa for rider and motorcycle; all meals; hotels; cooking equipment; expedition van; gasoline; tour guide.

Motorcycle Provisions:
You must bring your own four-stroke enduro motorcycle and proper cross-country riding apparel, including protection for knees, elbows, spine, etc.

Luggage Provisions:
Two jeeps accompany the tour to carry food, water, gasoline, and luggage. There is also the possibility for a few participants to make the trip in the jeep.

Special Notes:
This tour is for experienced endurance riders as well as beginners, despite the fact that it is a demanding trip, requiring a bit of physical and mental endurance.

NORTH AFRICA

Douala to Mombasa (Explo-Tours #M7)

"To think, I almost brought the Gold Wing."

Tour Operator:
Explo-Tours
Arnulfstraße 134
8000 Munich 19
WEST GERMANY

Contact: Mr. Josef Geltl
Phone: (49) 089-16-07-89
Telex: 1631 btxd/089161716 1+

Length of Tour:
4 weeks, covering approximately 5,000 km along the equator

Dates:
- November 18 through December 17, 1989

Trip Begins and Ends: Munich, West Germany

Highlights:
You'll need steady nerves for this trip. Follow ever-changing trails from the white sands of Limbet to the black sands of Mombasa. Roll through Cameroon on red dusty paths that become impassable mud trenches in a sudden tropical downpour. Push through the rain forest in Zaire. Cross one of Africa's largest rivers on a primitive raft. Perhaps you'll see members of the Bambuti tribe; these pygmies are the world's smallest people. From the slogging mud of the rain forest, you'll steam up mountains and zoom down the valleys of the Central African Replublic on your way to Africa's highest peak at Mt. Kilamanjaro. Unwind on the last run of tar road into Mombasa on the shores of the Indian Ocean.

Price (does not include motorcycle rental):
- Single rider, double occupancy .... 5,800 DM
- Motorcycle passenger, double occupancy .... 4,800 DM
- Supplement for single tent .... 100 DM

Price Includes:
Flights Munich to Douala and Nairobi to Munich; tour guide; food in Africa; tents and camping fees.

GUIDED TOURS – AFRICA & NEAR EAST

Not Included in Price:
Gasoline; food on ferry; drinks; or hotel accommodations.

Motorcycle Provisions:
Your motorcycle will be containerized and shipped from Munich to Douala and from Nairobi to Munich by sea as part of the tour cost. Rental available for 490 DM per week. New Yamaha XT 350, 27hp. Price includes mileage, insurance, fuel, and gas.

Luggage Provisions:
A van will accompany this tour to carry luggage.

Special Notes:
The common language of this tour is German. Guide also fluent in English and French. Clients come from throughout Europe. Physical and mental endurance, with endurocycle experience required for this trip.

Reader Discount:
A discount of 100 DM applies to this tour when you send in the Reader Discount Coupon.

AFRICA — Dunes Expedition

Tour Operator:
Wüstenfahrer
Bahnhofstraße 7e
8011 Baldham
WEST GERMANY

Contact: Mr. Thomas Troßmann or Mrs. Antje Vogel
Phone: (49) 81 06/77 99

"This sure is a big beach!"

Length of Tour: 3 weeks, approximately 3,500 km (of which 2,100 km is off-road)

Dates:
- September 30 through October 21, 1989
- January 27 through February 17, 1990

Trip Begins and Ends: Genoa, Italy

Highlights:
This tour leads through the middle of the great seas of sand, the Ergs. It is a trip as far from the well-known routes as one can think; a trip for the rider who wishes to see the unknown and untouched Sahara.

Price (does not include motorcycle rental):
• Single rider, double occupancy .... 3,570 DM
• Passenger, pillion or jeep, double occupancy .... 3,270 DM

Price Includes:
Round trip Genoa/Tunis/Genoa for rider and motorcycle; all meals; hotels; cooking equipment; expedition van; gasoline; tour guide.

Not Included in Price:
Sleeping bag; souvenirs; alcohol; cigarettes; and various Algerian entry charges.

Motorcycle Provisions:
You must bring your own four-stroke enduro motorcycle and proper cross-country riding apparel, including protection for knees, elbows, spine, etc.

Luggage Provisions:
Two jeeps accompany the tour to carry food, water, gasoline, and luggage. There is also the possibility for a few participants to make the trip in the jeep.

Special Notes:
This tour is for experienced endurance riders only. This is a demanding trip, requiring great physical and mental endurance.

EGYPT

Egypt Tour

Tour Operator: Sahara Cross
Landfridstraße 6
7910 Neu-Ulm 4
WEST GERMANY

Contact: Jürgen Greif
Phone: (49) 07307-31445

GUIDED TOURS – AFRICA & NEAR EAST

Length of Tour:	3 weeks, covering approximately 3,000 km (Cairo to Aswan and back)

Dates:
- October 7 through October 27, 1989
- November 4 through November 24, 1989
- February 3 through February 23, 1990
- March 3 through March 23, 1990
- March 31 through April 20, 1990
- October 6 through October 26, 1990
- November 3 through November 23, 1990

Trip Begins and Ends:	Munich, West Germany

Highlights:
Revel in an enduro paradise from Cairo to the head of the Nile River and back to Cairo. Battle sand and biting sandstorms from the limestone formations in the white desert to grandiose landscapes where yellow sand stretches from horizon to horizon. Camp in the oasis of Farafra. Bathe in its hot springs in the midst of the desert. Superior drivers press on to mountain desert. Trek through 150 kilometers of sand, stone, and gravel to Luxor. Journey over mountains and valleys to Aswan, head of the Nile River Valley. Leave the road for 30 kilometers of rough gravel riding to an ancient Roman fortress. Run through deep red granite gorges and over wadis, dry beds that become rushing streams in the rainy season. You'll persevere through rock and sand and desert heat for a motorcycling adventurer's thrills in the land of ancient pyramids.

Price (includes motorcycle rental):
- Single rider, double occupancy .... 4,090 DM
- Passenger, double occupancy .... 3,000 DM
- Passenger, riding in the luggage van .... 2,500 DM

Price Includes:
Round trip airfare Munich/Cairo/Munich; transfers; hotel accommodations with breakfast; tools and spare parts; lunch and dinner in desert camps; farewell banquet; experienced tour guide; medical treatment; damage insurance — covered up to 50 DM and over 1,000 DM (guest pays up to 1,000 DM for serious damage); baggage loss insurance.

Not included is gasoline (about 220 DM); lunch and dinner in Cairo, Karga, Luxor, and Safaga (total cost, about 100 DM); malaria pills for April and September.

Motorcycle Provisions:
Yamaha XT 500 is included in price of tour.

Luggage Provisions:
A van accompanies each tour to carry luggage.

Special Notes:
This tour is for experienced enduro riders only. It requires considerable physical stamina and will place exceptional demands on riders. The tour guide speaks fluent English as well as German. The last half-day will be spent cleaning the motorcycles before turning them in.

Reader Discount:
A discount of $25 applies to this tour when you send in the Reader Discount Coupon.

NORTH AFRICA

High Dunes and Deep Valleys: Algeria (Explo-Tours #M4)

Taking a break, Hoggar Mountains

Tour Operator:
Explo-Tours
Arnulfstraße 134
8000 Munich 19
WEST GERMANY
Contact: Mr. Josef Geltl
Phone: (49) 089-16-07-89
Telex: 1631 btxd/089161716 1+

GUIDED TOURS – AFRICA & NEAR EAST

Length of Tour: 3 weeks, covering approximately 4,000 km (1,800 rough km)

Dates:
- April 15 through May 6, 1989
- March 17 through April 7, 1990
- April 7 through April 28, 1990

Trip Begins and Ends: Genoa, Italy

Highlights:
Only 500 kilometers of asphalt before you thrust into the desert sand track of Algeria. Leave El Oued Oasis, pass Arab market villages and bear south across the dunes of the Great Western Plateau. Conquer the 600 meter sand dune. Storm off the barely visible track for even more challenging trails across the dunes. Brave the northern boundaries of Plateau of the Dead. Climb the high plateau for a stunning view of the Tassili Mountains, part of the Hoggar Range. Navigate the wadis that crease the high plateau. You'll visit an important center for oil pumping in In Amenas. Master the descent from the plateau; migrate across the Great Eastern Desert toward the oasis of El Oued and the beautiful shining Mediterranean.

Price (does not include motorcycle rental):
- Single rider, double occupancy .... 2,970 DM
- Motorcycle passenger, double occupancy .... 2,850 DM
- Surcharge for single tent .... 100 DM

Price Includes:
Round trip ferry Genoa to Tunis; tour guide; all meals in Africa; tents and camping fees.

Not Included in Price:
Gasoline; food on ferry; drinks; or hotel accommodations.

Motorcycle Provisions:
Your own motorcycle accompanies you round trip from Genoa to Tunis. Rental available for 490 DM per week. New Yamaha XT 350, 27hp. Price includes mileage, insurance, fuel, and gas.

Luggage Provisions:
A van will accompany this tour to carry luggage.

Special Notes:
The common language of this tour is German. Guide also fluent in English and French. Clients come from throughout Europe. Physical and

mental endurance, along with endurocycle experience is strongly suggested for this trip.

Reader Discount:
A discount of 100 DM applies to this tour when you send in the Reader Discount Coupon.

KENYA	**Jambo Kenya!** **The other Africa . . .**
Tour Operator:	Motorrad-Reisen Postfach 44 01 48 D-8000 Munich 44 WEST GERMANY Contact: Mr. Hermann Weil Phone: (49) 89 39 57 68 FAX: (49) 89 34 48 32 Telex: 5218511
U.S. Agent:	Motorrad-Reisen P.O. Box 591 Oconomowoc, WI 53066 Contact: Ms. Jean Fish Phone: 414-567-7548
Length of Tour:	10 days, covering approximately 750 miles

Dates:
- January 25 through February 4, 1989 (for reference)
- February 8 through February 17, 1989 (for reference)
- February 22 through March 3, 1989 (for reference)
- March 8 through March 17, 1989 (for reference)

Trip Begins and Ends:	Frankfurt, West Germany.

Highlights:
Begin your Kenya adventure with a full day in the capital city of Nairobi. Travel through the lush highlands. In the pasture lands, you'll ride past herds of antelope and zebra. Speed through acres of evergreen tea bushes with fragrant white blossoms. Journey through emerald valleys decorated

with crystalline lakes. Capture African game on film during your excursion to the game park. Watch the sun set over the cradle of civilization; tell stories around a campfire and listen for the roar of the regal lion. Visit a Massai village. Throughout your Kenya travels, you'll hear the word "Jambo" as cordial natives bring you their wishes for a good day.

Price (includes motorcycle rental):
- Two riders, double occupancy $4,400
- Single rider, double occupancy $2,400
- Supplement for single room occupancy .... $ 270

Price Includes:
Airfare to and from Frankfurt; motorcycle; fuel and oil; full-board and comfortable, modern accommodations (two nights in a camp with modern conveniences).

Motorcycle Provisions:
Yamaha XT 500 and XT 600.

Luggage Provisions:
Luggage van accompanies tour.

AFRICA	**The Jumbo Safari Rider Tour**
Tour Operator:	TransCyclist International CPO Box 2064 Tokyo, 100-91 JAPAN Contact: Mr. Volker Lenzner Phone: (81) 3-402-5385 FAX: (81) 3-402-5358
Length of Tour:	23 days, on- and off-road, covering approximately 7,000 km

Dates:
- April 13 through May 6, 1989
- April 12 through May 5, 1990 (approximate)

Trip Begins and Ends:	Johannesburg, South Africa

Highlights:

Experience the true African *Born Free* on TransCyclist's (TC) ultimate bike adventure: The Jumbo Safari Rider Tour. Enjoy clean spacious roadways with generous turnouts next to breathtaking views of a steamy wilderness. Bring your camera, there are plenty of photo opportunities. Big game graze along the side of the trail. Sounds, smells, and tastes from Africa will be deeply engraved in your memory. Have a chat with the friendly natives, children of the sun. Explore the remote areas in Southern Africa where you can still find the genuine Africa away from commercialization.

The Jumbo Safari Rider Tour is a challenge for the long-distance tourer and off-road enthusiast. Explore wild game reserves and Kalahari desert territory, riding as far as Windhoek in South West Africa (Namibia).

Price (includes motorcycle rental):
- Single rider, double occupancy from $2,500
- Passenger (four-wheel drive van), double occupancy from $1,500

Price Includes:
All hotels and bush camps; breakfasts and dinners; information packet; guiding; luggage transport; four-wheel drive van; airport transfers; game reserve visits; motorcycle rental. Not included: fuel, oil, lunch snacks, travel accident insurance, $500 U.S. refundable insurance bond.

Motorcycle Provisions:
BMW R80GS; other BMW's available.

Luggage Provisions:
Four-wheel drive van will carry luggage.

Special Notes:
International driver's license valid for motorcycle operation required by participants. You are advised to book well in advance. In addition to this tour, a standard Safari Rider Tour is operated year round. Prices range from $990 per rider for a seven-day tour (double occupancy), all inclusive except gas and lunches. Send a self-addressed, stamped envelope and one international reply coupon (available from the post office) when inquiring about the tour.

MOROCCO — Morocco Trailblaze

Tour Operator:	Wanderer's Expeditions, c/o Tee Mill Tours Ltd. 56 Tooting High Street London SW17 0RN ENGLAND Contact: Mr. Reg Thomas Phone: (44) 01-767-8739 FAX: (44) 01-682-0138 Telex: 945307
Length of Tour:	15 days

Dates:
- July 15 through July 29, 1989
- August 5 through August 19, 1989
- July 21 through August 4, 1990
- August 11 through August 25, 1990

Trip Begins and Ends:	London, England

Highlights:
Ferry to Morocco across the Strait of Gibraltar. Stop at Volubilis. Tour the ancient ruins of this Roman capital. In Fez, you'll have your first chance to see locally made carpets. Look for snake charmers and other exotic features of the marketplace. Climb the Atlas Mountains heading for a desert oasis. Camp and swim beneath the palm trees or laze in the sun. Hit the hard riding of the desert terrain on your way to Marrakech. Drive through a breathtaking mountain pass. Camp on the slopes of Mount Taubkal in the small village of Imlil. Trek into a Berber village and join the natives for traditional mint tea. Wind down with a run along the golden beaches, through Casablanca, Rabat, and Tangier before ferrying back to Spain to catch your flight to London.

Price (includes motorcycle rental):
- Single rider .... £ 999

Price Includes:
Airfare; all food; all camping equipment; motorcycle rental; spare parts; insurance for the motorcycle; personal accident and medical insurance during the trip.

Motorcycle Provisions:
Can-Am Bombardier, 250cc, two-stroke, all terrain bike is supplied. These motorcycles are used by the army and are light and easy to maneuver with good power and acceleration.

Backup:
A backup truck complete with driver/mechanic and cook follows the tour. Spare parts are available and the truck can carry disabled motorcycles or injured riders.

Special Notes:
Pillion passengers may come on this tour, provided the traveler ships his own motorcycle. Call agent for details.

Reader Discount:
A discount of $25 applies to this tour when you send in the Reader Discount Coupon.

White dessert! (photo by Explo-Tours)

NORTH AFRICA

Paris – Dakar Special
North Africa & the Sahara

Tour Operator:	Wanderer's Expeditions, c/o Tee Mill Tours Ltd. 56 Tooting High Street London SW17 0RN ENGLAND Contact: Mr. Reg Thomas Phone: (44) 01-767-8739 FAX: (44) 01-682-0138 Telex: 945307
Length of Tour:	22 days

Dates:
- December 17, 1989 through January 7, 1990
- January 22 through February 2, 1989

Trip Begins and Ends:	London, England

Highlights:
Travel the same route as the Trans-Sahara Trailblaze with an important detour that pushes farther into the desert to catch the action of the Paris – Dakar Rally. Trek through the fantastical Hoggar Mountains with their moonlike surface. Test your skills against the challenge of desert riding. Climb sand dunes; spin down the dry river beds. You'll have plenty to tell your friends after this adventure vacation!

Price (includes motorcycle rental):
- Single rider .... £ 1,595

Price Includes:
Airfare; all food; all camping equipment; motorcycle rental; spare parts; insurance for the motorcycle; personal accident and medical insurance during the trip.

Motorcycle Provisions:
Can-Am Bombardier, 250cc, two-stroke, all terrain bike is supplied. These motorcycles are used by the army and are light and easy to maneuver with good power and acceleration.

GUIDED TOURS – AFRICA & NEAR EAST 209

Backup:
A backup truck complete with driver/mechanic and cook follows the tour. Spare parts are available and the truck can carry disabled motorcycles or injured riders.

Reader Discount:
A discount of $25 applies to this tour when you send in the Reader Discount Coupon.

AFRICA   Sahara Without Borders

Tour Operator:	Wüstenfahrer Bahnhofstraße 7e 8011 Baldham WEST GERMANY Contact: Mr. Thomas Troßmann or Mrs. Antje Vogel Phone: (49) 81 06/77 99
Length of Tour:	Six weeks, covering approximately 6,600 km (of which 4,200 km is off-road)

Dates:
- November 25, 1989 through January 6, 1990
- March 24 through May 5, 1990

Trip Begins and Ends:	Genoa, Italy

Highlights:
This is the ultimate Sahara trip, the dream of everyone who has been infected by desert fever. You will cross right through the middle of the legendary Ténéré Desert in the state of Niger. Agadez, Bilma, Djado, and Djanet are the best known oases on this very special trip.

Price (does not include motorcycle rental):
- Single rider, double occupancy .... 5,420 DM
- Passenger, pillion or jeep, double occupancy .... 4,800 DM

Price Includes:
Round trip Genoa/Tunis/Genoa for rider and motorcycle; all meals; hotels; cooking equipment; expedition van; gasoline; tour guide.

Motorcycle Provisions:
You must bring your own four-stroke enduro motorcycle and proper cross-country riding apparel, including protection for knees, elbows, spine, etc.

Luggage Provisions:
Two jeeps accompany the tour to carry food, water, gasoline, and luggage. There is also the possibility for a few participants to make the trip in the jeep.

Special Notes:
This tour is for experienced endurance riders only. You must be able to ride in all conditions and terrains. This is a demanding trip, requiring physical and mental endurance.

NEAR EAST

Sinai Tour

"One snorkel for me and one for the bike."

Tour Operator:
Sahara Cross
Landfridstraße 6
7910 Neu-Ulm 4
WEST GERMANY

Contact: Mr. Jürgen Greif
Phone: (49) 07307-31445

Length of Tour:
14 days, approximately 1,500 km

Dates:
- April 1 through April 14, 1989
- April 15 through April 28, 1989
- September 2 through September 15, 1989

Trip Begins and Ends: Munich, West Germany

Highlights:

Watch the sun rise on the commanding peak of majestic Mt. Sinai. You'll always remember the wildness of this overpowering mountain world and the colorful array of rocks in the sunlight. Visit the Katherina monastery. Camp at spectacular beaches along the bays of the Sinai. In the Gulf of Aqaba, you'll snorkel in the world's most beautiful coral reefs. Alternate days of water sport with one- and two-day forays into the desert.

Price (includes motorcycle rental):

- Single rider, double occupancy .... 2,990 DM
- Passenger, double occupancy .... 2,200 DM
- Passengers riding in the luggage van .... 1,990 DM

Price Includes:

Round trip airfare; transfers; hotel accommodations with breakfast; tools and spare parts; lunch and dinner; farewell banquet; experienced tour guide; medical treatment; damage insurance — covered up to 50 DM and over 1,000 DM (guest pays up to 1,000 DM for serious damage); baggage loss insurance. Not included is gasoline.

Motorcycle Provisions:

Yamaha XT 500 is included in price of tour.

Luggage Provisions:

Luggage van accompanies tour.

Special Notes:

This tour is for experienced enduro riders only. It requires considerable physical stamina and will place exceptional demands on riders. The tour guide speaks fluent English as well as German.

Reader Discount:

A discount of $25 applies to this tour when you send in the Reader Discount Coupon.

EUROPE – NORTH AFRICA	16-Week, Trans-Africa Trailblaze
Tour Operator:	Wanderer's Expeditions, c/o Tee Mill Tours Ltd. 56 Tooting High Street London SW17 0RN ENGLAND Contact: Mr. Reg Thomas Phone: (44) 01-767-8739 FAX: (44) 01-682-0138 Telex: 945307
Length of Tour:	16 weeks

Dates:
- November 5, 1989 through February 25, 1990

Trip Begins:	London, England
Trip Ends:	Nairobi, Kenya

Highlights:
You'll talk about this trip for the rest of your life! Ride through a dozen countries. Conquer the vast Sahara; climb fantastic mountains; journey through rain forests and travel lush river valleys. Meet your backup truck in London and begin your expedition. Take a direct route through Europe, crossing at the Strait of Gibraltar to the duty-free port of Ceuta. Ride over the endless sand dunes of the great Sahara Desert. Climb to a height of 8,000 feet in the Hoggar Mountain Range where barren volcanic plugs suggest a desolate moonscape. You'll stop in towns as varied as the landscape — Ghardaia, a beautiful oasis where caravans congregate; In-Salah one of the hottest towns in the Sahara; Arlit, a uranium mining town built over the last 15 years; Agadez, long famous for its silversmiths.

Spend a total of 12 days in the game preserves of the fabulous National Parks. See herds of zebra, antelope, and elephants. Perhaps you'll sight a lion, a cheetah, rhino, or giraffe. Crawl through dense undergrowth of the Zaire jungle looking for the rare Mountain Gorilla, an enormous but gentle creature. Drift down the Zaire River with jungles on both sides. Trek into the rain forest to visit a Pygmy village. Stay overnight and accompany the villagers on an early morning hunt. See the source of the great River Nile. Climb beautiful Mt. Kilimanjaro. If you have satisfied your lust for adventure, end your trip in Nairobi. If you thirst for still more excitement, continue south on your own.

GUIDED TOURS – AFRICA & NEAR EAST   213

Price (does not include motorcycle rental):
• Single rider £1,500
• Food kitty contribution ....£ 350

Price Includes:
Guide, backup truck for spares and luggage, and cooking equipment. Guests bring their own camping gear.

Not Included in Price:
Airfare; visa fees; accommodations in hotels; personal, motorcycle and medical insurance (which is compulsory); gas and oil for your motorcycle; local tourist/camera taxes; guide and porter fees; and game park fees not met by the kitty.

Motorcycle Provisions:
Bring your own motorcycle to meet the truck in London, England or call agent about individual rental.

Backup:
A backup truck complete with driver/mechanic and cook follows the tour. Spare parts are available and the truck can carry disabled motorcycles or injured riders.

Reader Discount:
A discount of $25 applies to this tour when you send in the Reader Discount Coupon.

NORTH AFRICA	**Tassili to North Tenere (Explo-Tours #M1)**
Tour Operator:	Explo-Tours Arnulfstraße 134 8000 Munich 19 WEST GERMANY Contact: Mr. Josef Geltl Phone: (49) 089-16-07-89 Telex: 1631 btxd/089161716 1+
Length of Tour:	4 weeks, covering approximately 6,000 km (3,000 hard km)

Dates:
- February 17 through March 17, 1990

Trip Begins and Ends:
Genoa, Italy

Highlights:
You'll make the most of your time on this run into the sand dunes. Breeze into Tunisia on quiet roads leading directly to the edge of the desert. Cross the Plateau de Tedemait to a sandy area with tremendous dunes. Begin the evil cross-country trip; jolt over rocky corrugation with lots of deep sand; travel a barely visible ancient path with no markers except the Gara Kranfoussa Mountains. With luck, you'll navigate the labyrinth of dunes. Yellow sand gives way to black mountains. Fountains flow with brackish water. Take your own direction heading toward the southeast where a formidable wall of mountains and dunes seem to block your exit. You'll find a path over the dunes in the soft sand. Then you'll speed over a dry salt sea; climb steep mountains and return too soon to civilization.

Price (does not include motorcycle rental):
- Single rider, double occupancy .... 3,450 DM
- Motorcycle passenger, double occupancy .... 3,350 DM

Price Includes:
Ferry trip across Mediterranean; luggage from Munich to Tunis; tour guide; full meals; tents; camping fees; breakdown guarantee.

Not Included in Price:
Gasoline; food on ferry; or hotel accommodations.

Motorcycle Provisions:
Your own motorcycle accompanies you round trip from Genoa to Tunis. Rental available for 490 DM per week. New Yamaha XT 350, 27 hp. Price includes mileage, insurance, fuel, and gas.

Luggage Provisions:
A van will accompany this tour to carry luggage.

Special Notes:
The common language of this tour is German. Guide also fluent in English and French. Clients come from throughout Europe. Physical and mental endurance, along with endurocycle experience is strongly suggested for this trip.

Reader Discount:
A discount of 100 DM applies to this tour when you send in the Reader Discount Coupon.

GUIDED TOURS – AFRICA & NEAR EAST 215

AFRICA

Tenere: Central North Africa (Explo-Tours #M5)

Making camp, Hoggar Mountains

Tour Operator:
Explo-Tours
Arnulfstraße 134
8000 Munich 19
WEST GERMANY

Contact: Mr. Josef Geltl
Phone: (49) 089-16-07-89
Telex: 1631 btxd/089161716 1+

Length of Tour:
4 weeks

Dates:

Dates not available at time of publication. Contact Explo-Tours for 1989/1990 dates.

Trip Begins and Ends: Genoa, Italy

Highlights:

Conquer 7,000 kilometers of high desert plateau, mountains, gorges, wadis, and the endless sands of the Sahara on this enduro adventure. From the eerie Hoggar mountains where the landscape is cratered like the surface of the moon, descend to the deep sands, and the dry rivers with countless boulders, bumpy fields, and tight paths for kilometers at a time. Journey to the wide Tenere desert and pass through an endless corridor of sand dunes blocking the sun. Drive under towering escarpments of sand and rock with beautiful vistas on all sides. Glimpse ancient Tamrit as you speed across the Tassili Plateau in the shadow of Mount Afao. Follow the pipelines to In Amenas, a center of oil production. You'll master more difficult sand driving, more heat, and more sandstorms before you reach the shores of the Mediterranean.

Price (does not include motorcycle rental):
• Single rider, double occupancy .... 3,940 DM
Passengers are not permitted on this trip

Price Includes:
Round trip ferry from Genoa to Tunis; luggage transport from Munich; tour guide; all meals in Africa; tents and camping fees.

Not Included in Price:
Gasoline; food on ferry; drinks; or hotel accommodations.

Motorcycle Provisions:
Your own motorcycle accompanies you round trip from Genoa to Tunis. Rental available for 490 DM per week. New Yamaha XT 350, 27hp. Price includes mileage, insurance, fuel, and gas.

Luggage Provisions:
A van will accompany this tour to carry luggage.

Special Notes:
The common language of this tour is German. Guide also fluent in English and French. Clients come from throughout Europe. Physical and mental endurance, along with endurocycle experience is strongly suggested for this trip.

Reader Discount:
A discount of 100 DM applies to this tour when you send in the Reader Discount Coupon.

TENERIFE

Tenerife – Canary Island

Tour Operator: Motorrad-Reisen
Postfach 44 01 48
D-8000 Munich 44
WEST GERMANY

Contact: Mr. Hermann Weil
Phone: (49) 89 39 57 68
FAX: (49) 89 34 48 32
Telex: 5218511

U.S. Agent:	Motorrad-Reisen P.O. Box 591 Oconomowoc, WI 53066 Contact: Ms. Jean Fish Phone: 414-567-7548
Length of Tour:	7 days

Dates:
- January 20 through January 27, 1989 (for reference)
- January 27 through February 3, 1989 (for reference)
- February 3 through February 10, 1989 (for reference)
- February 10 through February 17, 1989 (for reference)
- February 17 through February 24, 1989 (for reference)
- February 24 through March 3, 1989 (for reference)
- March 10 through March 17, 1989 (for reference)
- March 17 through March 24, 1989 (for reference)
- March 24 through March 31, 1989 (for reference)
- April 7 through April 14, 1989
- April 14 through April 21, 1989

Trip Begins and Ends:	Tenerife, Canary Islands

Highlights:
Leave winter behind for this sun-drenched Canary Island, a land of extreme contrast. Begin your run at sea level, rolling through a banana plantation. Push on to the proud elevation of 3,717 meters on the rim of an extinct volcano. You'll drive through a varied terrain of lava fields, dirt paths, and sandy roads; over mountain passes; and on beaches beside the ocean. Taste local specialties ranging from a shepherd's cheese to a local drink that's a blend of rum and palm honey. You'll return to the same hotel each night, so your winter escape is totally carefree.

Price (includes motorcycle rental):
- Two riders, double occupancy $3,150
- Single rider, double occupancy $1,820
- Supplement for single room occupancy .... $ 540

Price Includes:
Tour guide, accommodations, full board, motorcycle, gasoline, and Gomera ferry.

Motorcycle Provisions:
BMW K75, K100, and R100GS

SPAIN, MOROCCO and ALGERIA — Trans-Sahara Trailblaze

Tour Operator:	Wanderer's Expeditions, c/o Tee Mill Tours Ltd. 56 Tooting High Street London SW17 0RN ENGLAND Contact: Mr. Reg Thomas Phone: (44) 01-767-8739 FAX: (44) 01-682-0138 Telex: 945307
Length of Tour:	15 days or 22 days

Dates:
15-day tour:
- November 19 through December 12, 1989
- December 3 through December 17, 1989
- January 14 through January 28, 1990
- January 28 through February 11, 1990

22-day tour:
- November 12 through December 3, 1989

Trip Begins and Ends:	London, England

Highlights:
Conquer the vast emptiness of the Sahara. You'll drive a variety of conditions from pebble wastelands to barren rocky mountains, through dry valleys called wadis, and endless stretches of hot yellow sand with dunes that run on forever. Camp in the desert and under the palm trees of the oasis. Stop in beautiful Ghardaia, a resting place for many caravans. Visit the bustling marketplace. Enjoy the beautiful date palm grove with white houses and mosques perched on the hillside. Before and after your desert battles, enjoy the sun and sea of Northern Africa.

Price (includes motorcycle rental):
- 15 days: Single rider, double occupancy .... £ 1,295
- 22 days: Single rider, double occupancy .... £ 1,595

Price Includes:
Airfare; all food; all camping equipment; motorcycle rental; spare parts; insurance for the motorcycle; personal accident and medical insurance during the trip.

GUIDED TOURS – AFRICA & NEAR EAST   219

Motorcycle Provisions:
Can-Am Bombardier, 250cc, two-stroke, all terrain bike is supplied. These motorcycles are used by the army and are light and easy to maneuver with good power and acceleration.

Backup:
A backup truck complete with driver/mechanic and cook follows the tour. Spare parts are available and the truck can carry disabled motorcycles or injured riders.

Special Notes:
Video of a previous Trans-Sahara Trailblaze is available. Send £10 refundable deposit for loan of a copy.

Reader Discount:
A discount of $25 applies to this tour when you send in the Reader Discount Coupon.

NORTH AFRICA	**Tunis to Douala (Explo-Tours #M6)**
Tour Operator:	Explo-Tours Arnulfstraße 134 8000 Munich 19 WEST GERMANY Contact: Mr. Josef Geltl Phone: (49) 089-16-07-89 Telex: 1631 btxd/089161716 1+

Dates:
• October 20 through November 14, 1989

Length of Tour:	23 days, approximately 5,500 km
Trip Begins:	Genoa, Italy
Trip Ends:	Munich, West Germany

Highlights:
Drive through desert, brush, and tropical forest from the Mediterranean to the Gulf of Guinea. In the Great Sahara, you'll feel as if your motor-

cycle stands still and the earth rotates under you. You'll lose your sense of perspective in the endless yellow sand of the dunes and feel as if you move in a third dimension. Navigate the perils of sand with conditions ranging from soft powder to hard pack. Plunge into the Nigerian brush. Ride through Yankari Game Reserve in the company of jungle apes. With luck, you'll spot elephants or lions. Cross smooth roads to the Cameroon border. Then a short but difficult ride on the muddy Malfe Road brings you to beautiful Cameroon highlands. Except for lush banana, mango, and avocado trees along the road, you'll believe you're in the Swiss Alps. You'll need endurance for this tour, but it is accessible to every good rider.

Price (does not include motorcycle rental):
- Single rider, double occupancy .... 4,950 DM
- Motorcycle passenger, double occupancy .... 4,450 DM
- Surcharge for single tent .... 100 DM

Price Includes:
Ship from Genoa to Tunis for cycle and driver; tour guide; transportation by air from Douala to Munich; all meals in Africa; tents and camping fees.

Not Included in Price:
Gasoline; food on ferry; drinks; or hotel accommodations.

Motorcycle Provisions:
Containerized shipping of your motorcycle from Douala to Munich by ship. A good enduro motorcycle is suggested for this trip. Rental available for 490 DM per week. New Yamaha XT 350, 27hp. Price includes mileage, insurance, fuel, and gas.

Luggage Provisions:
A van will accompany this tour to carry luggage.

Special Notes:
The common language of this tour is German. Guide also fluent in English and French. Clients come from throughout Europe. Physical and mental endurance, along with endurocycle experience is strongly suggested for this trip.

Reader Discount:
A discount of 100 DM applies to this tour when you send in the Reader Discount Coupon.

GUIDED TOURS – AFRICA & NEAR EAST 221

AFRICA

Tunis to Timbuktu to Abidjan (Explo-Tours #M2)

Some miles are slower than others.

Tour Operator:
Explo-Tours
Arnulfstraße 134
8000 Munich 19
WEST GERMANY

Contact: Mr. Josef Geltl
Phone: (49) 089-16-07-89
Telex: 1631 btxd/089161716 1+

Length of Tour: 4 weeks, covering approximately 6,000 km (1,300 hard km)

Dates:
Dates not available at time of publication. Call Explo-Tours.

Trip Begins: Genoa, Italy

Trip Ends: Munich, West Germany

Highlights:
Experienced drivers rack up 6,000 kilometers of trans-Sahara riding on this enduro tour. Propel yourself through terrain that includes 100 meter high sand hills, impressive mountain ranges, gorges, and rocky passes. Enter Africa through the Arabian bazaar of Tunis. Speed on paved road from oasis to oasis. Climb as high as 2,918 meters at Mt. Tahat in the Hoggar Mountains. Spin down dry river beds called wadis in barren desert country on your way to Timbuktu. Ford swamp lands of the Niger River basin. At the railhead of Kankan, head south across plateau country spotted with grazing antelope. Climb to Mt. Nzerekore, at the intersection of Liberia, Guinea, and the Ivory Coast. Finish your African odyssey at Abidjan, capital of the Ivory Coast.

Price (does not include motorcycle rental):
- Single rider, double occupancy .... 4,980 DM
- Motorcycle passenger, double occupancy .... 4,380 DM

Price Includes:
Ferry trip across Mediterranean; luggage from Munich to Tunis; tour guide; vehicle for baggage, passengers, water, equipment; full meals in Africa; tents; camping fees; breakdown guarantee.

Not Included in Price:
Gasoline; drinks; food on ferry; or hotel accommodations.

Motorcycle Provisions:
Your motorcycle will be containerized and shipped from Munich to Tunis, and from Abidjan to Munich by sea for free. When Explo-Tours receives your 400 DM deposit for space, they will tell you whether you have been placed.

Rental available for 490 DM per week. New Yamaha XT 350, 27hp. Price includes mileage, insurance, fuel, and gas.

Luggage Provisions:
A van will accompany this tour to carry luggage.

Special Notes:
The common language of this tour is German. Guide also fluent in English and French. Clients come from throughout Europe. Physical and mental endurance, along with endurocycle experience is strongly suggested for this trip.

Reader Discount:
A discount of 100 DM applies to this tour when you send in the Reader Discount Coupon.

High Sahara Dunes (photo by Explo Tours)

GUIDED TOURS – ASIA & INDONESIA

CHINA

China

Tour Operator:	Von Thielmann Tours P.O. Box 87764 San Diego, CA 92138 Contact: Ms. Gina Guzzardo Phone: 619-463-7788 or 619-291-7057 FAX: 619-291-4630 Telex: 910 335 1607 MESA SERV SDG
Length of Tour:	18 days
Dates:	May 15 through June 1, 1989
Trip Begins and Ends:	Los Angeles, California

Highlights:
Watch the panorama of China unfold from the seat of your motorcycle. Ride through the rural villages, peaceful and everlasting, toward the misty hills, through dense forests, and green rice fields. Gaze upon mile after mile of wall receding in each direction. Know the China of mulberry groves where silks are produced and the China of flooded rice fields. Earn the status of a visiting dignitary as a member of this motorcycle tour. You'll request special tours from the government official who escorts this American "sports team." Perhaps you'll visit an elementary school, a farm, or a factory — part of the revelation of modern China along with the ancient jewels of this civilization.

Price (includes motorcycle rental):
- Single rider, double occupancy $3,235
- Two people, double occupancy $5,970
- Single passenger, double occupancy $2,985
- Supplement for single room occupancy, Hong Kong only .... $ 184

Price Includes:
Chinese driver's license; visa application processing; airfare; motorcycle; hotel; sightseeing; transfers and almost all meals.

Motorcycle Provisions:
Touring motorcycles, two or four cylinders, dual seat, U.S. models. Mechanic accompanies the tour, with spare parts.

GUIDED TOURS – ASIA & INDONESIA 225

Luggage Provisions:
Support vehicle carries all luggage and offers pillion passengers a ride if tired.

Special Notes:
Special departures are being offered to groups of at least 10 persons. Many itineraries available for tours of one to three weeks duration. Most itineraries start in southern China and may include Hainan Island, Guilin, and Shanghai. Tours include option to visit Beijing and the Great Wall.

CHINA   **China: The Middle Kingdom**

A sawmill in China

Tour Operator: Motorrad-Reisen
                    Postfach 44 01 48
                    D-8000 Munich 44
                    WEST GERMANY

                    Contact: Mr. Hermann Weil
                    Phone: (49) 89 39 57 68
                    FAX: (49) 89 34 48 32
                    Telex: 5218511

U.S. Agent:	Motorrad-Reisen P.O. Box 591 Oconomowoc, WI 53066 Contact: Ms. Jean Fish Phone: 414-567-7548
Length of Tour:	14 days, covering approximately 870 miles

Dates:
- February 14 through February 28, 1989 (for reference)
- March 3 through March 18, 1989 (for reference)
- September 19 through October 3, 1989
- October 10 through October 24, 1989
- October 27 through November 11, 1989

Trip Begins:	Hong Kong
Trip Ends:	Peking, China

Highlights:
Begin your adventure in Hong Kong, on the doorstep of China. You'll have two days to familiarize yourself with chopsticks, cook shops, food stalls, and rice wine before you head on to Canton, capital of the south Chinese province. From the bustle of Canton's busy streets teeming with carts and bicycles, you'll travel increasingly narrower roads where sand replaces asphalt. Journey through tiny villages past laughing children and serene water buffalo. Climb a range of ridges and green mountain tops with endless Eastern horizons. Visit a Taoist temple. Stop in a mountain village. Tour a silk spinning mill or a jade cutter's shop. Bargain for exotic items in the noisy open-air market. Then leave your motorcycle back in Canton. Fly to Peking to visit the ancient wonder of the Great Wall, the Emperor's Palace, and the Forbidden City. You'll capture the full flavor of China, the tiny inaccessible village as well as the monuments of the ancient Orient.

Price (includes motorcycle rental):
- Two riders, double occupancy $7,995
- Single rider, double occupancy $4,150
- Supplement for single room occupancy .... $ 500

Price Includes:
Full board (typically Chinese, good and plenty); accommodations in double rooms; visa fees; fee for driver's test; sightseeing tours; translator

and escorting vehicle. Includes airfare from Germany to China and within the country.

Motorcycle Provisions:
BMW R80 rental included in the tour.

Luggage Provisions:
A van accompanies this tour to carry luggage.

Special Notes:
The nature of this trip is adventure, not relaxation or luxury.

KASHMIR

Expedition to Kashmir

Tour Operator:
Adventure Asia
1112 West Pender St. #603
Vancouver, B.C. V6E 2S1
CANADA

Contact: Mr. Bill Leininger
Phone: 606-687-7435

Length of Tour: 17 days

Dates:
• July 28 through August 13, 1989

Trip Begins:
Given dates represent the tour ending in New Delhi, India. Three days travel is required to reach New Delhi from North America. One day is required to reach India from Europe.

Trip Ends:
Given dates represent the tour ending in New Delhi, India. Two days travel is required to return to North America. One day of travel is required to return to Europe.

Highlights:
This tour will travel through regions of India that no other westerners have ridden. The ride will begin in the old British hill station of Simla. There you will rest and prepare for your expedition at the Woodville Palace Hotel — originally a Maharajah's palace that still incorporates the original decor.

During the first week of the tour, riders will face the challenges of operating the bikes over 17,000-ft. passes on the military road from Manali to Leh, the ancient capital of Ladahk. The terrain of this region is often described as "moonscape" and the site of a group of motorcycles speeding across it should be phenomenal.

At Leh, the tour will visit many temples and monasteries in this predominately Tibetan Buddhist area. Leh was once the gateway to Tibet and China and its bazaars were reputed throughout the world as being the most colorful.

A two-day ride from Leh will take the tour over another 17,000-foot pass, into the Kashmir Valley and on to Srinagar (also called Shangri La) where the group will spend three nights on the famous houseboats of Dal Lake. Srinagar and the bountiful Kashmir Valley are but two of the many highlights of the tour.

Near the end of your journey you'll travel south along the switchback mountain highways to Darmsala the home of the exiled Tibetan leader, the Dalai Lama. The last day of riding takes the group to Simla and the Woodville Palace Hotel. The tour then departs for New Delhi where you will have a farewell dinner before heading home.

Price (includes motorcycle rental):
- Single rider, double occupancy $3,995
- Pillion passenger, double occupancy $3,495
- Supplement for single room occupancy .... $ 845

Price Includes:
All of the tours are first class. In remote areas camping will replace hotels; in some places you will use good quality tourist class accommodations. Riding motorcycles is exciting but also tiring, consequently your hosts provide lots of meals with good food. Support vehicles carry luggage and spare equipment; the price also includes all airfare from the West Coast to New Delhi, accommodations, meals, guides, and transfers. When it is necessary to camp, all of the camping equipment is supplied and camps are pre-set, requiring no assistance from tour group.

Motorcycle Provisions:
Honda XL600R motorcycle, 1987 models 600cc equipped with extra fuel tanks (5 liters) and some lightweight carrying equipment.

Luggage Provisions:
Tour is supported by sweep vehicle carrying all luggage and personal belongings. There is sufficient room for sore riders to travel in the support vehicle.

MALAYSIA – BANGKOK, SINGAPORE

Far East Motorcycle Tour

A shrine in Malaysia

Tour Operator:
Edelweiss Bike Travel
Steinreichweg 1
A-6414 Mieming
AUSTRIA

Contact: Mr. Werner Wachter
Phone: (43) 05264/5690
FAX: (43) 05264/58533
Telex: 534158 (rkmiem)

U.S. Agent:
Armonk Travel
146 Bedford Road
Armonk, NY 10504

Contact: Ms. Linda Rosenbaum
Phone: 800-255-7451 or 914-273-8880

Length of Tour:	15 days, covering approximately 1,300 miles

Dates:
- April 8 through April 23, 1989
- Late January, 1990
- Early February, 1990
- Late February, 1990
- Early March, 1990
- Late March, 1990
- Early April, 1990
- Late April, 1990

Note: The dates for 1990 have not been finalized yet, but will be approximately in the ranges indicated. Contact Edelweiss for current schedules.

Trip Begins and Ends:	Los Angeles, California

Highlights:
Steep in the exotic charms of the Far East and travel some of the best motorcycle roads in the world. Ride past a jostling crowd of ox-drawn carriages, bicycles, and mopeds outside of Kuala Lumpur. Head into the

jungle on a roller coaster road that whips through 572 curves within a 30-mile loop. Waterfalls rush down mountains, and monkeys swing through lush jungle in this unspoiled land. Explore the jungle on foot by moonlight. Sleep in a tree house safe from tigers. Eat freshly caught, steamed fish. Take your pleasure in the sweeping turns of a 150-mile road built through the ancient Malaysian forest. Try parasailing on the South China Sea. Shop in Singapore and explore Bangkok.

Price (includes motorcycle rental):
- Single rider, from west coast, double occupancy $2,690
- Motorcycle passenger, from west coast, double occupancy $2,380

Note: Above prices are for scheduled trips. Prices for 1990 have not been finalized.

Price Includes:
Round trip Los Angeles/Kuala Lumpur (KL/Singapore/Bangkok – optional); tour information package; 13 nights hotel/lodge accommodation; breakfast and dinner for 13 days; transfers; sightseeing tours, admissions, boat rides; tour guide; tour gift.

Motorcycle Provisions:
Kawasaki KLR-650 enduro motorcycles with electric starter included in the price of the tour.

Luggage Provisions:
A luggage van accompanies tour.

ASIA/INDIA	**Goa and South Indian Coasts and Jungle by Royal Enfields**
Tour Operator:	Prima Klima Reisen GmbH Hohenstaufenstraße 69 1000 Berlin 30 WEST GERMANY Contact: Mr. Klaus Brass Phone: (49) 030 216 10 82/83 Telex: 186381 pkr d
Length of Tour:	3 weeks

Dates:
- November 26 through December 16, 1989
- February 10 through March 3, 1990
- March 3 through March 24, 1990

Trip Begins and Ends: Bombay, India

Highlights:
Ride '50s style British Royal Enfield Silver Bullet 350cc bikes built in India. Travel 2,000 kilometers through the Indian paradise: dreamlands, jungles, the old Portuguese colony of Goa. Travel with two guides (German and Indian), and a mechanic; stay in a variety of Indian-style hotels. Lots of adventure guaranteed on this trip.

Price (includes motorcycle rental):
- Per person .... 3,050 DM

Price Includes:
Round trip flight Frankfurt/Bombay/Frankfurt; (other cites cost a little more or less); all accommodations; transfers; insured motorcycle; two guides.

Motorcycle Provisions:
350cc Royal Enfields included in the tour price.

Luggage Provisions:
Each traveler is responsible for carrying his own luggage.

Special Notes:
The weather on this trip will be quite warm (28 to 40°C; 82 to 104°F); bring appropriate clothing. You will not need a large variety of clothing or equipment. Travelers should bear in mind that India is a Third World country, with its own culture and mentality. You should not expect western standards of service or reliability. As this trip is still in the planning stage, contact PKR after July 1989 for further details.

Reader Discount:
A discount between 50 DM and 150 DM applies to this tour when you send in the Reader Discount Coupon. Amount depends upon season, accommodation, and the motorcycle you book.

BALI — Motorcycle Vacation in Bali

Tour Operator: Bike Tours
Einsiedeleiweg 16
5942 Kirchhundem 4
WEST GERMANY

Contact: Ms. Eveline Veenkamp
Phone: (49) 2764-7824

Length of Tour: 19 days

Dates: Whenever you want to go.

Trip Begins and Ends: Amsterdam, Netherlands

Highlights:
Combine your hot, dusty Australia trip with a stopover in beautiful Bali. Here you can relax on the beach, or participate in one of the many festivals and processions throughout the island. This is a paradise of friendly, gentle people, with deep religious beliefs. Unlike the guided tours in this Directory, this is actually a trip to Bali where you can sightsee and travel on your own around the island on a motorcycle.

Price (includes motorcycle rental):
- Single rider .... 3,450 DM

Price Includes:
Hotel accommodations for 19 nights at Rita's House, a beautiful inn near Kuta Beach (single rooms, private bath, tea, and bananas); round trip airfare from Amsterdam; touring information; maps.

Motorcycle Provisions:
125cc to 250cc bikes provided

Luggage Provisions:
None needed. The traveler is based in one inn, free to visit other parts of the island as the urge arises.

GUIDED TOURS – ASIA & INDONESIA

JAPAN	**Nippon Week**
Tour Operator:	TransCyclist International CPO Box 2064 Tokyo, 100-91 JAPAN Contact: Mr. Volker Lenzner Phone: (81) 3-402-5385 FAX: (81) 3-402-5358
Length of Tour:	Five to 10 days, covering 500 to 1,000 km, depending upon rider's wishes

Dates:
- October 1990 (exact dates have not yet been set)

Trip Begins and Ends: Tokyo, Japan

Highlights:
See Madame Butterfly country by joining TransCyclist's (TC) exotic bike adventure through Japan. This tour takes you out of Tokyo's maze of concrete and steel into the hazy green mountains behind. Ride past majestic Mt. Fuji to Matsumoto and its old Samurai Castle. Scale up steep mountain passes to the Shogun town of Takayama in central Japan. Lake Biwa and beautiful Kyoto are next with glimpses of historical temples and modern geishas called "maiko." You'll take picturesque Route 9 through Tottori's countryside, aiming for the famous sand dunes near Tottori Town. Then, it's across Honshu to the old town of Kurashiki on the lovely Setonaikai Inland Sea. There'll be time to relax on your return to Tokyo via a comfortable Pacific Coastal ferry boat. During each day, you can define your own itinerary; the pace is highly informal. Ride solo or with others in your party, as you wish. Each day starts with a route orientation by your experienced guide. At night share your stories of the day with others on the tour over rice wine or soaking in a Japanese bath. Or both, if you can take it!

Price (10-day tour; includes motorcycle rental):
- Rider or passenger, two-up, double occupancy, per person $1,500

Price Includes:
Japanese accommodations; all breakfasts and dinners; motorcycle rental (250cc, two-up); insurance; ferry fees. Not included are: lunch, fuel, oil, tolls.

Motorcycle Provisions:
Choice of several kinds of 250cc motorcycles.

Luggage Provisions:
Travelers are expected to carry their own luggage on this tour.

Special Notes:
International driver's license valid for motorcycle operation required by participants. This tour requires a minimum of six participants. You are advised to book well in advance. Send a self-addressed, stamped envelope and one international reply coupon (available from the post office) when inquiring about the tour. Advised to travel lightly (bulky luggage must be stored in Tokyo). Larger displacement motorcycles can be obtained at increased cost provided the international driver's license of holder is accepted in Japan. (International driver's licenses of some nationals are not accepted, however they may still ride 250cc motorcycles.) This tour is under development and is expected to be in operation in 1990.

NEPAL — Nirvana In Nepal

Tour Operator:	Adventure Asia 1112 West Pender St. #603 Vancouver, B.C. V6E 2S1 CANADA Contact: Mr. Bill Leininger Phone: 606-687-7435
Length of Tour:	12 days

Dates:
- March 18 through March 30, 1989 (for reference only)
- April 15 through April 27, 1989
- May 6 through May 18, 1989
- October 7 through October 19, 1989
- November 11 through November 23, 1989
- December 2 through December 14, 1989

Trip Begins:
Given dates represent the tour originating in Kathmandu, Nepal. Three days travel is required to reach Nepal from North America. One day is required to reach Nepal from Europe.

Trip Ends:
Given dates represent the tour ending in Kathmandu, Nepal. Two days travel is required to return to North America. One day of travel is required to return to Europe.

Highlights:
Two weeks of contrasts that only exist in Nepal. The world's highest peaks, rain forests, grasslands, and jungles. A cultural melting pot of Nepalese, Indian, Tibetan, and international adventures.

This tour begins in Kathmandu where, for two full days, you experience the mystic allure that has entranced travelers for centuries. After visiting the ancient Durbar square and the cultural highlights of the city, venture out into the valley to see the enormous Stupa (shrine) of Swayambhunath, the city of Patan, Bhaktapur, and many fabulous viewpoints.

Depart Kathmandu to begin your expedition to Pokhara. During the next two days you will experience life in a Tibetan village, your first Dal Bhat meal, and explore a Hindu temple. Continuing on to Tansen, on what is considered the best road for sport touring in Nepal, you'll arrive at a mountain top retreat, the Srinagar Hotel, a photographer's dream come true.

Off again the next day to the birthplace of the prophet Buddha, a 2,000-year-old site, before arriving in the lush jungles of the Chitwan National Forest. Your two days at the lodge are coordinated by the resident naturalists taking advantage of current animal migrations, on elephant safaris.

Finally it's back to Kathmandu through the challenging switchback roads of the Raj Path, Nepal's first major paved road.

Price (includes motorcycle rental):
- Single rider, double occupancy $2,995
- Pillion passenger, double occupancy $2,495
- Supplement for single room occupancy ....$ 495

Price Includes:
West coast to Kathmandu return airfare, accommodations, meals, guides, all transfers, motorcycle and vehicle insurance. Meals consist of 80% western style, 20% local fare.

Motorcycle Provisions:
Honda XL600R, 600cc single cylinder, kick start, equipped with extra fuel tanks (5 liter), and some lightweight carrying equipment.

Luggage Provisions:
Tour is supported by sweep vehicle carrying all luggage and personal belongings. There is sufficient room for sore riders to travel in the support vehicle.

Equipment:
Riding gear should consist of type required for summer riding. Nepal is in the tropics and though you travel some high areas the only time it is near freezing is during late November and December. In the Terrai area the temperatures are very hot. Open face helmets are recommended, as are goggles, enduro style or sport touring jackets, pants, boots, and gloves.

Special Notes:
Eight millimeter video is available on riding in Nepal. Good for groups or clubs interested in promoting the tours for their membership or for fund raising.

NEPAL

Nirvana in Nepal

Tour Operator:
Edelweiss Bike Travel
Steinreichweg 1
A-6414 Mieming
AUSTRIA

Contact: Mr. Werner Wachter
Phone: (43) 05264/5690
FAX: (43) 05264/58533
Telex: 534158 (rkmiem)

U.S. Agent:
Armonk Travel
146 Bedford Road
Armonk, NY 10504

Contact: Ms. Linda Rosenbaum
Phone: 800-255-7451 or 914-273-8880

"I'll trade you the statue for the bike."

| Length of Tour: | 15 days, approximately 870 miles |

Dates:
- March 16 through March 31, 1989 (for reference only)
- April 13 through April 28, 1989
- May 4 through May 19, 1989
- November 9 through November 24, 1989
- November 30 through December 15, 1989

Trip Begins and Ends: Los Angeles

Highlights:
Thrill to the adventure and variety of Nepal. You'll herd rhinos from the back of an elephant. Track wild boars. Spot crocodiles in the river from your dugout canoe. Spend a night in a game blind hoping to spot the Royal Bengal tiger in the wild. Journey to magnificent Mount Everest, the world's tallest mountain. In the plains, you'll speed through fields as far as the eye can see, past grass huts and herds of water buffalo. Twist through the mountains on the torturous Raj Path with switchback turns ten at a time and views that open on misty peaks.

Price (includes motorcycle rental):
- Single rider, double occupancy $2,995
- Motorcycle passenger, double occupancy $2,495
- Supplement for single room occupancy ....$ 495

Price Includes:
Round trip airfare; motorcycle insurance; 14 nights hotel/lodge/camp accommodations; transfers; sightseeing; baggage handling; all meals in Nepal; American plan breakfasts in Hong Kong.

Motorcycle Provisions:
Honda XL600 R enduro motorcycle included in the price of the tour.

Luggage Provisions:
A luggage van accompanies this tour.

Special Notes:
This tour is offered and organized in cooperation with China Worldwide Travel, Inc.

ASIA, AUSTRALIA, NEW ZEALAND

Overland to Australia and New Zealand

Tour Operator:	Wanderer's Expeditions, c/o Tee Mill Tours Ltd. 56 Tooting High Street London SW17 0RN ENGLAND Contact: Mr. Reg Thomas Phone: (44) 01-767-8739 FAX: (44) 01-682-0138 Telex: 945307
Length of Tour:	34 weeks
Dates:	Starts April 1, 1990
Trip Begins and Ends:	Not determined as yet.

Highlights:
Contact agent for brochure and itinerary. This trip is being developed for next spring. You'll travel through Asia to Kathmandu then on to Burma. Alternatively, you may travel from India to Thailand by sea. From Thailand, journey to Malaysia and Singapore. Take a boat to Indonesia and Bali. Then you'll take another boat to Australia and New Zealand for the final leg of your odyssey. You'll supply your own bike and fuel. Wanderer's Expeditions supplies the backup truck and equipment.

Price (does not include motorcycle rental):
To be determined.

Special Notes:
Wanderer's Expedition will accept refundable deposit of £25 to secure a spot on the tour.

Reader Discount:
A discount of $25 applies to this tour when you send in the Reader Discount Coupon.

NEPAL AND CHINA — Ride from the Roof of the World

Tour Operator:	Adventure Asia 1112 West Pender St. #603 Vancouver, B.C. V6E 2S1 CANADA Contact: Mr. Bill Leininger Phone: 606-687-7435
Length of Tour:	15 days
Dates:	June 19 through July 3, 1989

Trip Begins:
Given dates represent the tour originating in Kathmandu, Nepal. Three days travel is required to reach New Delhi from North America.

Trip Ends:
Given dates represent the tour ending in Kathmandu, Nepal. Two days travel is required to return to North America. One day of travel is required to return to Europe.

Highlights:
As with all of Adventure Asia's programs the tour members will board a Royal Nepal 737 for the one-hour mountain flight to Tibet's capital, Lhasa. For the next four days the group will acclimate to the altitude of the Tibetan Buddhist population. Hundreds of pilgrims can be seen daily as they pay homage and worship at the many temples of Lhasa.

During your stay the tour will ride to ancient monasteries and sites within the Lhasa Valley area. On the ninth day of the tour the group will depart Lhasa for the overland journey to Nepal. The roads west of Lhasa are all dirt, which slowly traverse several 17,000-ft. passes. The landscape in these areas is stark. The snowcapped light brown hills with sparse grass stand out in vivid contrast to the clear blue of the high altitude sky. As you ride over passes it seems as though you can see hundreds of miles with the Himalayas filling the horizon. You'll spend evenings in towns with names like Shigatse and Tingri. There you will stay in modest hotels with simple amenities. One major highlight will be the 12th day when you ride to Rongbuk, the base camp of Mount Everest. Three days later, descend the Himalayan range and enter Nepal.

The countryside turns green and the population begins to increase as you near Kathmandu. You'll have completed one of the most fantastic journeys possible and will be one of an elite group of motorcyclists who have crossed the Tibetan plateau.

Price (includes motorcycle rental):
- Single rider, double occupancy $4,995
- Supplement for single room occupancy .... $ 875

Price Includes:
West coast to Kathmandu return airfare, accommodations, meals, guides, all transfers, motorcycle and vehicle insurance. Meals consist of 80% western style, 20% local fare.

Motorcycle Provisions:
Honda XL600R motorcycle, 1987 models, 600cc equipped with extra fuel tanks (5 liter) and some lightweight carrying equipment.

Luggage Provisions:
Tour is supported by sweep vehicle carrying all luggage and personal belongings. There is sufficient room for sore riders to travel in the support vehicle.

Equipment:
Riding gear should consist of type required for cool weather riding. The atmosphere and high altitude of Tibet make the air very dry; consequently dehydration is a major consideration. Open face helmets are recommended, as are goggles, enduro style or sport touring jackets, pants, boots, and gloves.

NEPAL	**Ride to the Roof of the World**
Tour Operator:	Adventure Asia 1112 West Pender St. #603 Vancouver, B.C. V6E 2S1 CANADA Contact: Mr. Bill Leininger Phone: 606-687-7435
Length of Tour:	15 days
Dates:	June 5 through June 19, 1989

Trip Begins:

Given dates represent the expedition originating in Kathmandu, Nepal. Three days travel is required to reach Kathmandu from North America. One day is required to reach Nepal from Europe.

Trip Ends:

Given dates represent the expedition ending in Kathmandu, Nepal. Two days travel is required to return to North America. One day of travel is required to return to Europe.

Highlights:

On October 5, 1987 Adventure Asia promoted an attempt to be the first motorcyclists to ride to Tibet and the base camp of Mount Everest. Turmoil in the capital city of Lhasa, at the time they were to go from Nepal to Tibet, caused authorities to close the border to their group and consequently end their expedition's hopes.

For the first time since that date all of the necessary pieces for the resumption of this expedition have fallen into place.

Imagine, starting in the mystical city of Kathmandu and riding a motorcycle with a full support crew to the border of Nepal and China, then riding up the face of the great Himalayan mountain range to the Tibetan plateau. This will be a first! No foreign motorcyclist has ever ridden his machine into Tibet. Once on the plateau, the group will ride to Rongbuk, the base camp of Mount Everest at over 16,000 ft. Following this you will continue to cross Tibet riding over several 17,000-ft. passes until reaching the capital, Lhasa. Finally you will visit the many famous landmarks of Lhasa including the Potala Palace.

Besides being an expedition full of first-ever events, this tour will require riders to be hardy individuals able to ride long distances on dirt roads at high altitudes. The Ride to the Roof of the World is most worthy of the term "expedition" and the members of this ride will have an accomplishment that will never be duplicated.

Price (includes motorcycle rental):

- Rider, double occupancy $4,995
- Supplement for single room occupancy ....$ 875

Price Includes:

West coast to Kathmandu return airfare, accommodations, meals, guides, all transfers, motorcycle and vehicle insurance. Meals consist of 80% western style, 20% local fare.

Motorcycle Provisions:

Honda XL600R motorcycle, 1987 models, 600cc equipped with extra fuel tank (5 liters) and some lightweight carrying equipment.

The tour will spend several days acclimating to the altitudes of the Tibetan Plateau. At this time the motorcycles will be re-jetted for operation at these severe altitudes.

Luggage Provisions:
Tour is supported by sweep vehicle carrying all luggage and personal belongings. There is sufficient room for sore riders, support personnel, friends, and family to travel in the support vehicle.

Equipment:
Riding gear should consist of type required for cool weather riding. The atmosphere and high altitude of Tibet make the air very dry. Consequently dehydration is a major consideration. Open face helmets are recommended, as are goggles, enduro style or sport touring jackets, pants, boots, and gloves.

CHINA	**The Silk Road Rider**
Tour Operator:	TransCyclist International CPO Box 2064 Tokyo, 100-91 JAPAN Contact: Mr. Volker Lenzner Phone: (81) 3-402-5385 FAX: (81) 3-402-5358
Length of Tour:	10 days, approximately 1,400 km by motorcycle (plus some by plane)

Dates:
1989:
- April 27 through May 6, 1989 (runs east to west)
- May 3 through May 12, 1989 (runs west to east)
- May 25 through June 3, 1989 (east to west)
- May 31 through June 9, 1989 (west to east)
- June 29 through July 8, 1989 (east to west)
- July 5 through July 14, 1989 (west to east)
- July 27 through August 5, 1989 (east to west)
- August 2 through August 11, 1989 (west to east)
- August 31 through September 9, 1989 (east to west)
- September 6 through September 15, 1989 (west to east)

GUIDED TOURS – ASIA & INDONESIA

1990:
- April 26 through May 5, 1990 (runs east to west)
- May 2 through May 11, 1990 (runs west to east)
- May 24 through June 2, 1990 (east to west)
- May 30 through June 8, 1990 (west to east)
- June 28 through July 7, 1990 (east to west)
- July 4 through July 13, 1990 (west to east)
- July 26 through August 4, 1990 (east to west)
- August 1 through August 10, 1990 (west to east)
- August 30 through September 8, 1990 (east to west)
- September 5 through September 14, 1990 (west to east)

Trip Begins and Ends: Beijing Airport

Highlights:

Two years of negotiations with various Chinese agents have finally borne fruit, and this exciting tour is ready to take off. TransCyclist (TC) believes it is the first genuine and regular motorcycle tour along the famous Silk Road. The Chinese agent operating this tour is an associate of the TC organization and a leader in his field.

In ancient times the Silk Road was the main trade route between Europe and China, on which the main and most desirable commodity exported from China was silk. What was and still is the throat of the Silk Road is the Hexi Corridor. On this tour you will explore the Hexi Corridor between Lanzhou on the east and Dunhuang on the west. See the precipitous Wu Qiao Ling (Black Scabbard Mountain) winding 1,200 km westward to Xing Xing Xia (the Star Gorge); the ice-capped Qilian Mountain Range to the south and enormous Tengri and Badanjilin Deserts to the north. The Corridor passes through prairies, deserts, mountains, and oases. While part of this area is desolate, as a whole it is rich both in agricultural products and natural resources and is famous for its majestic scenery.

A rustic, rugged experience by motorcycle!

Price (includes motorcycle rental):
- Group of 10 people or more, per person, double occupancy $2,200
- Group of six to nine people, per person, double occupancy $2,700

(The small motorcycles used on this trip preclude riding double; there is room in the luggage van for up to four people.)

Price Includes:

Beijing airport reception/farewell; welcome party; first day route and traffic orientation; all hotels (double occupancy); all meals in China; all public transportation in China (includes three domestic flights); Chinese driver's license; motorcycle rental; tour guide; camel or horse riding; all gasoline and oils; tourist admission fees.

Motorcycle Provisions:
Honda and Suzuki 85cc/125cc/250cc off-road touring motorcycles are included in the price of this tour.

Luggage Provisions:
A van accompanies the tour to carry luggage.

Special Notes:
International driver's license valid for motorcycle operation required by participants. If a minimum of 10 participants are not confirmed by the booking deadline for a particular trip (one month before departure), you may change your booking to another suitable departure date or join as a member of a smaller group. Minimum of six participants. You are advised to book well in advance. Some of the tour machines are motocross models and all participants need to be fit and experienced riders. Riding wear (helmet, boots, gloves, rain suit, etc.) must be provided by participants themselves. Send a self-addressed, stamped envelope and one international reply coupon (available from the post office) when inquiring about the tour.

NORTHERN THAILAND

Thailand Special

Tour Operator:	Wanderer's Expeditions, c/o Tee Mill Tours Ltd. 56 Tooting High Street London SW17 0RN ENGLAND
	Contact: Mr. Reg Thomas Phone: (44) 01-767-8739 FAX: (44) 01-682-0138 Telex: 945307
Length of Tour:	15 days and 22 days

Dates:
15-day tour:
- November 25 through December 9, 1989
- January 20 through February 3, 1990
- February 17 through March 3, 1990
- March 24 through April 7, 1990

22-day tour:

- December 12, 1989 through January 2, 1990 *
* This is a special 22-day trip designed to coincide with school holidays.

Trip Begins and Ends: Bangkok, Thailand

Highlights:
Explore the tropical jungles, raft on the rivers, and storm the beautiful rolling hills in the Golden Triangle which stretches between Burma and Laos. You'll be bused from the teeming metropolitan city of Bangkok to the charming regional capital, Chiang Mai. Journey through golden poppy fields. Roll past rice paddies worked by water buffalo. Glide through the teak forests dappled with sunlight. Stay overnight in a bamboo hut in a hill tribe village. Take a ride on an elephant. Visit Buddhist temples. Enjoy the friendly people of this most beautiful Oriental country. You'll receive a copy of the film of this trip as a memento.

Price (includes motorcycle rental):
- Single rider, double occupancy £1,290

Price Includes:
Air-conditioned coach between Bangkok/Chiang Mai; all accommodations including an overnight stay in a thatched hut; breakfast and evening meals; motorcycle rental; full medical and accident insurance during the trip.

Motorcycle Provisions:
Honda 125cc or equivalent.

Special Notes:
This is an active trip for adaptable, reasonably fit, and active people. Road insurance is not available to tourists.

Reader Discount:
A discount of $25 applies to this tour when you send in the Reader Discount Coupon.

Werner Wachter in Thailand (photo by Edelweiss Bike Travel)

GUIDED TOURS – AUSTRALIA

AUSTRALIA

Bike Tours Special '89

Tour Operator:
Bike Tours
Einsiedeleiweg 16
5942 Kirchhundem 4
WEST GERMANY

Contact: Ms. Eveline Veenkamp
Phone: (49) 2764-7824

Stopping to greet a friendly local

Length of Tour:	5 weeks, covering approximately 8,000 km; 300 km per day (5,000 km rough roads, trails)
Dates:	June 11 through July 15, 1989
Trip Begins:	Melbourne, Australia
Trip Ends:	Darwin, Australia

Highlights:
Enduro adventurers, pack your gear and head across 8,000 kilometers of Aussie road with 5,000 kilometers of extreme challenge. You'll need strength and experience to master the most difficult terrain in Australia. For five weeks, you'll travel the most beautiful and the loneliest paths of this continent. Course through the plains of the eastern states past herds of sheep and cattle. Stop at Alice Springs, the most northern outpost of civilization in the outback. Push on to legendary Ayers Rock. This mass of red sandstone rises for 948 meters from the desert floor and serves as the focus for the Aborigine's mystical dreaming culture. See the real Crocodile Dundee wrestle crocodiles in Kakadu National Park. Cross the Great Sandy Desert. Wind through endless coves on the shoreline from Broome to Darwin.

Price (includes motorcycle rental):
- Single rider .... 6,500 DM
- Vehicle passenger .... 2,850 DM

Price Includes:
Camping equipment (except sleeping bag); transfer from airport to camp; campground fees; tents; maintenance and repairs; food; fuel; and insurance. Cost approximately $125 AUS weekly.

Motorcycle Provisions:
Yamaha XT 600.

Luggage Provisions:
A van accompanies tour to carry all luggage.

Special Notes:
The principal language of this tour is German. English can be spoken if necessary.

AUSTRALIA

Boomerang Tour

Highton Manor and guests

Tour Operator:
Australian Motorcycle Touring
46 Greenways Road
P.O. Box 256
Glen Waverley, Victoria 3150
AUSTRALIA

Contact: Mr. Geoff Coat
Phone: (61) 3-233-8891
FAX: (61) 3-233-1407

Agent for UK and Europe:
Twickers World
22 Church Street
Twickenham TW1 3NW
ENGLAND
Phone: (44) 1-892-7606

Agent for USA and Canada:
Adventure Center Inc.
5540 College Avenue
Oakland, CA 94618
Phone: 415-654-1879

Length of Tour:
8 days, covering 1,414 miles

Dates:
1989:
- April 10 through April 17, 1989
- April 24 through May 1, 1989
- November 6 through November 13, 1989
- November 20 through November 27, 1989
- December 4 through December 11, 1989

1990:
- January 1 through January 8, 1990
- January 15 through January 22, 1990
- January 29 through February 5, 1990
- February 12 through February 19, 1990
- February 26 through March 5, 1990
- March 12 through March 19, 1990
- March 26 through April 2, 1990
- April 9 through April 16, 1990
- April 23 through April 30, 1990
- November 5 through November 12, 1990
- November 19 through November 26, 1990
- December 3 through December 10, 1990

Trip Begins and Ends: Melbourne, Australia

Highlights:
From the heights of the Snowy Mountains to the sweeping beaches of the Pacific Ocean, delight in Australia's best motorcycle roads. Average about 200 miles per day with plenty of time to sightsee, photograph, and enjoy Australia's unique wildlife. In Healesville, you'll pet kangaroos and befriend koalas and wombats at one of the world's great wildlife parks. Whip through switchbacks and hairpin curves that rival the European Alps on the scenic climb up Mt. Buffalo. Ride to the top of the Snowies, dipping down from time to time to several dams and lakes in the giant hydroelectric project. Visit Canberra, the country's capital, constructed in the virgin bush by American architect Walter Burley Griffin. Speed over the grassy hills of South Gippsland to see the penguin parade on Phillip Island when these tuxedo-clad birds return from their fishing grounds to their burrows. Return to stately Melbourne, your departure point for the Boomerang Tour.

Price (includes motorcycle rental):
- Single rider, double occupancy ....$2,400 AUS
- Passenger, double occupancy ....$1,200 AUS
- Security deposit of $500 AUS for riders over the age of 25 (credit card accepted), refunded upon return of undamaged motorcycle.

Price Includes:
Accommodations for seven nights; seven breakfasts; seven dinners (includes wine/beer); and a get-acquainted Australian barbecue the night before the tour starts. Gas and oil are also included.

Not Included in Price:
Personal accident insurance (available through travel agent); lunch; snacks; nor personal items. Motorcycle helmets and rain gear, which may be rented for $10 AUS per item for duration of tour.

Motorcycle Provisions:
Nearly new BMW Model R80 sports touring bikes are provided as part of the price; they are fitted with a windshield, and lockable luggage cases.

Luggage Provisions:
Travelers are expected to carry their own luggage on their bikes.

Special Notes:
Deposit of $200 AUS needed to secure reservation on tour; balance due 30 days prior to tour commencement. If reservation canceled within 30 days prior to tour, 50% refund; if within seven days prior to tour, no refund.

AUSTRALIA

East Coast Tour

On top of the bottom of the world

Tour Operator:
Bike Tours
Einsiedeleiweg 16
5942 Kirchhundem 4
WEST GERMANY

Contact: Ms. Eveline Veenkamp
Phone: (49) 2764-7824

Length of Tour:
3 weeks, covering approximately 5,000 km; 300 km per day

Dates:
- March 12 through April 1, 1989 (for reference only)
- December 17, 1989 through January 6, 1990

- January 14 through February 3, 1990
- February 11 through March 3, 1990
- March 11, 1990 through March 31, 1990

Trip Begins and Ends:	Melbourne, Australia

Highlights:
Escape winter. Head for the beach and summer weather in Australia. Sprint over 6,000 kilometers of Aussie road from the spectacular mountain world to the edge of the primitive outback and along the endless Pacific coast. Take a diving expedition to the marvels of the Great Barrier Reef. Enjoy Australia's exceptional surfing. From Melbourne you'll wander through the mountainous world of Victoria, New South Wales, and Queensland to splendid Paradise Falls. Speed through the planes of Bogong National Park to Mt. Kosciusko, Australia's highest peak. Visit Croajingalong National Park with the 100-meter-high sand dune. Drive to the southernmost tip of Australia for spectacular ocean views. Wind through countless bays on the southern tip of Australia.

Price (includes motorcycle rental):
- Single rider .... 2,650 DM
- Motorcycle passenger .... 950 DM
- Vehicle passenger .... 1,850 DM

Price Includes:
Camping equipment (except sleeping bag); transfer from airport to camp; campground fees; tents; maintenance and repairs.

Not Included in Price:
Food, fuel, insurance. Cost approximately $125 AUS weekly.

Motorcycle Provisions:
Yamaha XT 600.

Luggage Provisions:
A luggage van accompanies this tour.

Special Notes:
The principal language of this tour is German. English can be spoken if necessary.

AUSTRALIA

Gold Coast to Cairns: Amazing Queensland

Mossman and Cape Tribulation from the Rex Highway

Tour Operator:	Australian-American Mototours RR1 Box 38 Waitsfield, VT 05673 Contact: Craig or Kerry Keown Phone: 802-496-3837
Length of Tour:	21 days, covering approximately 2,000 miles (the average rider drives over 3,000 miles on this tour)

Dates:
1989:
- April 8 through April 29, 1989
- May 6 through May 27, 1989 (time reserved for custom tours; to be arranged)
- September 2 through September 23, 1989
- September 30 through October 21, 1989 (this trip runs in the reverse direction: Cairns to Gold Coast)

1990:
- April 7 through April 28, 1990
- May 5 through May 26, 1990 (time reserved for Cairns to Gold Coast or custom tours, depending upon interest)
- September 1 through September 22, 1990
- September 29 through October 20, 1990 (Cairns to Gold Coast)

GUIDED TOURS – AUSTRALIA

Trip Begins and Ends: Brisbane (Toowoomba) to Cairns or Cairns to Brisbane, Australia

Highlights:
Enjoy open Aussie hospitality on this three-week tour of Queensland's 2,500 miles of sunny coastline. From the glittering casinos of the Gold Coast to the Great Barrier Reef, you'll love the green mountains, white beaches, and blue water of Australian paradise. Relax and pamper yourself. Work on your tan on Fraser Island with 100 miles of isolated beach. Visit Jupiters on the Gold Coast, the southern hemisphere's largest casino. Shop for opals. Cruise tropical rain forest and spectacular scenery where mountains and reef meet the shoreline. On Gillies Highway, whirl through 365 hairpin turns in 17 kilometers. Spend a day on the America's cup contender Gretel in Whitsunday Islands. Take days to snorkel, scuba, and dive off the Great Barrier Reef. A spectacular float plane flight to the reef is included.

Price (does not include motorcycle rental):
- Single rider, double occupancy $3,195
- Supplement for single room occupancy .... $ 400

Price Includes:
Round trip airfare from U.S.A. west coast; 21 nights accommodation; airport transportation, luggage transportation; personalized guide service; daily briefing; maps; all breakfasts and dinners upon arrival in a new location; Whitsunday Island cruise on Gretel; and flight to reef.

Not Included in Price:
Gas, oil, insurance, some meals, and spending money.

Motorcycle Provisions:
Rent various BMW models, ranging from $750 AUS for an R65LS to $1,200 AUS for a K100. A $500 AUS damage deposit is required with rentals; it is refunded when the motorcycle is returned without damage. A few other types of motorcycle are available with special arrangement.

Luggage Provisions:
A van accompanies this tour to carry luggage.

GUIDED TOURS – AUSTRALIA

AUSTRALIA	**The GP Oz Rider Tour**
Tour Operator:	TransCyclist International CPO Box 2064 Tokyo, 100-91 JAPAN Contact: Mr. Volker Lenzner Phone: (81) 3-402-5385 FAX: (81) 3-402-5358
Length of Tour:	9 days, approximately 2,250 km

Dates:
- April 5 through April 13, 1989
- Similar dates for 1990

Trip Begins and Ends:	Sydney, Australia

Highlights:

This trip is arranged out of Sydney (the most scenic city in Australia) and combines the Oz Rider Tour with a free visit to the first Australian Grand Prix on Phillip Island near Melbourne. The itinerary includes two and one-half days riding to the Grand Prix, three days watching the event (practice, qualifying, Superbike races, sidecar races, second round of 125/250/500cc road race championships), and then a return to Sydney via a different inland route over another two and one-half days. You'll have one full day at the end to see beautiful Sydney and do some shopping. A bus will follow the same route and will share the same lunch and overnight stops. Participants will be able to travel by bus or motorcycle or change and only ride one way.

Price (includes motorcycle rental):
- Rider both ways, double occupancy .... $2,155 AUS
- Rider one way (bus other way), double occupancy .... $1,810 AUS
- Passenger (bus or motorcycle), double occupancy .... $1,260 AUS

Price Includes:

All food; entrance fees; camping fees; motorcycle rental; bus fare; camping equipment and hotel fees; gasoline and oil; guide service. NOTE: discounts available to groups of 10 or more.

Motorcycle Provisions:

Yamaha 250/600/XJ750/900 and BMW 100 available.

Luggage Provisions:
The bus will carry luggage.

Special Notes:
International driver's license valid for motorcycle operation required by participants. You are advised to book well in advance. In addition to the tour described above, there is also a standard seven-day (or longer) guided or self-guided Oz Rider Tour operational year round. Prices range from $1,300 AUS per rider, double occupancy (all inclusive except for gas and lunches). Send a self-addressed, stamped envelope and one international reply coupon (available from the post office) when inquiring about the tour.

AUSTRALIA	Kangaroo Caper
Tour Operator:	Beach's Motorcycle Adventures, Ltd. 2763 West River Parkway P.O. Box 36 Grand Island, NY 14072-0036 Contact: Mr. Rob Beach Phone: 716-773-4960 FAX: 716-773-0783 Telex: 6854139 GIBCO UW
Length of Tour:	22 days

Dates:
- April 8 through April 30, 1989
- April 7 through April 29, 1990
- April 6 through April 28, 1991

Trip Begins and Ends:	Los Angeles, California

Highlights:
The itinerary for this trip concentrates on the state of New South Wales, which offers a sampling of almost everything great in Australia. In the north one finds subtropical weather; in the south the Australian Alps and over 1,300 kilometers of coastline. One half of the riding will be on or near the coast. The other half is through the mountains, bushlands, vineyards, farmlands, and rain forests of New South Wales.

After arriving at Sydney airport, ride through the Blue Mountains, the Golden West, the Hunter River Valley, up the Holiday Coast through the New England area, and down the southeastern coast of New South Wales. Visit Canberra, the capital of Australia, and (after returning the motorcycle in Sydney) fly up the coast to Townsend to visit the Great Barrier Reef before returning home.

Price (does not include motorcycle rental):
- Per person, double occupancy $3,600
- Supplement for single room occupancy . . . .$ 250

Price Includes:
Round trip airfare from/to Los Angeles on Qantas; all hotels; all morning and evening meals; maps; tour jackets; tote bags and a trip to the Great Barrier Reef.

Motorcycle Provisions:
BMW motorcycles with saddlebags are available for rental for $700.

Luggage Provisions:
A van accompanies each tour to carry luggage.

Reader Discount:
A discount of $50 applies to this tour when you send in the Reader Discount Coupon.

"If only these 'roos could drive." (Geoff Coat, Aus MCT)

AUSTRALIA

Melbourne to Darwin and Darwin to Melbourne

"When I say go, head for Burger King."

Tour Operator:	Bike Tours Einsiedeleiweg 16 5942 Kirchhundem 4 WEST GERMANY Contact: Ms. Eveline Veenkamp Phone: (49) 2764-7824
Length of Tour:	3 weeks, covering approximately 5,000 km; 300 km per day

Dates:

Melbourne to Darwin:
- April 9 through April 29, 1989
- August 27 through September 16, 1989
- April 8 through April 28, 1990

Darwin to Melbourne:
- May 7 through May 27, 1989
- July 30 through August 19, 1989
- September 24 through October 14, 1989
- May 6 through May 26, 1990

Trip Begins and Ends:	Melbourne to Darwin or Darwin to Melbourne, Australia

Highlights:

Bisect the Australian continent with this run from Melbourne to Darwin. Start in Melbourne where the climate is as temperate as Ireland. Follow the Great Ocean Road along sandy bays and fantastical rock formations. Breathtaking views open at every turn of the road. Roar onto the legendary Stuart Highway that runs 3,000 miles hell-bent for Darwin. Travel the deserted roads of the outback past herds of sheep and cattle with eucalyptus trees marking the landscape. See koalas and kangaroos in the wild. Go through Coober Pedy, a desert town where people live in dugouts — comfortable apartments carved into soft boulders. Discover the variety of the Land Down Under with climates that range from mild in the south to tropical in the north.

Price (includes motorcycle rental):
- Single rider, double occupancy .... 2,650 DM
- Motorcycle passenger, double occupancy .... 950 DM
- Vehicle passenger, double occupancy .... 1,850 DM

Price Includes:
Camping equipment (except sleeping bag); transfer from airport to camp; campground fees; tents; maintenance and repairs.

Not Included in Price:
Food, fuel, insurance. Cost approximately $125 AUS weekly.

Motorcycle Provisions:
Yamaha XT 600.

Luggage Provisions:
A van accompanies tour to carry all luggage.

Special Notes:
The principal language of this tour is German. English can be spoken if necessary.

AUSTRALIA

Melbourne to Perth and Perth to Melbourne

No problem with traffic here

Tour Operator:
Bike Tours
Einsiedeleiweg 16
5942 Kirchhundem 4
WEST GERMANY

Contact: Eveline Veenkamp
Phone: (49) 2764-7824

Length of Tour:
3 weeks, covering approximately 5,000 km; 300 km per day

Dates:
Melbourne to Perth:
- October 22 through November 11, 1989

Perth to Melbourne:
- November 19 through December 9, 1989

Trip Begins and Ends:
Melbourne to Perth or Perth to Melbourne, Australia

Highlights:
Only enduro enthusiasts in good shape should take this tour in the Australian spring. You'll travel two of the loneliest paths of Australia. Expert drivers find no boundaries in the bush country. Storm primitive deserts and barren steppes. Course down Gunbarrel Highway through Gibson and Great Victoria deserts. This is the most isolated path in the country. Water, gas, and food will be transported in a tagalong van. Spend a week camping under the starry skies of the outback. Emerge from the bushland after seven days of freedom from the constraints of civilization.

Price (includes motorcycle rental):
- Single rider .... 2,650 DM
- Motorcycle passenger .... 950 DM
- Vehicle passenger .... 1,850 DM

Price Includes:
Camping equipment (except sleeping bag); transfer from airport to camp; campground fees; tents; maintenance and repairs.

Not Included in Price:
Food, fuel, insurance. Cost approximately $125 AUS weekly.

Motorcycle Provisions:
Yamaha XT 600.

Luggage Provisions:
A van accompanies tour to carry all luggage.

Special Notes:
The principal language of this tour is German. English can be spoken if necessary.

"It's beer from here on, mates." (photo by Bike Tours)

AUSTRALIA	**Mulga Tour**

Tour Operator:
Australian Motorcycle Touring
46 Greenways Road
P.O. Box 256
Glen Waverley, Victoria 3150
AUSTRALIA

Contact: Mr. Geoff Coat
Phone: (61) 3-233-8891
FAX: (61) 3-233-1407

Agent for UK and Europe:
Twickers World
22 Church Street
Twickenham TW1 3NW
ENGLAND
Phone: (44) 1-892-7606

Agent for USA and Canada:	Adventure Center Inc. 5540 College Avenue Oakland, CA 94618 Phone: 415-654-1879

Length of Tour:	10 days

Dates:

1989:
- May 8 through May 17, 1989
- May 22 through May 31, 1989
- June 5 through June 14, 1989
- June 19 through June 28, 1989
- July 3 through July 12, 1989
- July 17 through July 26, 1989
- July 31 through August 9, 1989
- August 14 through August 23, 1989
- August 28 through September 6, 1989
- September 11 through September 20, 1989
- September 25 through October 4, 1989
- October 9 through October 18, 1989
- October 23 through November 1, 1989

1990:
- May 7 through May 16, 1990
- May 21 through May 30, 1990
- June 4 through June 13, 1990
- June 18 through June 27, 1990
- July 2 through July 11, 1990
- July 16 through July 25, 1990
- July 30 through August 8, 1990
- August 13 through August 22, 1990
- August 27 through September 5, 1990
- September 10 through September 19, 1990
- September 24 through October 3, 1990
- October 8 through October 17, 1990
- October 22 through October 31, 1990

Trip Begins and Ends:	Melbourne, Australia

Highlights:

Penetrate the desiccated heart of the driest continent on the planet. Discover the real Australia. From desert outback to a motorcyclist's dream on the Great Ocean Road, you'll get an unequaled picture of the past and present of the Land Down Under. Visit Sovereign Hill, a recreation of an

1850's gold mining town. See the center of present-day mining country at Broken Hill. Ride across the blinding white salt pans of Lake Frome in the remote Flinders Range at the end of civilization. Roll down the vine-covered hills in Barossa Valley, world famous wine country. Ride through wheat fields and pine forest to Mount Gambier and its renowned Blue Lake. Twist along Great Ocean Road past the Cliffs of the Twelve Apostles and the Bay of Islands.

Price (includes motorcycle rental):
- Single rider, double occupancy .... $3,000 AUS
- Passenger, double occupancy .... $1,500 AUS
- Security deposit of $500 AUS for riders over the age of 25 (credit card accepted), refunded upon return of undamaged motorcycle.

Price Includes:
Accommodations for nine nights; nine breakfasts; nine dinners (includes wine/beer); and a get-acquainted Australian barbecue the night before the tour starts. Gas and oil are also included.

Not Included in Price:
Personal accident insurance (available through travel agent); lunch; snacks; nor personal items. Motorcycle helmets and rain gear, which may be rented for $10 AUS per item for duration of tour.

Motorcycle Provisions:
Nearly new BMW Model R80 sports touring bikes are provided as part of the price; they are fitted with a windshield, and lockable luggage cases.

Luggage Provisions:
Travelers are expected to carry their own luggage on their bikes.

Special Notes:
Deposit of $200 AUS needed to secure reservation on tour; balance due 30 days prior to tour commencement. If reservation canceled within 30 days prior to tour, 50% refund; if within seven days prior to tour, no refund.

AUSTRALIA

Outback Tour One, Outback Tour Two, Outback Tour Three

"Faster. I think that 'roo is gaining on us."

| Tour Operator: | Top Gear Tours
Southern Skies Travel
P.O. Box 109
Mornington, Victoria 3931
AUSTRALIA

Contact: Ms. Liz Sannen
Phone: (61) 59 751 505
FAX: (61) 59 751 599 |

Length of Tour:
- Outback Tour One: 10 days, nine nights
- Outback Tour Two: seven days, six nights
- Outback Tour Three: seven days, six nights

Dates:
Outback One:
- Starts every second Tuesday, May 2, 1989 to October 17, 1989
- Starts every second Tuesday, May 1, 1990 to October 16, 1990

Outback Two and Three:
- Starts every Tuesday, May 2, 1989 to October 17, 1989
- Starts every Tuesday, May 1, 1990 to October 16, 1990

| Trips Begins and Ends: | Tullamarine Airport, Melbourne, Australia |

Highlights, Outback Tour One:
This tour is a combination of Tours Two and Three but also included is a jog to the north into Queensland, the fourth state you'll visit, along with the very best of the outback. (See descriptions below.)

Highlights, Outback Tour Two:
From Melbourne fly northwest to Adelaide. The tour then travels up the longest river system in Australia. Start out along the shore of the Murray River, which winds through irrigated orchards before it moves across the rolling plains. Here you'll see sheep, kangaroos, and emus. You may even see some of the gun shearers in action. The tour visits a mining city, and then for contrast an almost ghost town. White Cliffs is another town with a difference; it is all underground to escape the intense heat of summer. After seeing an opal mine in action, wind back toward Adelaide through wine growing country. There will be plenty of opportunities to sample the best.

Highlights, Outback Tour Three:
From Adelaide, travel north through Port Augusta and on to the Stony Desert. You will visit Woomera, the site of Australia's rocket testing, and Coober Pedy, an opal town built underground so even the beer is always cool. Then you'll visit a camel ranch, where the cowboys ride old BMW bikes. Test your bike for speed at your next stop, Lake Eyre, the dry lake bed site of Donald Campbell's land speed record. Head south through the cattle towns of Marree and Leigh Creek; visit Wilpena Pound, a natural amphitheater in the Flinders Ranges. And what more natural way to finish the tour than to visit the wineries before returning back to Adelaide.

Highlights, All Tours:
All outback tours include some camping, often with no other people around for miles and miles and under the brightest stars you can imagine. After rain in the outback the desert becomes a sea of wild flowers for just a few days. Sit around the campfire drinking billy tea and swapping stories. This is what cycle touring is really all about.

Price (includes motorcycle rental):
Single rider, double occupancy:
- Outback Tour One: $2,050
- Outback Tour Two: $1,625
- Outback Tour Three: $1,625
- Extra mandatory cost for transfers to/from airport, first and last nights hotel accommodation: ....$ 200

Note: Any Top Gear tours can be combined; to get the total price add the individual tour prices, then add a $200 surcharge cost for transfers, and first and last nights accommodation.

Price Includes:
Nightly accommodations in country hotels and motels or camping; breakfast and dinner each day; welcome dinner; farewell barbecue; transfers between airport and Melbourne hotel for first and last nights accommodation, transfers between Adelaide airport and start of tour; tour guide; all camping equipment.

Motorcycle Provisions:
An insured Honda NX 650 is included with the price.

Luggage Provisions:
A van accompanies each tour to carry luggage.

Special Notes:
Desert areas can be cold at night so warm clothing is advisable. Motorcycle helmets are mandatory. Top Gear reserves the right to substitute tours if insufficient numbers are booked on any tour.

Departure dates for the outback tours (Tuesday mornings) are planned to allow American visitors time to leave most parts of the U.S. on Saturday, to arrive in Melbourne on Monday morning (having lost a day passing the international date line), and have a day to recuperate from jet lag before flying on to Adelaide Tuesday morning.

Reader Discount:
A discount of $30 applies to this tour when you send in the Reader Discount Coupon.

Spectacular vistas at every turn

AUSTRALIA	**Victoria One, Victoria Two, Tasmania One**
Tour Operator:	Top Gear Tours Southern Skies Travel P.O. Box 109 Mornington, Victoria 3931 AUSTRALIA Contact: Ms. Liz Sannen Phone: (61) 59 751 505 FAX: (61) 59 751 599
Length of Tour:	7 days, 6 nights

Dates:
Victoria One & Two:
- Starts every Tuesday, November 7, 1989 to April 17, 1990
- Starts every Tuesday, November 6, 1990 to April 16, 1991

Tasmania:
- Starts every Monday, November 6, 1989 to April 16, 1990
- Starts every Monday, November 5, 1990 to April 15, 1991

Trips Begin and End:	Tullamarine Airport, Melbourne, Australia

Highlights, Victoria One:
This trip encompasses everything that is different about Australia. First tour the old sea ports, winding coastal roads, and rugged cliffs. Then drive inland to country towns and caves, an outback farm, vineyards, across the desert to a bustling mining city, and for contrast an almost ghost town. Finally journey through the mountains to the site of Australia's revolution (failed) and back to Melbourne. Don't think this can't be done in seven days! As the Australians say, "no worries".

Highlights, Victoria Two:
This tour shows you the other side of Victoria, both geographically and scenically. It takes in the island famous for its wildlife and equally a motorcycle Grand Prix circuit living together in harmony. You will pass through various national parks, then over Australia's highest mountain to the headwaters of the largest river. See the strangest pub, then up onto the high plains, and down into gentle valleys along winding roads that are a motorcyclist's delight. Everywhere, you will see the strange wildlife for which Australia is famous.

Highlights, Tasmania One:
This trip journeys across the Bass Strait to the island state of Tasmania where Australia's convict heritage began. The roads are great for riding, the scenery always different, and the wildlife is unique to this island. The seafood specialities of the island include lobster, shrimp, scallops, abalone, and sea trout. There will even be time for a boat trip through a wilderness area.

Price (includes motorcycle rental):
Single rider, double occupancy
- Victoria One: $1,700
- Victoria Two: $1,700
- Tasmania: $1,900
- Extra mandatory cost for transfers, first and last nights accommodation, with dinner and breakfast: .... $ 200

Note: Any Top Gear Victoria or Tasmania tours can be combined; to get the total price add the individual tour prices, then add the $200 cost for transfers, first and last nights accommodation only once, not for each tour.

Price Includes:
Six nights country hotels; breakfast and dinner each day; welcome dinner; farewell barbecue; transfer from airport to Melbourne hotel; tour guide.

Motorcycle Provisions:
An insured Honda NX 650 is included with the price.

Luggage Provisions:
A van accompanies each tour to carry luggage.

Special Notes:
Departure dates for the Victoria tours (Tuesday mornings) are planned to allow American visitors time to leave most parts of the U.S. on Saturday, to arrive in Melbourne on Monday morning (having lost a day passing the international date line), and have a day to recuperate from jet lag before starting to ride on Tuesday morning.

Because of the need to mesh with a ferry schedule, the Tasmanian tours must begin on Monday mornings. American travelers will therefore have to leave the U.S. on Friday, in time to arrive in Melbourne on Sunday and start the trip on Monday.

Top Gear reserves the right to substitute tours if insufficient numbers are booked on any tour. Helmets are mandatory.

Reader Discount:
A discount of $30 applies to this tour when you send in the Reader Discount Coupon.

AUSTRALIA

The Wonders of New South Wales

"When the big hand is on 12 and..."

Tour Operator:

Australian-American Mototours
RR1 Box 38
Waitsfield, VT 05673

Contact: Craig or Kerry Keown
Phone: 802-496-3837

Length of Tour:
21 days, covering approximately 2,300 miles (although the average rider drives over 3,500 miles on this tour).

Dates:
- October 28 through November 18, 1989
- October 27 through November 17, 1990

Trip Begins and Ends: Brisbane (Toowoomba), Australia

Highlights:
Take in the friendly Aussie welcome of New South Wales on this three week loop through the home of Australia's first settlement. Begin in Toowoomba, Australia's largest inland city and then travel south for memorable mountain riding and a sampling of the world's finest beaches — including Byron Bay, Australia's most easterly point. Visit Coff's Harbor and the original convict settlement of Port Macquarie. Wander over the scenic roads of Tuncurry/Forster and then head for the heart of the wine making district, the famous Hunter Valley. You'll sample the vintages of over 20 renowned wineries. You'll travel by bus for this part of the tour. Then it's on to the mysterious Blue Mountains and Katoomba for breathtaking vistas before boarding a train into Sydney, Australia's largest city. See the sights of this great city before returning to Katoomba and departure for the Snowy Mountains of Banjo Paterson fame. Retrace your steps inland to the upper Hunter region. You'll have a chance for more wine tasting before you return to Toowoomba through the fascinating New England district. Follow the original paths of the early explorers over winding mountain passes and gaze with awe on the 1,000-foot waterfalls that bear their names.

Price (does not include motorcycle rental):
- Single rider, double occupancy $3,195
- Supplement for single room occupancy .... $ 400

Price Includes:
Round trip airfare from U.S.A. west coast; 21 nights accommodation; airport transportation, luggage transportation; personalized guide service; daily briefing; maps; all breakfasts and dinners upon arrival in a new location; Whitsunday Island cruise.

Not Included in Price:
Gas, oil, insurance, some meals, and spending money.

Motorcycle Provisions:
Rent various BMW models, ranging from $750 AUS for an R65LS to $1,200 AUS for a K100. A $500 AUS damage deposit is required with rentals; it is refunded when the motorcycle is returned without damage. A few other types of motorcycle are available with special arrangement.

Luggage Provisions:
A van accompanies this tour to carry luggage.

On the road, outside Riva, Italy (photo by Barbara Laurent)

GUIDED TOURS - NEW ZEALAND

NEW ZEALAND — The Kiwi Rider

Tour Operator:	TransCyclist International CPO Box 2064 Tokyo, 100-91 JAPAN Contact: Mr. Volker Lenzner Phone: (81) 3-402-5385 FAX: (81) 3-402-5358

Length of Tour:
- 7-day Deluxe tour, covering approximately 1,100 km
- 14-day Standard tour, covering approximately 2,000 km

Dates, Seven-Day Deluxe Tour:

1989:
- April 30 through May 6, 1989
- September 10 through September 16, 1989
- November 5 through November 11, 1989
- November 26 through December 2, 1989
- December 17 through December 23, 1989
- December 31, 1989 through January 6, 1990

1990 (the following dates are approximate):
- January 14 through January 20, 1990
- January 28 through February 3, 1990
- February 11 through February 17, 1990
- February 25 through March 3, 1990
- March 11 through March 17, 1990
- March 25 through March 31, 1990
- April 29 through May 5, 1990
- September 9 through September 15, 1990
- November 4 through November 10, 1990
- November 25 through December 1, 1990
- December 16 through December 22, 1990
- December 30, 1990 through January 5, 1991

Dates, 14-Day Standard Tour:

1989:
- April 18 through May 1, 1989
- November 14 through November 27, 1989
- December 6 through December 19, 1989

1990 (the following dates are approximate):
- January 9 through January 22, 1990
- February 20 through March 5, 1990
- March 20 through April 2, 1990
- April 17 through April 30, 1990
- November 13 through November 26, 1990
- December 5 through December 18, 1990

Trip Begins:	Christchurch, New Zealand
Trip Ends:	Auckland, New Zealand

Highlights:

This tour reveals one of the great travel secrets left in the world. Enjoy New Zealand's amazing diversity of scenery still unspoiled by tourism. Experience the native Maori culture and the well-preserved Victorian towns. Meet people of genuine friendliness. Ride through a landscape of breathtaking fjords and volcanoes. Take a dip in a rejuvenating hot spring. Sample the rich food of New Zealand. On these tours, you'll travel a leisurely 300 kilometers per day, giving you plenty of time to meet the Kiwis and get to know them. Spend one morning on an operating sheep farm and another white-water rafting through rapids and gorges. Enjoy the Southern Alps with crystalline lakes, glaciers, and snowcapped peaks punctuating the Alpine settings. Return through awesome mountain scenery to the resort of Queenstown on the shores of Lake Wakatipu, and then on to the salt air of the southern Pacific and back to Auckland.

Price (includes motorcycle rental):

Seven-Day Deluxe Tour:
- Single rider, double occupancy .... $1,495 NZ
- Passenger, double occupancy .... $1,295 NZ

14-Day Standard Tour:
- Single rider, double occupancy .... $1,995 NZ
- Passenger, double occupancy .... $1,595 NZ

Note: A $400 NZ insurance bond is required when renting the motorcycle; refundable when motorcycle is returned free of damage.

Price Includes:

All hotels; breakfast and dinner each day; motorcycle rental and insurance; transport from Christchurch airport; maps; route guides; and tour guide. Does not include gasoline or lunches. You should add about $30 NZ to $50 NZ per day for gasoline, lunch, snacks, etc.

Motorcycle Provisions:
Choice of BMW R65, R80, or R100 for riders over age 25; Japanese makes (Yamaha 440, 550, 650) for those under age 25. Motorcycle rental is included with the tour price.

Luggage Provisions:
Travelers are expected to carry their luggage on their motorcycle. Pack lightly.

Special Notes:
International driver's license valid for motorcycle operation required by participants. Only Deluxe tours include touristic extras (i.e., Cessna joy flight, white-river rafting, etc.). Tour price based on minimum of five participants. You are advised to book well in advance. Tour participants must be at least 21 years of age (at least 25 for machines over 750cc). Send a self-addressed, stamped envelope and one international reply coupon (available from the post office) when inquiring about the tour.

NEW ZEALAND — Maori Meander

Tour Operator:	Beach's Motorcycle Adventures, Ltd. 2763 West River Parkway P.O. Box 36 Grand Island, NY 14072-0036 Contact: Mr. Rob Beach Phone: 716-773-4960 FAX: 716-773-0783 Telex: 6854139 GIBCO UW
Length of Tour:	22 days, approximately 2,600 miles

Dates:
- March 12 through April 2, 1989 (for reference only)
- March 11 through April 1, 1990
- March 10 through March 31, 1991

Trip Begins and Ends:	Los Angeles, California

Highlights:
This tour begins in Christchurch and winds its way down to Auckland. Averaging 150 to 200 miles a day, each day's ride allows plenty of time to

sightsee, to relax and to get an in-depth look at both of the islands that make up New Zealand. A number of overnight stays on privately-owned farms allows participants a far greater contact with the inhabitants than would be available otherwise.

A complete itinerary and a collection of excellent maps are provided, giving total freedom to tour participants to choose their own daily routes. Attractions included in the tour price are: jetboat rides, a scenic flight to Fox Glacier, white-water rafting, and a choice of sightseeing cruises.

As always, there will be a Beach on the tour. Both Rob and Bob spend the winter months staring out the window at the piles of snow around western New York and dream of the tour to New Zealand.

Price (does not include motorcycle rental):
- Per person, double occupancy $3,600
- Supplement for single room occupancy ....$ 250

Price Includes:
Round trip airfare from/to Los Angeles on Air New Zealand; all hotels; all morning and evening meals; maps; tour jackets; tote bags and additional surprises.

Motorcycle Provisions:
BMW R-series and Japanese motorcycles are available for rental for $600, including insurance. The renter is responsible for the first $500 NZ of any damage to the motorcycle in the event of an accident.

Luggage Provisions:
A van accompanies each tour to carry luggage.

Reader Discount:
A discount of $50 applies to this tour when you send in the Reader Discount Coupon.

NEW ZEALAND

New Zealand

Volcano in Tongariro National Park

Tour Operator:	Von Thielmann Tours P.O. Box 87764 San Diego, CA 92138 Contact: Ms. Gina Guzzardo Phone: 619-463-7788 or 619-291-7057 FAX: 619-291-4630 Telex: 910 335 1607 MESA SERV SDG
Length of Tour:	19 days
Dates:	March, October
Trip Begins and Ends:	Los Angeles, California

Highlights:
South and North Island. A paradise for motorcyclists. Scenery ranging from Alpine country to tropical rain forests.

Price (includes motorcycle rental):
- Single rider, double occupancy $2,985
- Two people, double occupancy $5,970
- Single passenger, double occupancy $2,985
- Supplement for single room occupancy .... $ 680

Price Includes:
Round trip airfare from Honolulu; hotel accommodations; breakfast daily; plus other meals; sightseeing; transfers; Inter-Island Ferry.

Motorcycle Provisions:
Rental motorcycles available (touring type).

Luggage Provisions:
Support vehicle will carry the luggage.

NEW ZEALAND	**New Zealand 14-Day Tour**
Tour Operator:	South Pacific Motorcycle Tours Ltd. 18 King Edward St. P.O. Box 158 Masterton NEW ZEALAND Contact: Glen and Maureen Bull Phone: (64) 59-84490
Reservations and Information:	A.A. Travel (Wairarapa) Ltd. P.O. Box 457 Masterton NEW ZEALAND Phone: (64) 59-82222 FAX: (64) 59-82485 Telex: NZ 3982
U.S. Agent:	New Zealand Central Reservations Office 6033 W. Century Blvd., Suite 1270 Los Angeles, California 90045 Phone: 800-351-2323 (outside California) 800-351-2317 (within California) FAX: 213-215-9705
Length of Tour:	14 days, approximately 2,000 miles

Dates:
- March 7 through March 20, 1989 (for reference only)
- March 31 through April 13, 1989 (for reference only)
- April 17 through April 30, 1989
- May 9 through May 22, 1989

Tours arranged during winter months if requested:
- September 5 through September 18, 1989
- October 3 through October 16, 1989
- November 7 through November 20, 1989
- November 30 through December 13, 1989

Trip Begins and Ends:	Wellington, New Zealand

Highlights:
Tour beautiful, unspoiled New Zealand with an intimate group of no more than six motorcycles. See the thundering Huka Falls. Attend a traditional Maori hangi and concert. Learn more about the Polynesian culture of these native New Zealanders. Experience the wonderland of geysers, bubbling mud pools, and crystal clear lakes in Rotorua. Visit the world famous glow worm caves at Waitomo, which George Bernard Shaw called the eighth wonder of the world. Ferry across magnificent Marlborough Sounds. Twist through the majestic Southern Alps. Take a guided walk on Fox Glacier. Begin and end your trip with a home-cooked dinner at your tour operator's home. You'll learn to expect this kind of hospitality in friendly New Zealand.

Price (does not include motorcycle rental):
- Two riders, double occupancy $4,744
- Single rider, double occupancy $2,372
- Supplement for single room occupancy .... $ 447
- Motorcycle rental .... $ 702

Price Includes:
Accommodations in first-class motels on bed and breakfast basis; gas and oil; tour information package; daily briefing; transportation costs to/from Wellington; ferry fares; tours through National Wildlife Centre and Waitomo Caves; guided walk on a glacier, and a traditional Maori hangi and concert.

Motorcycle Provisions:
Gold Wing touring motorcycles (GL400 series are also available). Guests also have the option of shipping their own motorcycle to use on the tour.

Luggage Provisions:

A fully equipped 11-seater escort coach and trailer will accompany all tours. The coach will carry any passenger who tires of riding, all excess baggage and purchases, and is in constant radio contact with the tour leader.

Special Notes:

Weather conditions vary. As a precaution pack your wet weather gear as well as helmet, sunglasses, and bathing suit. As a guide to personal spending, South Pacific Motorcycle Tours recommends $72 per day to cover lunch, dinner, side tours, and souvenirs, etc. They can accommodate individual or group needs for shorter or longer tours of New Zealand.

NEW ZEALAND

New Zealand Tour

Tour Operator:	Pancho Villa Moto-Tours 9437 E.B. Taulbee El Paso, TX 79924 Contact: Mr. Skip Mascorro Phone: 915-757-3032 FAX: 915-562-1505
Length of Tour:	16 days

Dates:
- March 28 through April 12, 1989 (for reference)
- March 27 through April 11, 1990

Trip Begins:	Auckland, New Zealand
Trip Ends:	Christchurch, New Zealand

Highlights:

New Zealand, a country about the size of California, but with a population of only three million, is a motorcyclist's paradise. Void of traffic and filled with magnificent scenery, New Zealand offers a broad range of sensory stimuli: gorgeous mountains, lush forests, huge sheep farms, and the beautiful Pacific Ocean. You'll travel at a leisurely pace on this tour and have plenty of time to mingle with the Kiwis and get to know them. You'll stay overnight at the home of a rural New Zealand farming family and possibly go on a midnight rabbit hunt or help work the sheep dogs. Best of all, you'll sample the famous New Zealand hospitality.

Price (includes motorcycle rental):
- Single rider, double occupancy $3,349
- Two people (one bike), double occupancy $5,995
- Supplement for single room occupancy .... $ 395

Price Includes:
Airfare round trip Los Angeles to Auckland, New Zealand; necessary transfers in Los Angeles, Auckland, and Christchurch; motorcycle rental and insurance for 14 days; hotel accommodations for 13 nights including the farm stay (double occupancy); at least 24 meals; a tour escort; road logs, maps, and information; Cook Strait ferry crossing; Milford Sound launch tour; Queensland gondola ride with dinner; Pancho Villa T-shirt; and a followup vehicle to carry luggage.

Motorcycle Provisions:
Rental of a Yamaha XV 1100 or XJ 900, with necessary insurance, is included with the tour price.

Luggage Provisions:
A followup vehicle will travel with the group to carry luggage.

Special Notes:
Contact Pancho Villa Moto-Tours if you want to modify your trip to include other destinations while outside the U.S.

Reader Discount:
A discount of $25 applies to this tour when you send in the Reader Discount Coupon.

NEW ZEALAND

Two-Week Tour of New Zealand

Tour Operator:	Te Waipounamu Motorcycle Tours P.O. Box 673 Christchurch NEW ZEALAND Contact: Mr. John Rains Phone: (64) 03 794 320 or (64) 03 427 503 FAX: (64) 03 842 345
Length of Tour:	14 days, approximately 2,800 miles

Dates:
- November 7 through November 20, 1989
- December 5 through December 18, 1989
- January 16 through January 29, 1990
- February 13 through February 26, 1990
- March 13 through March 26, 1990

Trip Begins and Ends:	Christchurch, New Zealand

Highlights:
The pace of this tour through the unspoiled New Zealand countryside is fairly relaxed. Cruise through vineyards and orchards on switchback roads to the water-filled extinct volcano which became Lake Taupo. In the town of Napier, stay in a historic hotel, right in the middle of all sorts of interesting thermal attractions. The town will also be your base for shopping, walking, trout fishing, and deer stalking. You'll have to tear yourself away, and start your ride down past three volcanoes toward Wanganui on the southwest coast. From there, go south to Wellington, and take the ferry across Cook Strait to Picton. Wend your way back through fishing villages to Christchurch. John Rains, your tour guide, aims to provide good value for your money and plenty of variety on his tours. Groups are generally small, often only four or five motorcycles, so you'll have a good chance to get to know your riding companions.

Price (does include motorcycle rental):
- Single rider, double occupancy .... $2,395 NZ
- Passenger, double occupancy .... $2,095 NZ

Note: A $500 NZ insurance bond is required upon renting the motorcycle; refundable when motorcycle is returned free of damage.

Price Includes:
Accommodations for 13 nights in hotels, motels, and New Zealand farm stays with local people; breakfast and dinner each day; ferry crossings; transport from Christchurch airport; maps; route guides; and tour guide. According to John Rains, the accommodations are "very good, not ostentatious or flashy". Does not include gasoline.

Motorcycle Provisions:
Choice of: BMW R-series 800cc and 1000cc models; Yamaha 750cc; Honda 400cc and 500cc models

Special Notes:
Tour participants must be at least 21 years of age (at least 25 for machines over 750cc).

Visitors to Maori village (photo by von Thielmann Tours)

MOTORCYCLE RENTAL AGENCIES

Motorcycle rentals are more widely available in Europe and other areas outside this country, than in the United States. Availability of motorcycle rental programs will be a key ingredient in the future growth of motorcycle touring. We applaud Harley Owners Group's rental program and hope that more associations and individuals follow their lead. By next year's publication, we hope there will be more U.S. entries in this section.

Aloha Funway Rentals

1982 Kalakaua
Honolulu, HI 96815

Contact:
Mr. Ross Murphy, Sales Representative
Phone: 808-945-3677 or 800-367-2686
FAX: Not available
Telex: Not available

Prices (Motorcycles):
- Kawasaki 305 LTD: $35 per day; $89 for 3 days; $183 per week.
- Kawasaki 454 LTD: $40 per day; $102 for 3 days; $210 per week.
- Kawasaki 600 ZL: $47 per day; $120 for 3 days; $246 per week.
- Kawasaki EX500: $55 per day; $140 for 3 days; $288 per week.
- Kawasaki 600ZX Ninja: $70 per day; $178 for 3 days; $367 per week.
- Harley Sportster 1100: $70 per day; $178 for 3 days; $367 per week.
- Harley Low Rider 1340: $80 per day; $204 for 3 days; $420 per week.

Prices (Motorscooters):
- Honda 150 Elite: $30 per day; $76 for 3 days; $157 per week.
- Honda 250 Elite: $35 per day; $89 for 3 days; $183 per week.

Price Includes:
Unlimited mileage; limited liability insurance. Free courtesy van pickup and return. Free directions and maps. Japanese-speaking agents.

Deposit Required:
Cash security deposit depends upon the motorcycle. It ranges from $150 to $800 for up to two days rental; $250 to $1,000 for up to four days rental; $350 to $1,200 for one week rental. Credit cards accepted for the security deposit.

Insurance Arrangements:
Aloha Funway Rentals is self-insured under Hawaii state law for no-fault insurance to state mandated minimum amounts. Its liability is limited to those amounts. You may purchase from Aloha Funway Rentals a Collision Damage Waiver (CDW), which will reduce your personal liability for damage done to the motorcycle. Some age groups will be required to purchase the CDW as a condition of renting a motorcycle from Aloha Funway Rentals. No medical insurance is provided to renters by Aloha Funway Rentals.

Accessories:
Some models have fairings and windshields. None have saddlebags.

Special Requirements:
Renter must be at least 21 years of age (25 years for renters of 600ZX Ninja), have driver's license valid for motorcycle operation, and demonstrate driving ability to Aloha Funway Rentals. Drivers and passengers must wear eye protection (state law). Passengers under 18 years of age must wear a helmet (state law).

Reservations:
Strongly advised. Aloha has good supply of motorcycles but it is always more certain to make arrangements in advance.

Other services:
Aloha Funway Rentals also rents snorkeling equipment, bicycles, mopeds, and exotic cars.

American Motorcycle Rentals and Sales, Inc.

10924 Portal Drive
Los Alamitos, CA 90720

Contact:
Mr. Wayne Murphy
Phone: 213-594-8901 or
714-821-1590
FAX: Not available
Telex: Not available

Hours:
Monday through Saturday, 9 a.m. to 6 p.m.; Sunday by appointment.

Motorcycles Available:
Various types from dual-purpose 350cc to 1500cc street touring; availability subject to change.

Prices:
- One-half day: $35 to $75
- One day: $50 to $110
- Two days: $85 to $180
- Three days: $100 to $225

- Four to six days: $120 to $300
- Seven to eight days: $144 to $360
- Two weeks: $150 to $375
- Three weeks: $200 to $450
- Four weeks: $260 to $525

Price Includes:
Free 100 miles per day; add $.10 per mile thereafter. Free instructions for safe riding.

Deposit Required:
Security deposit is $250 per unit, depending on size. Major credit cards (VISA, MC, AMEX) or cash required. Also $50 or credit card imprint held 90 days to cover traffic tickets. Note $35 will be withheld from deposit if bike is not returned cleaned.

Insurance Arrangements:
Renter is responsible for their own insurance.

Accessories:
Helmets offered free to renters. Tank bags and soft saddle bags available. No windshields on bikes. Special clothing not supplied; renter is responsible for their own.

Special Requirements:
Primary renter must be at least 18 years of age and have driver's license valid for motorcycle operation. Learner's permit acceptable for California residents on half-day rental only.

Reservations:
Recommended. With limited supply, newest units rented first. Deposit of $50 per vehicle required to confirm reservation (returnable with 10-day notice). Checks accepted if received 14 days in advance.

Other Services:
- Tours to west coast races. Write or call for rates and tour dates. Tour bookings must be made at least two months in advance. Deposit of 50% is required to hold your reservation.
- Motorcycle parts and accessories.
- Service on all makes and models.

Arrow Rentals

159 Greyhound Lane
Streatham
London SW16 5NJ
ENGLAND

Contact:
Mr. Russell L. Stutely
Phone: (44) 1-677-7733
FAX: (44) 1-677-7670
Telex: Not available

Motorcycles Available:
Honda GL1200 or 1100 Aspencade; Honda VT500E; Kawasaki GT550; other sport motorcycles and non-touring machines also available. Inquire of Arrow for rates on non-touring bikes, available at competitive rates.

Prices (per week):
- Honda GL1200 or 1100 Aspencade (1988-89) £200
- Honda VT500E (1988) £100
- Kawasaki GT550 (1988-89) £100

Notes:
15% Value Added Tax and insurance will be added to these rates. Payments can be made by cash, travelers checks, bankers draft, or credit card (Access, VISA, or American Express).

Price Includes:
Free mileage.

Deposit Required:
Deposit of £50 is required; refundable upon returning the motorcycle undamaged.

Insurance Arrangements:
Compulsory full comprehensive insurance arranged by Arrow through their broker. Charges will depend upon the individual renting the motorcycle. Arrow cannot provide insurance for any driver with drunk driving convictions. Arrangements can also be made for insurance coverage for European continent ("green card" insurance required).

288 MOTORCYCLE RENTAL AGENCIES

Accessories:
Top boxes and side bags are installed on all touring motorcycles. Clothing and helmets can be rented or purchased upon request at discount prices, with advance notice.

Special Requirements:
Renters must have adequate identification and driver's license validated for motorcycle operation (American or international driver's license is acceptable).

Reservations:
Strongly advised. You will have a better chance of getting the model you want by giving Arrow advance notice of your schedule.

Other Services:
- With group rentals, Arrow Rentals can arrange for coach transfer of the group between the airport and the motorcycle rental office.
- Hotel reservations for renters as they are passing through London.

Bosenberg Motorcycle Excursions

Bosenberg Motorcycle Excursions

Mainzer Straße 54
D-6550 Bad Kreuznach
WEST GERMANY

Contact:
Mr. Leon A. Heindel
Phone: (49) 671-67580
FAX: Not available
Telex: Not available

U.S. Agent:

Around the Globe Travel, Ltd.
1417 North Wauwatosa Avenue
Milwaukee, WI 53213

Contact:
Mr. Walt Weber
Phone: 800-234-4037 or
414-257-0199 (WI or Canada)

Hours:

Motorcycles are available from May through October. The operating hours of the rental centers are: Monday through Friday from 9 a.m. to 1 p.m. and 2:30 p.m. to 6 p.m. and on Saturday mornings from 9 a.m. to 1 p.m. The rental centers are closed on Sundays and the following dates because of German holidays: May 4 and May 25, June 17, and August 15.

Description:

Bosenberg Motorcycle Excursions has arranged for the individual rental of BMW motorcycles in the Frankfurt and Munich, West Germany areas. The motorcycle rental centers are reached easily by public transportation from the airports and train stations in both cities. They strongly recommend you book your motorcycle as soon as you know your travel plans. The earlier you submit an application, the greater your chances of getting the exact model you want. For the high demand periods of June through August, list a second rental period. Only after your booking application and deposit are received, can your request for a motorcycle rental be coordinated and a confirmation sent to you by return mail. If no motorcycles are available for your indicated choices and rental period, your entire deposit will be refunded promptly.

Bosenberg Motorcycle Excursions acts as your agent to coordinate the rental of a BMW motorcycle based on your model choices and rental time frame.

Motorcycles and Rates:

The following rental rates are used for individual rental under the Travel on Your Own program and for scheduled excursions with Bosenberg Motorcycle Excursions (which use the Frankfurt rate only). The rates are priced per day in U.S. dollars for the specified models and rental period.

Rental Motorcycle Daily Rates

	– One to 14 Days –		– 15 to 60 Days –		Extra
	Frankfurt	Munich	Frankfurt	Munich	KMs
R80/R80RT	$71	$85	$61	$73	$0.40
R80GS	$79	$95	$67	$80	$0.50
R100RS/R100RT	$81	$97	$69	$83	$0.50
K75/K75C	$87	$104	$77	$92	$0.60
K100/K100RS/K100RT	$111	$133	$99	$119	$0.60

Price Includes:

Each rental day includes 200 kilometers (124 miles) at the daily price. Mileage over this daily rate will be charged at $.40 to $.60 per kilometer, depending upon the model. Rentals used for Bosenberg scheduled excursions will have unlimited mileage at no extra charge. Your BMW motorcycle rental features the following:
- English language rental contract.

- International motor insurance card (i.e., "green card") that provides third party liability insurance with a 2,000,000 DM ceiling (approximately $1,100,000) and, for the motorcycle itself, a collision and comprehensive insurance with a deductible of 1,000 DM (approximately $600).
- Two BMW travel cases, with tool pouch and first aid kit.
- Owner's manual and a BMW European service handbook.

When your motorcycle reservation is confirmed, you will receive instructions that explain fully, with the use of detailed maps, where your hotel and the motorcycle rental center is located. From the Frankfurt International Airport or the Riem Airport in Munich, you will receive detailed descriptions on how to use the local transportation system to arrive at your final destination. Your hotel will be within walking distance of the rental centers.

Deposit Required:
To confirm a reservation Bosenberg requires a $150 rental deposit, made in your name and credited against your total rental cost. When signing for your motorcycle, a security deposit of $600 must be left at the rental center. Upon return of your undamaged motorcycle, your security deposit will be refunded.

Methods of Payment:
Credit cards (American Express and VISA), travelers checks, or cash may be used for payment.

Insurance Arrangements:
It is not possible to offer any type of rider/co-rider insurance coverage such as accident, medical disability, or life insurance with any motorcycle rental. Contact your travel agent for information. Numerous insurance firms offer these coverages at a nominal cost. The peace of mind that it offers will improve the quality of your vacation.

Accessories:
At the Frankfurt rental center it is possible to rent riding gear (i.e., helmet, leather riding suit, and a wet weather suit) at a nominal cost, or to purchase all your required items. At the Munich rental center, it is not possible to purchase or rent riding gear. As part of your information packet, you will be informed of motorcycle clothing stores in the area.

Special Requirements:
You are only permitted to pick up and sign for a motorcycle on the day AFTER your arrival on an international air flight.

Reservations:

To sign up for a rental motorcycle under the Travel on Your Own program, you must complete a booking application provided by Bosenberg. Your deposit must accompany your application.

Other Services:

- Travel kit, which will be at your rental center, that includes a country map, regional tourist information, and other useful information upon your arrival. Included are brochures that describe Biker's Hotels in Austria. These hotels have special events and prices that attract touring motorcyclists from throughout Europe. For instance, the Hotel Solaria in Obertauern, just south of Salzburg, will give each of their guests a roadbook that highlights day trips of the surrounding areas. Don't miss out on the superb Austrian hospitality.
- If requested on your booking application, hotel accommodations for your designated arrival and departure dates will be made for you in the vicinity of the rental center.

Special Notes:

It is also possible to schedule a one-way rental between the two rental stations. This special arrangement will cost $200.

California MotoTours

2170 Avenida de la Playa #B
La Jolla, CA 92037

Booking Agent:

Ms. Izabella Miram, Terra Tours
Phone: 800-444-9554 or
619-454-9551
FAX: 619-454-3549
Telex: 495-0609

Motorcycles Available:

Cruiser Style Motorcycles:
- Yamaha Virago, 500cc
- Suzuki Intruder, 700cc
- Yamaha Maxim, 750cc

Sport Bike:
- Kawasaki EX 500

Larger Touring Motorcycles:
- BMW R80RT, 800cc
- Honda Sabre V65, 1100cc
- Honda Gold Wing, 1200cc

Prices:
- Yamaha Virago: $43 per day with 100 free miles, plus $.14 for each extra mile; $600 for 14 days; $650 for 17 days.
- Suzuki Intruder: $43 per day with 100 free miles, plus $.14 for each extra mile; $700 for 14 days; $750 for 17 days.
- Yamaha Maxim: $50 per day with 100 free miles, plus $.14 for each extra mile; $750 for 14 days; $800 for 17 days.
- Kawasaki EX 500: $43 per day with 100 free miles, plus $.14 for each extra mile; $700 for 14 days; $750 for 17 days.
- BMW R80RT: $68 per day with 100 free miles, plus $.18 for each extra mile; $850 for 14 days; $925 for 17 days.
- Honda Sabre V65: $58 per day with 100 free miles, plus $.18 for each extra mile; $750 for 14 days; $800 for 17 days.
- Honda Gold Wing: $84 per day with 100 free miles, plus $.20 for each extra mile.

Price Includes:
Liability insurance. Free 100 miles per day; mileage charge thereafter.

Deposit Required:
Security deposit is $500 per motorcycle. Cash or travelers checks required.

Insurance Arrangements:
Rental price includes liability coverage ($100,000) and collision damage with $500 deductible.

Accessories:
Some motorcycles have windshields and/or saddle bags. Inquire at time of rental to get details.

Special Requirements:
Renter must be at least 21 years of age and have driver's license valid for motorcycle operation.

Reservations:
Must be made 90 days in advance, as the supply of motorcycles is limited.

Other services:
California MotoTours also operates guided tours of the United States southwest.

Harley Owners Group (H.O.G.) – Fly & Ride Program

Description:
H.O.G. operates a Fly & Ride program in nine different locations around the world to offer the opportunity for year-round motorcycling vacations. To make reservations, call the H.O.G. office listed below. From the rental location, you may travel anywhere you wish, except Mexico. Rental vehicles must be picked up and returned to the Harley-Davidson agent in that location. Pick-up and drop-off times must coincide with the operating hours of those businesses. Vehicle must be returned to the same location where it was picked up.

H.O.G. Office:	Harley Owners Group P.O. Box 453 Milwaukee, WI 53201 Contact: H.O.G. representatives Phone: 800-258-2464 (800-242-2464 in Wisconsin; 416-741-5510 in Canada; call collect at 414-935-4522 in Alaska and Hawaii) FAX: 414-935-4977 Telex: Not available
Frankfurt Agent:	Harley-Davidson Motor Company Raunheim Industriestraße 7 Frankfurt WEST GERMANY
Miami Agent:	Harley-Davidson, Inc. of Miami 7701 NW Seventh Avenue Miami, FL 33150
Vancouver Agent:	Trev Deeley Motorcycles, Ltd. 606 East Broadway Vancouver, B.C. V5T 1X6 CANADA
Reno Agent:	Harley-Davidson of Reno 3180 Mill Street Reno, NV 89502

MOTORCYCLE RENTAL AGENCIES

Tempe Agent:	Chosa's Harley-Davidson, Inc. 617 South Hayden Road Tempe, AZ 85281
Orlando Agent:	Dick Farmer's Harley-Davidson of Orlando, Inc. 46 North Orange Blossom Trail Orlando, FL 32805
Boston Agent:	Cycle Craft Co., Inc. 1813 Revere Beach Parkway Everett, MA 02149
Honolulu Agent:	Cycle City Ltd. Honolulu Harley-Davidson Sales 2965 North Nimitz Highway Honolulu, HI 96819
Los Angeles Agent:	Harley-Davidson of Glendale 3717 San Fernando Road Glendale, CA 91204
Hours:	These agents are open at various business hours. Contact the H.O.G. office for details.

Motorcycles Available:
Several different models of Harley-Davidson motorcycle are available at each location. Models usually include: FLTs, FLHTs, and FXRTs. Preferences for specific models will be allowed on a first come, first served basis. The number of machines available is limited. Make your reservations early.

Prices:
Rates are $50 per day (for 24 hours), with $100 minimum; $250 per week (seven days). A 20% discount is given for rentals of four weeks or more.

Price Includes:
Insurance (see below); free mileage; state and local taxes.

Deposit Required:
A 50% deposit is required to hold your reservation; the remaining 50% must be received at least three weeks before motorcycle is to be picked up.

Insurance Arrangements:
H.O.G. provides liability insurance up to $10,000 per person, but not more than $20,000 per accident, and property damage up to $5,000. Renter is responsible for the first $250 of any physical damage to the rent-

al vehicle, and the first $1,000 loss due to theft. A waiver of the $1,000 responsibility for theft loss can be purchased for $5 per day or $25 per week. Insurance limits may differ in various locations.

Methods of Payment:
Payment must be made by check at the Harley Owners Group office in Milwaukee.

Accessories:
Normal equipment found with each motorcycle.

Special Requirements:
Fly & Ride is available only to H.O.G. members. Motorcycle rider and passenger must wear a D.O.T. approved safety helmet at all times. Vehicle will be provided with a full tank of gas and oil. Additional gas or oil needed en oute must be provided by the renter.

Reservations:
All reservations must be made through the Harley Owners Group office in Milwaukee at least three weeks in advance of the pickup date. No reservation is confirmed until the deposit is received.

Other services:
The Harley Owners Group offers a number of other benefits to its members.

Motorrad Spaett, KG

Rüdesheimerstraße, 9
8000 Munich 21
WEST GERMANY

Contact:
Mr. Paul Spaett or office
Phone: (49) 089-57937-38
FAX: (49) 089-57017-69
Telex: 5216823 mosp

Motorcycles Available:
Various types from 50cc city bikes to 350cc dual-purpose bikes to 1500cc street touring bikes. All motorcycles are Honda or Yamaha. All motorcycles are new.

Prices:
- One day: 59 DM to 319 DM
- One week: 5 times daily rate
- Two weeks: 9 times daily rate
- Three weeks: 13 times daily rate
- Four weeks: 17 times daily rate
- Five weeks: 21 times daily rate
- Six weeks: 25 times daily rate

Price Includes:
Unlimited mileage.

Deposit Required:
Security deposit of 1,500 DM per unit. Major credit cards (Diners, American Express) or cash required.

Insurance Arrangements:
All vehicles are fully insured for comprehensive damage, with deductible of 1,500 DM (that is, you pay the first 1,500 DM of any damage caused by you; the insurance pays above that). An exclusion to the deductible amount is not possible. It is possible to travel to other European countries, but in case of damage you will have to arrange and pay for transport of youself and the motorcycle back to Munich.

Accessories:
Tank bags and clothing can be rented. Windshields are available only on touring bikes. Helmets can be rented for a small charge. Supply is limited.

Special Requirements:
Primary renter must be at least 18 years of age for motorcycle under 50hp, and at least 21 years of age for motorcycle over 50hp. Renters need a passport and driver's license validated for motorcycle operation. German or American driver's license is acceptable, as is international driver's license validated for motorcycle operation.

Reservations:
Reservations must be made at least four weeks in advance. Inventory of motorcycles is limited.

Other services:
- Motorcycle parts, service, and accessories.
- Guided tours to Turkey.

Moturis, Ltd.

MOTURIS

P.O. Box 1294
CH 8058 Zurich Airport
SWITZERLAND

Office: Kirchgasse 22
8302 Kloten
SWITZERLAND

Contact:
Ms. Conny Miro
Phone: (41) 01/814-09-61
FAX: (41) 01/814-14-79
Telex: 829 380 USAT CH

Rental Locations:
United States: New York, Miami, Los Angeles. Canada: Vancouver.

Motorcycles Available:
- Honda Gold Wing, 1300cc, four-cylinder, shaft driven, AM/FM cassette radio, top and saddle bags, fairing, and windshield.
- BMW R80RT, 800cc boxer engine, two-cylinder, shaft driven, luggage carrier, luggage case, fairing, and windshield.
- Yamaha Maxim XJ 750, four-cylinder, shaft driven, saddle bags, windshield.

Prices:
- Honda: $72 per day plus $.20 per mile over 100 miles; CDW insurance $12 per day; VIP insurance $16 per day.
- BMW: $58 per day plus $.18 per mile over 100 miles; CDW insurance $10 per day; VIP insurance $14 per day.
- Yamaha: $42 per day plus $.14 per mile over 100 miles; CDW insurance $8 per day; VIP insurance $12 per day.
- Penalty for change in confirmed reservation: $25 for each change beyond the first.
- Penalty for cancellation of reservation: up to 31 days prior to rental date, $100; 30 days or less prior to rental date, 100% of rental price.
- Penalty for late drop-off: $30 per hour; $300 per day.
- Surcharge for cleaning the motorcycle, if it is returned dirty, $50.
- Surcharge for drop-off at different location, $300.

Price Includes:
Free 100 miles per day; mileage charge thereafter. Free transfer from airport to rental location.

Deposit Required:
Security deposit is $2,500 per unit without CDW or VIP insurance. With CDW insurance, security deposit is $500. With VIP insurance, security deposit is $100. Major credit cards (VISA, MC, AMEX), cash, or travelers checks required.

Insurance Arrangements:
Rental price includes liability coverage ($100,000 in U.S.) and collision damage with $2,500 deductible. A Collision Damage Waiver (CDW) can be purchased to reduce the collision damage deductible to $500. Or, Vacation Interruption Protection (VIP) insurance can be purchased to reduce the collision damage deductible to $100.

Accessories:
Camping equipment is offered to renters at $50 per person. Neither helmets nor any special clothing are available from Moturis; renter is responsible for his own.

Special Requirements:
Minimum rental is seven days. Renter must be at least 21 years of age and have driver's license valid for motorcycle operation.

Reservations:
Must be made well in advance, as the supply of motorcycles is limited. Contact Zurich office.

Other services:
Moturis also offers campers and trailers for rent.

Pancho Villa Moto-Rentals

9437 E.B. Taulbee
El Paso, TX 79924

Contact:
Mr. Skip Mascorro
Phone: 915-757-3032
FAX: 915-562-1505
Telex: Not available

| Hours: | 8:30 a.m. to 5:30 p.m. Monday through Saturday |

Motorcycles Available:

A variety of Harley-Davidson full-dress touring machines; other makes and models including a limited supply of Honda Gold Wings, Yamaha Ventures, and various sport machines. All range from 1984 to current year models. Call for updated inventory. Over thirty to choose from.

Prices:

Each unit is graded on one of three levels depending on year, model, and condition. Prices range from $45 to $85 per day with six days minimum rental. Ask about discounts for groups of six or more motorcycles.

Price Includes:

Free 150 miles per day. Only $.15 per mile over 150 miles per day.

Deposit Required:

Ranges from $200 to $600 cash or major credit card depending on category of motorcycle rented. Security deposit is refunded when the unit is returned undamaged.

Insurance Arrangements:

Riders from the U.S. or Canada should make their own arrangements through their personal carrier. Pancho Villa Moto-Rentals will provide the renter with the necessary data for obtaining coverage.

Accessories:

Renters are expected to provide their own riding helmet and apparel. Full touring motorcycles will have wind screens and protective fairings as well as luggage accommodations. A limited selection of soft luggage is available for sport machines.

Special Requirements:

Each rider must be a licensed motorcyclist with at least three years riding experience, and must be 25 years or older. Riders and passengers must sign a standard release of liability.

Reservations:

Riders are urged to allow at least 15 working days to permit ample time for processing insurance (when applicable). Riders and passengers must sign a standard release of liability.

Other services:

Escorted motorcycle tours of Old Mexico, New Zealand, U.S., and Canada. Dual purpose motorcycle expeditions. Volume sales of used motorcycles to foreign markets. Processing of vehicle permits and visas for Mexico.

Scootabout Motorcycle Centre

59 Albert Embankment
London SE1 7TP
ENGLAND

Contact:
Mr. C.S.C. Ram, Director
Phone: (44) 01-582-0055
FAX: (44) 01-735-7818
Telex: Not available

Hours: Monday through Friday, 9 a.m. to 6 p.m.; Saturday 9 a.m. to 2 p.m.

Motorcycles Available:
Various types from mopeds to 750cc street touring machines. The larger machines are most suitable for touring and are maintained to high standards by Scootabout mechanics. In the event of a breakdown or tire puncture, the Automobile Association (AA) service (included in rental fee) provides for free assistance or transport of the machine anywhere in the U.K.

Prices:

	Per Day	Per Week
Moped (min. age 18)	£10.95	£54.50
Honda CG125 (min. age 18)	£12.95	£64.50
Honda CD250 (min. age 21)	£16.50	£82.50
Suzuki GN250 250 (min. age 21)	£16.50	£82.50
Honda VT500 (min. age 21)	£19.95	£99.50
Kawasaki GT750 (min. age 25)	£25.00	£125.00

Note: two new machines will be introduced to the Scootabout fleet in 1989: the Honda Revere NTV600 and the Kawasaki GTR1000. Contact Scootabout for availability and rates.

Monthly rate: 25% discount from weekly rate.

All prices subject to 15% Valued Added Tax.

Price Includes:
Insurance; unlimited mileage; open-faced helmet; luggage carrier; AA membership. Rental fee payable in advance at the start of the rental period. Not included: gas and oil required during the trip.

Deposit Required:
Security deposit is £100, payable by: cash, check with bank card, VISA, Access/Mastercard, American Express, and travelers checks.

Insurance Arrangements:
Liability and collision insurance for driving in the U.K. included in the price. Renter is responsible for the first £250 of damage to the motorcycle in the event of an accident. If you want to take the motorcycle to Europe, you need "green card" insurance, which costs about £25 per week (or part) and which Scootabout can arrange. AA Continental Cover is also needed; price is £27.50 for one to ten days and £34.50 for 11 to 31 days.

Accessories:
Open-faced helmets offered free to renters. A selection of full-face helmets, clothing, and accessories are available for rent at very reasonable rates.

Special Requirements:
Renter must have driver's license validated for motorcycle operation and be of minimum age listed above. International driver's license validated for motorcycle operation preferred.

Reservations:
Recommended. With limited supply, it is desirable to reserve a machine early. Scootabout needs details of time, dates, and type of machine desired. Reservation requires money order or credit card in the sum of £20 to secure a confirmed reservation. The deposit will be applied to the rental charge.

Other Services:
- Motorcycle sales, service, repairs, accessories.

South Pacific Motorcycle Tours Ltd.

AA Travel (Wairarapa) Ltd.
Chapel Street, Masterton
NEW ZEALAND

Contact:
Mr. Glen Bull
Phone: (64) 59 82222
FAX: (64) 59 82485
Telex: NZ 3982

Hours: Monday through Friday: 8 a.m. to 6 p.m.

Motorcycles Available:
Various Honda Gold Wing models, or 400cc Hondas.

Prices:
$54 per day plus $.10 per mile. Free instruction on New Zealand traffic laws if required.

Deposit Required: $200

Insurance Arrangements:
$360 bond is payable on delivery of motorcycle. This bond is refunded at end of rental period if no damage has been sustained, or insurance claim made. Third Party coverage, (i.e., damage to another person's property) is included in above. Renter is responsible for his insurance on riding clothes, and medical insurance.

Accessories:
Machines are equipped with fairings and pannier equipment. Renter is responsible for his own helmet and clothing.

Special Requirements:
Primary renter must be at least 23 years of age and have international driver's license and passport.

Reservations:
Essential. If booking by mail, allow at least one month for return of confirmation.

Other services:
Personally conducted tours with full back-up facilities are available, length of tour tailored to group requirements. South Pacific Motorcycle Tours of-

fers advice and assistance in planning trips, and will supply free tour maps and brochures. South Pacific will meet you at Wellington Airport and transport you to Masterton for collection of your rental motorcycle. Accommodations can be arranged if requested.

Te Waipounamu Motorcycle Tours

	P.O. Box 673 Christchurch NEW ZEALAND Contact: Mr. John Rains Phone: (64) 03 794 320 or (64) 03 427 503 FAX: (64) 03 842 345 Telex: Not available
Booking Agent:	Starquest World Tours 1120-87 Avenue S.W. Calgary, Alberta T2V 0W1 CANADA Phone: 403-252-4641 FAX: 403-229-2788
Booking Agent:	Schnieder Reisen Schomburgst 120 2000 Hamburg 50 WEST GERMANY Phone: (49) 40 38 02 06 33 FAX: (49) 40 38 89 65
Booking Agent:	Mr. Volker Lenzner TransCyclist International CPO Box 2064 Tokyo, 100-91 JAPAN Phone: (81) 3-402-5385 FAX: (81) 3-402-5358

Motorcycles Available:
- BMW R-series 800cc and 1000cc models; side bags, fairing, and windshield.
- Yamaha XV750; side bags, fairing, and windshield.
- Honda GL400 and GL500 models; side bags, fairing, and windshield.

Prices:
(Prices are in New Zealand dollars, for one-week period)
- BMW R-series 800cc and 1000cc models or Yamaha 750 cc: $395 NZ plus $.13 NZ per km.
- Honda 400cc and 500cc models: $325 NZ plus $.13 NZ per km.

Deposit Required:
Security deposit is $500 NZ per unit; will be refunded if motorcycle is returned without damage.

Insurance Arrangements:
Rental price includes liability coverage.

Accessories:
Helmet, gloves, and rain suits are available for rent at a nominal cost.

Special Requirements:
Renter must be at least 21 years of age (25 years of age for larger motorcycles) and have driver's license valid for motorcycle operation. Te Waipounamu reserves the right to decline to rent to anyone for any reason.

Reservations:
Should be made in advance, as the supply of motorcycles is limited.

Other services:
Te Waipounamu also runs guided tours of New Zealand and can offer considerable assistance in planning your trip, arranging accommodations, and suggesting routes in New Zealand.

Tours, S.R.L.

VENEZUELA EN MOTOCICLETA
Venezuela on bike

Edif. Res. Los Sauces
Entrada A, Piso 8, Apto. 1
Valencia
VENEZUELA

Contact:
Mr. Werner Glode or Mr. Martin Glode
Phone: (58) 41-213007 (office) or (58) 41-213752 (home)
FAX: (58) 41-342950
Telex: (58) 41-45116

Motorcycles Available:
Yamaha RD 350 LC

Prices:
$30 per day; $180 per week

Security Deposit:
A deposit equal to the full value of the motorcycle is required; refunded when the bike is returned free of damage.

Motorcycle Insurance:
Liability insurance provided by Tours S.R.L.; insurance for the motorcycle itself is not available in Venezuela.

Helmets:
Riders are expected to bring their own.

Reservations:
Must be made in advance as there is a limited number of machines.

Other Services:
• Guided tours of Venezuela.

Von Thielmann Tours

P.O. Box 87764
San Diego, CA 92138

VON THIELMANN TOURS

Contact:
Ms. Gina Guzzardo
Phone: 619-463-7788 or
619-291-7057
FAX: 619-291-4630
Telex: 910 335 1607 MESA SERV SDG

Motorcycles Available:
Touring, sports, and chopper type motorcycles. From approximately 400cc to 1200cc.

Prices:
Germany: from approximately $45 per day and up, depending on size. Minimum rental is three days. Flat rates available, including mileage.

California: from approximately $48 per day plus $5 per day for insurance. Minimum rental is two weeks. Includes 2,000 free miles per week.

Deposit Required:
Germany, $600; California, $500.

Insurance Arrangements:
Included is liability insurance and comprehensive insurance with a deductible.

Other Services:
- Guided tours.

MOTORCYCLE SHIPPING FACILITIES

In response to inquiries from several travel agencies and prospective overseas travelers, we have identified two companies that will help you ship motorcycles. Of course, most ships and ferries that carry automobiles will also carry motorcycles if they are properly secured. Some tour operators will arrange for shipment of motorcycles as part of their total service menu for clients. See the Tour Operator section for details. Please let us know if you find other companies that offer motorcycle shipping services.

Admiral Cruises, Inc.

P.O. Box 010882
Miami, FL 33101

Contact: Your local travel agent

Description:
Admiral Cruises operates the cruise ship Stardancer between Vancouver, British Columbia and several ports in Alaska (allowing disembarkation at Skagway); also between Los Angeles and several ports in Mexico (allowing disembarkation at Puerto Vallarta or Mazatlan). A great vacation idea is to combine a cruise with local touring on your own by motorcycle. Contact Admiral Cruises or your local travel agent for specific dates, prices, and vehicle arrangements.

Overseas Brokers, Inc.

111 Great Neck Road
Great Neck, NY 11021

Contact: Mr. Doron Weissman, President
Phone: 800-752-1102 or 516-773-6100
Telex: 4937607 OVBR UI

Description:
Overseas Brokers, Inc. offers transport of motorcycles and other equipment between points in the U.S. and anywhere in the world. They have handled many domestic and international shipments by air as well as by sea. They handle crating and all other aspects of motorcycle transport. They are experts in the documentation necessary for shipping motorcycles temporarily overseas (for competition or tours) to avoid trade duties.

In 1987 they handled the shipment of 13 motorcycles for the U.S. motorcycle team to and from Poland for the International Six-Day Enduro (ISDE) competition, without a single problem.

As the prices and details are dependent upon the destination of your trip and other factors, contact Overseas Brokers for more specific information.

RIDES AND RALLIES IN THE U.S.

In this section we have listed only rallies of national scope that have attracted at least 5,000 attendees in the past. At least three of these rallies are endorsed by local civic organizations such as the Chamber of Commerce, showing that motorcycle touring enthusiasts can be desirable visitors and important to the economy of an area.

In addition to the major events described here, there are countless gatherings held throughout the year for motorcycling enthusiasts. *Rider* and *Road Rider* magazines are good sources of information about touring activities. For those interested in more local events, participation in clubs and associations provide excellent opportunities to network.

Americade '89 East

Rally Sponsor:	Americade, Inc. P.O. Box 2205K Glens Falls, NY 12801
	Contact: Mr. William Dutcher, President Phone: 518-656-3696 (24-hour taped hotline)

Location:
Lake George, New York. Headquarters is Roaring Brook Ranch/Resort.

Dates: June 6 through June 10, 1989 (Tuesday through Saturday)

Main theme:
Fun! A gathering place for touring riders on all brands of motorcycle.

Background:
The world's largest touring rally, in 1988 it drew over 25,000 touring enthusiasts from across America and Canada, plus Japan and Europe. In 1983 Bill and Gini Dutcher started Aspencade East in Lake George. Approximately 3,000 attended that event. In 1986 they changed the name to Americade to better describe the scope of this rally. That year it drew about 15,000. Dutcher spent about 25 years in the motorcycle industry, working for Bultaco, Can-Am, and Harley-Davidson. He believed that a multi-brand touring rally with a multitude of activities could be hosted successfully in one community without moving around annually, as many other rallies do. The growth of the Lake George rally, every year in the same community, supports this philosophy.

Highlights:
Activities include: demo rides from the six major manufacturers (Honda, BMW, Harley-Davidson, Kawasaki, Suzuki, and Yamaha); steamboat cruises with live music, dancing, and buffet; or harness race evening with live music and barbecue; over $20,000 in door prizes including a 1989 Honda Gold Wing, Time-Out camper trailer, Kompact Kamp cargo trailer, and thousands of dollars in daily door prizes; TourExpo, the world's largest exposition of touring products; poker run; bike and rider judging with over 100 trophies; field events; light show; mini tours; touring videos; music and dancing nightly; top quality rally pin, patch, decal, and 60-plus-page, full color official program. Also, seminars by industry experts, Honda's riding fitness adventure (combination poker run and safety train-

ing); treasure hunt, where a motorcycle is not necessary to participate, and dozens of other activities.

Exhibitors and Special Events:
TourExpo traditionally draws more touring product exhibitors than any other trade show in North America. Many exhibitors offer discounts or special services: tire manufacturers who offer free mounting and tire checking, oil distributors who offer free oil changes with the purchase of oil, and all kinds of pinstripers, etchers, leather craftsmen, and chrome specialists who distribute goodies. Huge parade followed by BMW barbecue. There is a special door prize drawing for members of the American Motorcyclist Association.

Lodging Arrangements:
Lake George has sleeping accommodations for over 20,000 within a 15-minute drive. There are hundreds of small motels and dozens of campgrounds. There are even three state campgrounds nearby. Motel rates range from $25 per night up to approximately $80 per night. For a vacation community, the rates are fairly reasonable.

Reservations can be made either through the Lake George Regional Convention and Visitors Bureau (LGRCVB) (call 518-668-4617), or directly to one of the motels or campgrounds. LGRCVB's brochure is included with the standard Americade information package.

Contrary to popular rumor, there is always space available *somewhere*. One month before the event, most of the nearby accommodations are taken, so you may have to drive 15 minutes or more. Sometimes space becomes available in the Roaring Brook headquarters shortly before the rally, when some industry personnel cancel out. It's worth a call to Roaring Brook.

Price:
$40 for riders and $35 for passengers pre-registering (must be received by April 30, 1989). After May 1 the price is $50 for riders and $45 for passengers. Price for day trippers is $10.

Special Notes:
Americade East (and West) are, once again, the only national touring events, as recognized by the American Motorcyclist Association. In *Road Rider* magazine's writeup on the 1988 event, editor Bob Carpenter noted, "In an era when rallies try to outdo each other, Americade Lake George has emerged as King of the Rallies."

June in Lake George tends to be 75° days, 65° nights. However, 10 degrees higher or lower is not uncommon. Sundown comes about 8:30 p.m. so there are lots of hours for riding the interesting back roads of the area. Be sure to bring your camera and a smile.

Americade '89 Rockies

Rally Sponsor:	Americade, Inc. P.O. Box 2205K Glens Falls, NY 12801
	Contact: Mr. William Dutcher, President Phone: 518-656-3696 (24-hour taped hotline)
Location:	Estes Park, Colorado
Dates:	September 4 through September 8, 1989 (Monday through Friday)

Main theme:
Fun! An end-of-season gathering point for riders on all motorcycle brands, from both sides of North America.

Background:
Americade Rockies started in 1987 to give western U.S. riders the opportunity to enjoy Americade in a magnificent environment close to home. After reviewing a half-dozen possible sites in Colorado and Wyoming, the Dutchers selected Estes Park because it had the best combination of scenic roads, level parking, friendly town, spacious headquarters, and a variety of accommodations. Also, the eastern slope of the Rockies had a lower likelihood of rain in the fall than the western slope.

Highlights:
Activities include: demo rides from the six major manufacturers (Honda, BMW, Harley-Davidson, Kawasaki, Suzuki, and Yamaha); mini tours of the Rockies; chuck wagon dinner and western show, or country music dinner theater; TourExpo, the big touring trade show; poker run; field events; bike judging; over 100 trophies; light show bonfire; touring videos; live entertainment; top quality rally pin, patch, decal; and large full color program. Also, $20,000 in door prizes including brand new Honda Pacific Coast touring motorcycle, Time-Out camper trailer, Kompact Kamp cargo trailer, and thousands of dollars in daily door prize drawings.

Exhibitors and Special Events:
Although TourExpo is not as large as the eastern event, scores of pinstripers, etchers, leather craftsmen, chrome, oil, and tire distributors and dozens of other exhibitors will be present. During the Thursday night light show and bonfire, a special bagpipe band will play. Musical entertainment is a large part of the Americade experience, with music during the

opening celebration, throughout the event, and at the awards ceremony on Friday. Parade through Estes Park to fairgrounds and the BMW barbecue. There is a special door prize drawing for members of the American Motorcyclist Association.

Lodging Arrangements:

There is a wide variety of motels and campgrounds in Estes Park. Prices start around $25 a night and go up to approximately $55 a night. YMCA rooms in Estes Park tend to be rustic.

Reservations are handled by the Estes Park area Visitors Center (call 800-44-ESTES), or through the YMCA of the Rockies (Americade Rockies headquarters).

Price:

$35 for riders and $30 for passengers pre-registering (must be received by June 30, 1989). After July 1 the price is $45 for riders and $40 for passengers. Price for day trippers is $10.

Special Notes:

This western cousin of the eastern Americade is the only other 1989 national touring rally, as recognized by the American Motorcyclist Association.

Running across the middle of Rocky Mountain National Park is Trail Ridge Road, the highest continuous paved highway in North America, 12,200 feet in altitude. This provides a variety of special weather challenges, but is one of the most beautiful and memorable roads in the world. People with a heart condition should exercise caution. One should always pack a variety of clothing, at 12,000 plus feet the weather can turn cold very suddenly. However, September weather in Estes Park tends to be 75° days, and 45° nights. This is a dry climate, so both the heat and the cold are quite pleasant. Be sure to bring your camera, sunglasses, longies, and a smile!

Black Hills Motor Classic

Rally Sponsor:

Jackpine Gypsies Motorcycle Club
P.O. Box 504
Sturgis, SD 57785

Contact:
Mr. Neil Hultman
Phone: 605-347-2556

314 RIDES AND RALLIES IN THE U.S.

Location: Sturgis, South Dakota, in the Black Hills of southwestern South Dakota.

Dates:
- August 7 through August 13, 1989
- August 6 August 12, 1990 (the 50th year)

Main theme:
To promote motorcycling events and activities for all motorcycle enthusiasts. Come celebrate the 49th year of this open rally — for all types of motorcyclists and all brands of motorcycles.

Background:
Every year during the second week in August the Black Hills vibrate with the sound of cycles — sounds generated by one of the oldest open rallies in existence today: The Black Hills Motor Classic. The Classic is organized by two non-profit organizations, the Sturgis Area Chamber of Commerce and the Jackpine Gypsies Motorcycle Club.

Both the Classic and the Jackpine Gypsies Motorcycle Club were founded in 1937 by Mr. J.C. "Pappy" Hoel, the local Indian motorcycle dealer. The rally in Sturgis began with a half-mile race at the city fairgrounds with a $200 purse provided by Hoel and several local business people. This successful race became the annual event each year. The Jackpine Gypsies also promoted a one-day tour to Mt. Rushmore National Memorial, and in later years, as rally attendance increased, added a second tour to Devils Tower, Wyoming.

The 1988 rally drew an estimated 60,000 to 65,000 people. What will 1989 bring?!

Highlights:
Tours to the Mt. Rushmore National Memorial and to Devils Tower, Wyoming are offered; poker run; the Custom Chrome Hill Climb; and the Third Annual Big Daddy Rat Custom Chopper Trike and Motorcycle Show. Races include: the 600cc Miller Draft National Championship Short Track Race; the U.S. Western Regional Half Mile Championship Race; the Pro-Am Short Track Race; the Pro-Am Half Mile; the Vintage TT and Half Mile Races for pre-1972 motorcycles; and the Sturgis Third Annual Harley National Dragstrip Finals.

Exhibitors and Special Events:
A wide range of vendors set up on both sides of Main Street during rally week: aftermarket accessories, parts, sheepskin, jewelry, leathers, etc. Products bearing the rally's official logo help support the event by donating 10% of the product price to the rally.

And perhaps you may even see some of the major motorcycle manufacturers there . . . like maybe Harley-Davidson, BMW, and Honda? Maybe there will be a few bikes available for demo rides? Arrangements still were being made with potential exhibitors when this Directory went to press.

Lodging Arrangements:

The rally organizers provide a listing of motels and campgrounds in the Sturgis area. Phone numbers of four Northern Hills Area Chambers of Commerce may also be provided for lodging and tourist information. Contact the Black Hills Motor Classic at P.O. Box 504 in Sturgis for more information.

Price:

A registration fee of $12 per person is charged for each of the following events:
- Poker Run
- Tour to Mt. Rushmore National Memorial
- Tour to Devils Tower. For the two tours, the $12/person covers any entrance fees to the parks, a noon meal, and emergency road service, if needed. All registration for the tours and poker run takes place at Rally Headquarters on Main Street. You may register as soon as you arrive in town, or up to 30 minutes prior to the start of each event.

Special Notes:

Sturgis is located in the beautiful Black Hills of South Dakota, one of the most scenic areas in the country. Plan to spend several days taking in the beauty. Visit the Indian Museum of North America at Crazy Horse Mountain near Mt. Rushmore. Tour the Homestake Gold Mine. Be cautious on the curving roads of the Black Hills. Bring your camera and have a good time!

1989 International CLASSIC

Rally Sponsor:	BMW Motorcycle Owners of America P.O. Box 489 Chesterfield, MO 63006-0489 Contact: Mr. D.N. Douglass, Managing Director , Phone: 314-537-5511
Location:	York, Pennsylvania
Dates:	July 27 through July 30, 1989

Main theme:	International gathering of BMW enthusiasts

Background:
1973 marked the date of the first BMW Motorcycle Owners of America (BMW MOA) National Rally, an event organized to bring together all BMW enthusiasts from around the country to kick tires and swap stories. This annual event is the largest rally sponsored by BMW MOA and has grown to become an international gathering. Approximately 6,000 members/people attended in 1988.

The 1989 rally will be at the York County Agricultural Society fairgrounds, which covers 120 fenced acres.

Highlights:
Factory technical seminars; motorcycle safety, education, and skills classes; maintenance seminar; motorcycle competitive skilled events; tours of historic sites; vintage BMW motorcycle judging, with awards; field events (non-competitive) for riders: 2 km Fun Run (foot race); 10 km Serious Run; kite flying contest; volleyball; music and dancing.

This year's rally will draw about 7,000 riders from as far away as Great Britain, Europe, Canada, and Japan.

Exhibitors and Special Events:
There will be more than 50 aftermarket vendors, along with BMW of North America.

Lodging Arrangements:
York County has lots of motel rooms available. The city of York wants to help BMW MOA and their room-providers, so they've asked to coordinate your motel/hotel room reservations. Please contact the York County Convention & Visitors Bureau, P.O. Box 1229, York, PA 17405, 717-848-4000. They will send you a list and map of accommodations available; you should designate your three choices, and confirmations will be returned to you.

Price:
For registration by June 1: $18 per adult. For registration at the gate: $22 per adult.

Special Notes:
York is a National Historic Landmark, and not far away, in south central Pennsylvania, is the home of the Pennsylvania Dutch. The city of York offers attractions from museums to wineries. Gettysburg is 30 miles away; Washington, D.C. is 100 miles; the Blue Ridge Parkway is 75 miles west of York.

Rider Rally East

Rally Sponsor:	*Rider* Magazine P.O. Box 4000 Agoura, CA 91301 Contact: Mr. Marvin Miller, Rally Director Phone: 800-234-3450 or 818-991-4980
Location:	Richmond, Kentucky
Dates:	May 25 through May 29, 1989
Main theme:	Tour the Blue Grass country

Background:
This will be the third rally sponsored by *Rider*. Their two *Rider's Roamin' Wyoming Rallies* were such a smashing success they decided to have an event in Richmond, Kentucky so that rally enthusiasts in the east won't miss out. Quite simply, popular demand asked for an eastern rally, and here it is. More than 5,000 enthusiasts are expected to attend.

Highlights:
Trade fair; guided scenic and historic tours; CMA services; daily bike judging; charity poker run; safety seminar; daily field events; Best of Show judging; barbecue; entertainment; touring bike giveaway, a Kawasaki Voyager 12; factory demonstration rides; Memorial Day parade.

Exhibitors and Special Events:
Trade Fair, with six major manufacturers plus over 50 accessory vendors. Field events will be conducted on the specially built driving range constructed and maintained just for this purpose by the State of Kentucky.

Lodging Arrangements:
Eight motels, dorm rooms, seven campgrounds with 800 sites within 10 to 35 miles from Richmond, Kentucky. Call motels directly for reservations. For reservation of dorm rooms at Eastern Kentucky University, contact: Special Programs at 606-622-1224. For further information call Richmond Tourist Department, 606-623-0758.

Price:
$50 per person for Rider subscriber/club members and spouses. $55 per person for non-club members.

Special Notes:
Bring your state flag for the Memorial Day Parade.

Rider Rally West

Rally Sponsor:	*Rider* Magazine P.O. Box 4000 Agoura, CA 91301 Contact: Mr. Marvin Miller, Rally Director Phone: 800-234-3450 or 818-991-4980
Location:	Reno, Nevada
Dates:	August 27 through August 31, 1989
Main theme:	Tour Lake Tahoe country

Background:
This will be the fourth rally sponsored by *Rider*. As 2,000 people attended the '88 rally in Cody, Wyoming, they project this year's event will receive over 3,000 participants.

Highlights:
Trade fair; seminars; motorcycle judging; field events; charity poker run; entertainment; great mini tours; factory demonstration rides; touring bike giveaway, a Kawasaki Concours; Grand Parade.

Exhibitors and Special Events:
Trade fair. There will be five major manufacturers plus over 50 accessory vendors.

Lodging Arrangements:
Once you've registered for the rally, *Rider* will furnish you with a list of nearby motels and accommodations.

Price:
$45 per person for *Rider* subscribers/club members and spouses. $50 per person for non-members. After July 1, 1989: add $5 for each category.

Special Notes:
Rally headquarters will be in the Holiday Inn on Sixth Street. Bring your state flag for the Grand Parade.

V-Daze V

Rally Sponsor:	Venture Touring Society 1615 South Eastern Avenue Las Vegas, NV 89104
V-Daze	Contact: Mr. Joe Schaerer, Executive Director Phone: 702-457-6657
Location:	Hot Springs, Arkansas
Dates:	June 26 through July 1, 1989

Main theme:
Come share the Venture Touring Society (VTS) tradition of friendship and fun.

Background:
V-Daze is an annual convention for VTS members and friends to get together. This event is open to the public.

Future V-Daze plans are to alternate the rally site on a four-year rotating basis between the states of Wyoming, Arkansas, Michigan, and New Mexico.

Highlights:
MRC course; field events; poker runs; big barbecue; boat rides; minitours; TourXpo; seminars; clinics; demos; bike show and judging; light show and parade; picnic in the park at Magic Springs, a theme and ride park; special benefit concert for Make a Wish Foundation; and much more.

Exhibitors and Special Events:
Over 50 vendors will be exhibiting products ranging from accessories to insurance.

Special events:
- Music Mountain Jamboree Show
- Belle of Hot Springs Poker Run

• Saturday Charity Poker Run

Lodging Arrangements:
A list of hotels/motels and campgrounds is available. Reservations may be made by contacting the Housing Bureau at 800-543-BATH. Discounts available for VTS and American Motorcyclist Association (AMA) members.

Price:
Early registrants receive a discount and become eligible for a pre-registration prize. Registration must be postmarked before June 1, 1989 for these discounted fees:
- VTS members: $42 for rider; $38 for passenger
- AMA/VTS Booster: $45 for rider; $40 for passenger
- Other delegates: $47 for rider; $43 for passenger
- Children (12 & under): No charge

When registering after June 1, 1989, add $5 to all fees. V-Daze will be open to the public daily. Contact VTS for more information on daily admission.

Special Notes:
The altitude of Hot Springs rises 307 to 1,450 feet; June to July temperature averages 80 degrees; there are 47 hot springs; beautiful lakes and marvelous roads. Also, local attractions include Magic Springs, a family fun park; museums; Music Mountain Jamboree, and the famous Hot Springs Bath House Row.

Wing Ding XI

Rally Sponsor:	Gold Wing Road Riders Association, Inc. 3035 West Thomas Road Phoenix, AZ 85017 Contact: National headquarters (see above) Phone: 602-269-1403
Location:	Dane County Exposition Center, Madison, Wisconsin
Dates:	July 31 through August 3, 1989

Main theme:
"3 Ring Wing Ding." This year's Greatest Show on Two Wheels will be fun, it will be festive . . . it will be a real circus in both features and format.

Background:
wing-ding, n. (earlier whing-ding) Slang) 1. an event, action, party, celebration, etc., that is very festive, lively, unrestrained, etc. 2. something very striking, exciting, etc. of its kind.

The first Wing Ding was held in 1979 as a celebration; an opportunity for the members of the Gold Wing Road Riders Association (GWRRA) to share, on a national level, the camaraderie and fellowship for which the organization is known.

Phoenix, Arizona, Steamboat Springs, Colorado, Lake of the Ozarks, Missouri, Knoxville, Tennessee, and Snowmass Village, Colorado have over the course of the past ten years hosted this annual event. The 1989 edition marks the start of the second decade of Wing Ding, and by all indications, this year's activities in Madison will set the standards by which all future events will be measured.

Highlights:
Trade show; dance; event pin; seminars; talent show; door prize ticket; parade; field events; poker run; bike judging; and many other riding and non-riding opportunities; grand prize drawing for 1989 Honda Gold Wing. The big top will be the Coliseum building, a veritable pleasure palace of Gold Wing goodies and accessories. Step into the Forum building and be entertained and informed by your choice of meetings and seminars. Take a leisurely stroll down the midway, and test your relationship with Lady Luck. Peanuts, popcorn, cotton candy, hot dogs, and lemonade are but a few of the gourmet delights that will tempt the most sophisticated palate. Relax . . . have fun . . . enjoy!

Exhibitors and Special Events:
Approximately 200 exhibitors will represent a full complement of original equipment manufacturers and accessory suppliers.

Lodging Arrangements:
Lodging information will be sent to each person, upon registering with GWRRA.

Price:
For GWRRA members: early registration (if postmarked before June 15, 1989) is $35; Late registration is $40; on-site registration is $45. For non-members and guests: $50 before June 15; $55 after June 15; and $60 on site.

INTERNATIONAL WEATHER CHART

To give you a sense of what kind of weather to expect on your travels we've listed several cities throughout the world with their average high and low seasonal temperatures, and relative humidity. It is always possible to find a place to ride your motorcycle. If the weather doesn't suit you, move on down the road.

Table entries are:
Average high temperature/Average low temperature, Relative humidity
   (Temperature is given in degrees Fahrenheit)
   (Relative humidity is in percent)

City	Jan–Mar	April–June	July–Sept	Oct–Dec
Arctic Bay, Canada	-14/-28, 0%	27/12, 80%	47/35, 81%	2/-10, 82%
Vancouver, B.C.	44/34, 78%	64/46, 63%	73/54, 62%	48/39, 84%
New York, NY	38/24, 58%	68/53, 54%	80/66, 60%	51/37, 60%
San Francisco, CA	59/47, 66%	63/51, 62%	65/53, 70%	63/51, 60%
Monterrey, Mexico	72/52, 59%	87/68, 51%	92/72, 57%	71/55, 60%
Buenos Aires, Arg.	83/63, 63%	64/47, 74%	60/43, 74%	76/56, 60%
Caracas, Venezuela	77/56, 62%	80/62, 71%	79/61, 75%	77/60, 66%
London, England	44/36, 72%	62/47, 57%	71/56, 62%	50/42, 78%
Innsbruck, Austria	40/24, 58%	68/46, 43%	75/54, 52%	46/ 0, 65%
Lugano, Switz.	48/31, 52%	69/50, 53%	80/60, 51%	51/38, 59%
Belgrade, Yug.	42/29, 67%	73/54, 51%	83/62, 46%	51/39, 71%
Moscow, U.S.S.R.	22/ 8, 66%	66/46, 43%	72/53, 55%	35/26, 79%
Oslo, Norway	30/19, 74%	61/43, 52%	70/53, 61%	38/31, 83%
Rome, Italy	55/42, 64%	74/56, 54%	86/67, 43%	61/49, 66%
Madrid, Spain	52/36, 62%	70/50, 49%	85/63, 35%	55/42, 65%
Bordeaux, France	51/36, 73%	69/48, 60%	78/56, 60%	55/40, 80%
Ankara, Turkey	42/26, 67%	73/49, 38%	87/59, 25%	57/37, 52%
Cameron Highlands, Malaysia	72/55, 73%	74/58, 79%	72/56, 76%	71/57, 81%
Beijing, China	39/18, 50%	81/55, 49%	86/68, 74%	48/28, 56%
Katmandu, Nepal	67/39, 68%	86/61, 61%	83/68, 84%	74/45, 78%
Bangkok, Thailand	91/72, 55%	93/77, 64%	90/76, 66%	87/72, 65%
Darwin, Australia	90/77, 72%	91/73, 47%	89/70, 45%	94/78, 58%
Melbourne, Australia	78/57, 50%	62/47, 62%	59/43, 60%	71/51, 52%
Christchurch, NZ	69/53, 60%	56/40, 69%	52/36, 66%	66/47, 64%
In Salah, Algeria	75/47, 34%	99/69, 23%	111/82,19%	80/53, 38%
Douala, Cameroon	86/74, 75%	86/73, 79%	80/71, 84%	84/73, 80%

INDEX

A
A.A. Travel (Wairarapa) Ltd., 27, 277
Admiral Cruises, Inc., 308
Adriatic Sea, 127, 168, 181
Adventure Asia, 2, 227, 234, 239 – 240
Adventure Center Inc., 5, 249, 262
Aegean Sea, 189
Alaska, 41
Alaska Motorcycle Tours, Inc., 3, 42
Algeria, 192, 194 – 195, 199, 202, 208 – 209, 212 – 213, 215, 218 – 219, 221
Aloha Funway Rentals, 284
Alps, 31, 119, 121 – 122, 125 – 127, 129 – 130, 132, 135, 138, 142 – 144, 146 – 147, 150, 157, 159, 176, 188
Americade '89 East, 310
Americade '89 Rockies, 312
Americade, Inc., 310, 312
American Motorcycle Rentals and Sales, Inc., 285
American Motorcyclist Association, 108
Andes, 99, 101 – 102, 105
Andorra, 142
Apennines, 185
Appalachian Mountains, 69, 74
Arches National Park, 62
Argentina, 98
Armonk Travel, 15, 44, 132, 152, 162, 164, 166, 229, 236
Around the Globe Travel, Ltd., 9, 125, 138, 140, 288
Arrow Rentals, 287
Atlas Mountains, 206
Australia, 238
    New South Wales, 249, 252, 255 – 256, 261, 264
    Northern Territory, 248, 258
    Queensland, 252, 254
    South Australia, 258 – 259, 261, 264
    Victoria, 248 – 249, 252, 255, 258 – 259, 261
    Western Australia, 259
Australian Grand Prix, 255
Australian Motorcycle Touring, 5, 249, 261
Australian-American Mototours, 4, 253, 269
Austria, 119, 123, 126 – 127, 129, 132, 135, 138, 142, 146, 149, 153, 158, 164

B
Baja, 58, 76
Bali, 232, 238
Banff National Park, 46, 55
Beach's Motorcycle Adventures, Ltd., 6, 109, 122, 256, 274
Beach, Elizabeth L., 6
Beach, Rob, 6, 280
Beach, Robert D., 6
Belgium, 134
Big Sur, 60 – 61
Bike Tours, 7, 50, 55, 67, 232, 248, 251, 258
Bike Tours Unlimited, 8, 80, 178
Bjorkvist, Lars, 11
Black Forest, 137
Black Hills Motor Classic, 313
Black Sea, 163, 176, 178, 190
Blackwood, David, 24
Blue Ridge Mountains, 69
BMW Motorcycle Owners of America, 315
Bosenberg Motorcycle Excursions, 9, 125, 138, 140, 288
Bryant, Jan, 28
Bryant, Terry, 28
Bryce Canyon National Park, 58, 62, 70
Bugaboo Mountains, 47
Bull, Glen, 27, 302
Bull, Maureen, 27
Burma, 238

C
California MotoTours, 10, 58 – 60, 62, 291
Cameroon, 194, 197, 220
Canada
    Alberta, 45, 47, 49, 303
    British Colombia, 293, 297
    British Columbia, 43, 45, 47, 49 – 50, 53, 55, 67
    Yukon Territory, 43, 50, 55
Canary Islands, 217
Caribbean, 84, 94, 96, 99, 104
Carpenter, Bob, 311
Cascade Range, 68
Caucasus Mountains, 163
Central African Republic, 194, 197
China, 224 – 225, 239, 242
Chosa's Harley-Davidson, Inc., 294
Coach House Tours, 12, 113

INDEX

Coat, Geoff, 5
Coat, Maxene, 5
Copper Canyon, 76, 79, 86, 92
Corsica, 172
Crosby, Graeme, 22
Cycle City Ltd. Honolulu, 294
Cycle Craft Co., Inc., 294
Cyprus, 175

D

Dagiel, Gary, 26
Darwin to Melbourne, 258
Daytona International Bike Week, 65
Death Valley National Monument, 67, 72
del Bondio, Christoph, 31
Denali National Park, 42
Desmond Adventures, Inc., 13, 118, 120
Desmond, Thomas, E., 13
Dick Farmer's Harley-Davison of Orlando, Inc., 294
Dolomites, 119, 124, 126, 132, 148, 186
Douglass, D.N., 315
Dutcher, Gini, 310
Dutcher, William, 310, 312

E

Edelweiss Bike Travel, 14, 43, 132, 151, 162, 164, 166, 229, 236
Egypt, 199, 210
England, 108 – 109, 111 – 113, 212, 287, 300
Evans, Jack, 12
Evans, Pam, 12
Explo-Tours, 16, 192, 194, 197, 201, 213, 215, 219, 221

F

Fish, Jean, 20
France, 17, 121, 123, 130, 132, 134, 137, 140, 142, 144, 159, 172, 212
French, Les "Gringo", 18

G

Gara Kranfoussa Mountains, 214
Germany, Federal Republic of, 118, 123, 125, 128 – 130, 132, 137, 140 – 141, 146 – 147, 150, 153, 158, 165, 288, 293, 303, 306
Glacier National Park, 46
Glode, Martin, 33, 305
Glode, Werner, 33, 305
Gold Wing Road Riders Association, Inc., 320
Goodman, Flori, 37
Goodman, Warren, 37
Grand Canyon, 58, 62, 68, 70, 72, 74
Great Barrier Reef, 252, 254, 257
Great Motorcycle Adventures, 18, 79, 90, 94

Great Smoky Mountains, 69
Greif, Jürgen, 25
Guinea, 221
Gulf of Mexico, 65, 96
Guzzardo, Gina, 35, 306

H

Harley Owners Group, 293
Harley-Davidson Motor Company, 293
Harley-Davidson of Glendale, 294
Harley-Davidson of Reno, 293
Harley-Davidson, Inc. of Miami, 293
Heindel, Leon A., 9, 288
Himalayas, 227, 234, 236, 239 – 240
Hoel, J.C. "Pappy", 314
Hoggar Mountains, 193, 202, 208, 212, 221
Hong Kong, 226
Fritz Horvarth Trial-Tours, 17
Horvarth, Fritz, 17
Huasteca Canyon, 91
Hultman, Neil, 313
Hungary, 164
Huske, Roland, 10

I

India, 227, 230, 238
Indonesia, 232, 238
Ireland, Republic of, 111
Isle of Man, 108, 113 – 114
Italy, 119, 121, 123, 126, 132, 142, 144, 146, 148, 160, 172, 178, 180, 184, 186
Ivory Coast, 192, 221

J

Jackpine Gypsies Motorcycle Club, 313
Jamaica, 83
Japan, 233
Jasper National Park, 49, 55
Jesse, Al, 30
Josef Geltl, 16

K

Kananaskis Mountains, 46
Kashmir, 227
Kenya, 194, 197, 203, 212
Keown, Craig, 4
Keown, Kerry, 4

L

Leininger, Bill, 2
Lenzner, Volker, 29, 34, 303
Liechtenstein, 123, 146
Loch Ness, 108, 110, 115
Luxembourg, 133, 156

M

Malaysia, 229, 238
Mali, 221
Manton, Tom, 2
Mascorro, Skip, 22, 298
McDonnell, Duke, 3
McDonnell, Timothy, 3
Mediterranean, 131, 144, 169, 172, 174, 178, 184, 190, 192, 194, 202, 206, 214 – 215, 219, 221
Mesa Verde National Park, 64
Mexico, 76 – 77, 79 – 80, 82, 84, 86 – 88, 90, 92, 94 – 95
mhs Motorradtouren GmbH, 19, 49, 112, 115, 133, 135, 142, 144, 155 – 157, 159, 167, 169, 172, 180, 184
Millard, Steve, 32
Miller, Marvin, 317 – 318
Millette, Karin, 13
Miram, Izabella, 10, 291
Miro, Conny, 297
Moar, Nicholas, 24
Monte Carlo, 121, 131, 160
Morocco, 206, 208, 212, 218
Motorrad Spaett, KG, 21, 176, 187, 295
Motorrad-Reisen, 20, 71, 130, 137, 147, 149, 153, 183, 186, 203, 216, 225
Moturis, Ltd., 297
Mount Fuji, 233
Mount McKinley, 42, 51
Mount Sinai, 211
Murphy, Ross, 284
Murphy, Wayne, 285

N

Napa Valley, 61
Nepal, 234, 236, 238 – 240
New South Wales, 269
New Zealand, 238, 272, 274, 276 – 277, 279, 281, 302 – 303
New Zealand Central Reservations Office, 27, 277
Niagara Falls, 74
Niger, 193 – 194, 209, 212 – 213, 215, 219
Nigeria, 194, 220
Nile River, 200
1989 International CLASSIC, 315
Norway, 152

O

Overseas Brokers, Inc., 308

P

Pancho Villa Moto-Rentals, 298

Pancho Villa Moto-Tours, 22, 76 – 77, 82, 86, 88, 92, 95, 279
Paris – Dakar Rally, 208
Perniciaro, Vic, 8
Peru, 101
Peterborough Rally, 108
Poland, 166
Portugal, 181
Prima Klima Reisen GmbH, 23, 174, 230

Q

Queensland, 253, 265

R

Raedisch, Karl, 33
Rains, John, 29, 303
Rains, Maria, 30
Ram, C.S.C., 300
Rentals, 4, 7, 21, 24, 32
Rider Magazine, 317 – 318
Rider Rally East, 317
Rider Rally West, 318
Rocky Mountain Moto Tours Ltd., 24, 45, 47
Rocky Mountains, 43, 45, 47, 49, 55, 62, 64, 68, 73 – 74
Rosenbaum, Linda, 15, 229

S

Sahara, 31, 194, 196, 199, 201, 206, 208 – 209, 212 – 213, 215, 218 – 219, 221
Sahara Cross, 25, 199, 210
San Juan Mountains, 62
Sannen, Liz, 28
Sardinia, 172
Schaerer, Joe, 319
Schellhorn, Herbert, 19
Schellhorn, Wolfgang, 19
Schmidt, Peter, 23
Schnieder Reisen, 29, 303
Scootabout Motorcycle Centre, 300
Scotland, 17, 108, 110 – 111, 116
Selkirk Mountains, 47
Sequoia National Park, 60
Seymour Mountains, 54
Shipping, 7, 9 – 10, 21, 32, 34, 36 – 37
Sierra Madre Mountains, 76, 79, 82, 85, 89 – 90, 92
Sierra Nevada Mountains, 60
Singapore, 230, 238
Smoky Mountain Motorcycle Vacations, 26, 68
Snowy Mountains, 250
South Africa, 204
South Pacific Motorcycle Tours Ltd., 27, 277, 302

326 INDEX

Southern California Motorcycling Association, 72
Southern Skies Travel, 28, 264, 267
Soviet Union, 162, 164, 166
Spaett, Josef, 21
Spaett, Paul, 21, 295
Spaett, Peter, 21
Spain, 17, 141, 181, 212, 218
Starquest World Tours, 29, 303
Stutely, Russell L., 287
Sweden, 152
Switzerland, 118, 120, 123, 131 – 132, 142, 144, 146, 159

T

Tanzania, 194, 197, 212
Tasmania, 268
Te Wai Tours West, 30
Te Waipounamu Motorcycle Tours, 29, 281, 303
Team Aventura, 31, 101, 190
Tee Mill Tours Ltd., 32, 52, 66, 73, 206, 208, 212, 218, 238, 244
Terra Tours, 10, 58 – 59, 61 – 62, 291
Thailand, 229, 238, 244
Thomas, Reg, 32
Tibet, 241
Top Gear Tours, 264, 267
Tours
  Abidjan to Agadez to Tunis (#M3), 192
  AlpenTour™ East, 118
  AlpenTour™ West, 120
  Alpine Adventures, 122
  Alpine and Dolomites Excursion, 125
  Alpine Countries, 127
  Alpine Wandervogel Rider, 128
  Alps and Southern France, 130
  Alps: East and West, 132
  AMA's EuroTour, 108
  Arctic Tour, 43
  Ardennes (a gourmet tour), 133
  Argentina, 98
  Austria — Suzuki Test Drives, 135
  Best of Baja Tour, 76
  Best of the West, 58
  Best Winter in Africa (#M6 + #M7), 194
  Big Sky Tour, 45
  Bike Tours Special '89, 248
  The Black Forest, 137
  BMW Holiday Week, 138
  Boomerang Tour, 249
  British Bat, 109
  British Isles, 111
  Bugaboo Tour, 47
  California "Left Bank" Tour, 60
  California Grand Tour, 59
  Canada, 49

Tours (continued)
  Castles and Grapes Excursion, 140
  Central Sahara, 195
  China, 224
  China: The Middle Kingdom, 225
  Colonial 10-Day Tour, 77
  Colorado and the Best of the West, 62
  Copper Canyon Trail Ride, 79
  Corsica and Sardinia, 172
  Cyclecruise™ to Mexico's Riviera, 80
  Cyprus, 174
  Destination Spain, 141
  The Dolomites, 142
  Douala to Mombasa (#M7), 197
  Dual Purpose Expedition to the Sierra Madres, 82
  Dunes Expedition, 198
  East Coast Tour, 251
  East Turkey, 176 – 177
  Egypt Tour, 199
  Enduro High Alps Tour, 144
  England and Wales, 112
  Expedition to Kashmir, 227
  Fairbanks to Vancouver, 50
  Far East Motorcycle Tour, 229
  First Motorcycle Tour of the Caucasus, 162
  Fly 'N' Bike – Canada – 1989, 52
  Goa and South Indian Coasts and Jungle by Royal Enfields, 230
  Gold Coast to Cairns: Amazing Queensland, 253
  Grand Alpine Tour, 146
  High Alpine Circular Trip, 147
  High Dunes and Deep Valleys: Algeria (#M4), 201
  The Inca Rider, 99
  The Indian Badlands Rider, 63
  Isle of Man TT Races, 114
  Isles of Man "Insiders" Tour, 113
  Jamaica, 83
  Jambo Kenya! The other Africa..., 203
  The Jumbo Safari Rider Tour, 204
  Kangaroo Caper, 256
  The Kiwi Rider, 272
  Los Pancho Rider, 84
  Magic Austria, 149
  Maori Meander, 274
  Mardigras 1990 in Mazatlan, 86
  Melbourne to Darwin, 258
  Mexico, 87
  Midsummer's Night Tour, 151
  Mini-Chihuahua Tour, 88
  Monterreys' Cascade Cola de Caballo Trail Ride, 90
  Morocco Trailblaze, 206
  Motorail™ Tour: New Orleans and Daytona Beach, 65
  Motorcycle Vacation in Bali, 232

INDEX 327

Tours (continued)
  Mulga Tour, 261
  New Zealand, 276
  New Zealand 14-Day Tour, 277
  New Zealand Tour, 279
  Nippon Week, 233
  Nirvana in Nepal, 234, 236
  Outback Tour One, 264
  Outback Tour Three, 264
  Outback Tour Two, 264
  Overland to Australia and New Zealand, 238
  Paris – Dakar Special, 208
  Peru, 101
  Piggybike™ Tour of Italy, 178
  Ride America, 66
  Ride from the Roof of the World, 239
  Ride to the Roof of the World, 240
  Romantic Castles: Landscape and Wines of the Danube Valley, 153
  Sahara Without Borders, 209
  San Francisco to Vancouver, 67
  Scotland, 115
  Sicily and Southern Italy (a gourmet tour), 180
  The Silk Road Rider, 242
  Sinai Tour, 210
  16-Week, Trans-Africa Trailblaze, 212
  Smoky Mountains, 68
  Southwest U.S.A., 70
  Soviet Union, 164
  Spain and Portugal, 181
  Surprise Tours, 155
  Tasmania One, 267
  Tassili to North Tenere (#M1), 213
  Tenere: Central North Africa (#M5), 215
  Tenerife – Canary Island, 216
  Thailand Special, 244
  The GP Oz Rider Tour, 255
  The Wonders of New South Wales, 269
  Tour of the Baltic Countries, 166
  Trans-Sahara Trailblaze, 218
  Tunis to Douala (#M6), 219
  Tunis to Timbuktu to Abidjan (#M2), 221
  Turkey – 15 Day Tour, 183
  Tuscany (a gourmet tour), 184
  Tuscany: The Magic Spell of Italy, 186
  Two-Week Tour of New Zealand, 281
  U.S.A. The Great American Dream: The New World, 71
  United States, 42
  USA Four Corners Motorcycle Tour, 72
  USA Motorcycle Tour, 73
  Vancouver Coach Road Rider, 53
  Vancouver to Fairbanks, 55
  Vancouver to San Francisco, 67
  Venezuela: East, West and the Andes, 102
  Venezuela: The Northeast, 103
  Venezuela: The West and the Andes, 105

Tours (continued)
  Victoria One, 267
  Victoria Two, 267
  Weekend in Luxembourg (a gourmet tour), 156
  Weekend in Southern Bavarian Alps and Austria, 157
  West Coast of Mexico with Copper Canyon Excursion, 92
  West Turkey, 187, 189
  West Turkey and East Turkey, 190
  Western Alps Tour, 159
  Yucatan Peninsula Dual Sport/Road Trip, 94
  Yucatan Tour, 95
  Yugoslavia, Dalmatia – Suzuki Test Drives, 167
  Yugoslavia, Istra – Suzuki Test Drives, 169
Tours, S.R.L., 33, 102 – 103, 105, 305
Trans-Sahara Trailblaze, 208
TransCyclist International, 29, 34, 53, 63, 84, 99, 128, 204, 233, 242, 255, 272, 303
Trev Deeley Motorcycles, Ltd., 293
Troßmann, Thomas, 38
Tunisia, 192, 194 – 195, 198, 201, 209, 214 – 215, 219, 221
Turkey, 176 – 177, 183, 187, 189 – 190
Twickers World, 5, 249, 261

U

United States
  Alaska, 43, 50, 55
  Arizona, 70, 294
  Arkansas, 319
  California, 58 – 59, 61 – 62, 65 – 67, 70 – 71, 73, 285, 291, 294, 297, 306
  Colorado, 62 – 63, 312
  Florida, 65, 73, 293 – 294, 297
  Hawaii, 284, 294
  Kentucky, 317
  Louisiana, 65
  Maine, 73
  Massachusetts, 294
  Nevada, 58, 62, 67, 70 – 71, 293, 318
  New Mexico, 63
  New York, 297, 310
  North Carolina, 69
  South Dakota, 74, 314
  Texas, 298
  Utah, 58, 62, 67, 70 – 71
  Washington, 73
  Wisconsin, 293
  Wyoming, 68
Upper Volta, 193

V

V-Daze V, 319
Veenkamp, Eveline, 7

Venezuela, 99, 102, 104, 305
Venture Touring Society, 319
Victoria, 267
Vogel, Antje, 38
Von Thielmann Tours, 35, 70, 83, 87, 98, 111, 114, 141, 146, 177, 189, 224, 276, 306
Von Thielmann, Michael, 36
Vosges Mountains, 137, 140

W

Wachter, Coral, 16
Wachter, Werner, 15
Wales, 108, 112
Wanderer's Expeditions, 206, 208, 212, 218, 238, 244
Washington, 68
Waterton National Park, 45
Weber, Walt, 9, 288
Weidner, Kurt, 7
Weil, Hermann, 20
Weissman, Doron, 308
Westberg, Kjell, 11
Westberg, Maria, 11
Wilk, Gerhard, 10
Wing Ding XI, 320
Wisconsin, 320
World Motorcycle Tours, 37, 127, 181
Wüstenfahrer, 38, 195, 198, 209

Y

Yellowstone National Park, 68, 74
Yoho National Park, 49
Yosemite National Park, 60, 70, 72
Yucatan Peninsula, 94, 96
Yugoslavia, 127, 146, 167, 169

Z

Zaire, 194, 197, 212
Zion National Park, 58, 62